CEOE

50-51

OSAT

Elementary
Education

Teacher Certification Exam

By: Sharon Wynne, M.S
Southern Connecticut State University

"And, while there's no reason yet to panic, I think it's only prudent that we make preparations to panic."

XAMonline, INC.

Boston

To obtain permission(s) to use the material from this work for any purpose including workshops or seminars, please submit a written request to:

XAMonline, Inc.
21 Orient Ave.
Melrose, MA 02176
Toll Free 1-800-509-4128
Email: info@xamonline.com
Web www.xamonline.com
Fax: 1-781-662-9268

Library of Congress Cataloging-in-Publication Data

Wynne, Sharon A.
   OSAT Elementary Education Fields 50 -51 / Teacher Certification / Sharon A.   Wynne. -2nd ed.
   ISBN 978-1-58197-794-3
   1. OSAT Elementary Education Fields 50-51.   2. Study Guides.
   3. CEOE   4. Teachers' Certification & Licensure.   5. Careers

Disclaimer:
The opinions expressed in this publication are the sole works of XAMonline and were created independently from the National Education Association, Educational Testing Service, or any State Department of Education, National Evaluation Systems or other testing affiliates.

Between the time of publication and printing, state specific standards as well as testing formats and website information may change that is not included in part or in whole within this product. Sample test questions are developed by XAMonline and reflect similar content as on real tests; however, they are not former tests. XAMonline assembles content that aligns with state standards but makes no claims nor guarantees teacher candidates a passing score. Numerical scores are determined by testing companies such as NES or ETS and then are compared with individual state standards. A passing score varies from state to state.

Printed in the United States of America   œ-1

CEOE: OSAT Elementary Education Fields 50-51
ISBN: 978-1-58197-794-3

Table of Contents

DOMAIN II.   **LANGUAGE ARTS**

COMPETENCY 7.0   UNDERSTAND SKILLS AND STRATEGIES INVOLVED IN WRITING FOR VARIOUS PURPOSES

COMPETENCY 8.0   ANALYZE WRITTEN WORK IN RELATION TO ITS STATED PURPOSE; EVALUATE AREAS IN NEED OF IMPROVEMENT; AND REVISE WRITTEN TEXTS FOR STYLE, CLARITY, AND ORGANIZATION

COMPETENCY 9.0   APPLY KNOWLEDGE OF ENGLISH GRAMMAR AND MECHANICS IN REVISING TEXTS

<u>DOMAIN III.</u>   <u>SOCIAL STUDIES</u>

DOMAIN IV.   **MATHEMATICS**

DOMAIN V.   SCIENCE

COMPETENCY 25.0   UNDERSTAND THE INTERRELATIONSHIPS AMONG THE PHYSICAL AND LIFE SCIENCES AND THE CONNECTIONS AMONG SCIENCE, TECHNOLOGY, AND SOCIETY

COMPETENCY 26.0   UNDERSTAND THE PRINCIPLES OF LIFE SCIENCE, AND USE THIS UNDERSTANDING TO INTERPRET, ANALYZE, AND EXPLAIN PHENOMENA

Great Study and Testing Tips!

What to study in order to prepare for the subject assessments is the focus of this study guide but equally important is *how* you study.

You can increase your chances of truly mastering the information by taking some simple, but effective steps.

Study Tips:

1. <u>Some foods aid the learning process</u>. Foods such as milk, nuts, seeds, rice, and oats help your study efforts by releasing natural memory enhancers called CCKs (*cholecystokinin*) composed of *tryptopha*n, *choline*, and *phenylalanine*. All of these chemicals enhance the neurotransmitters associated with memory. Before studying, try a light, protein-rich meal of eggs, turkey, and fish. All of these foods release the memory enhancing chemicals. The better the connections, the more you comprehend.

Likewise, before you take a test, stick to a light snack of energy boosting and relaxing foods. A glass of milk, a piece of fruit, or some peanuts all release various memory-boosting chemicals and help you to relax and focus on the subject at hand.

2. <u>Learn to take great notes</u>. A by-product of our modern culture is that we have grown accustomed to getting our information in short doses (i.e. TV news sound bites or USA Today style newspaper articles.)

Consequently, we've subconsciously trained ourselves to assimilate information better in <u>neat little packages</u>. If your notes are scrawled all over the paper, it fragments the flow of the information. Strive for clarity. Newspapers use a standard format to achieve clarity. Your notes can be much clearer through use of proper formatting. A very effective format is called the <u>*"Cornell Method."*</u>

> Take a sheet of loose-leaf lined notebook paper and draw a line all the way down the paper about 1-2" from the left-hand edge.

> Draw another line across the width of the paper about 1-2" up from the bottom. Repeat this process on the reverse side of the page.

Look at the highly effective result. You have ample room for notes, a left hand margin for special emphasis items or inserting supplementary data from the textbook, a large area at the bottom for a brief summary, and a little rectangular space for just about anything you want.

3. Get the concept then the details. Too often we focus on the details and don't gather an understanding of the concept. However, if you simply memorize only dates, places, or names, you may well miss the whole point of the subject.

A key way to understand things is to put them in your own words. If you are working from a textbook, automatically summarize each paragraph in your mind. If you are outlining text, don't simply copy the author's words.

Rephrase them in your own words. You remember your own thoughts and words much better than someone else's, and subconsciously tend to associate the important details to the core concepts.

4. Ask Why? Pull apart written material paragraph by paragraph and don't forget the captions under the illustrations.

Example: If the heading is "Stream Erosion", flip it around to read "Why do streams erode?" Then answer the questions.

If you train your mind to think in a series of questions and answers, not only will you learn more, but it also helps to lessen the test anxiety because you are used to answering questions.

5. Read for reinforcement and future needs. Even if you only have 10 minutes, put your notes or a book in your hand. Your mind is similar to a computer; you have to input data in order to have it processed. *By reading, you are creating the neural connections for future retrieval.* The more times you read something, the more you reinforce the learning of ideas.

Even if you don't fully understand something on the first pass, *your mind stores much of the material for later recall.*

6. Relax to learn so go into exile. Our bodies respond to an inner clock called biorhythms. Burning the midnight oil works well for some people, but not everyone.

If possible, set aside a particular place to study that is free of distractions. Shut off the television, cell phone, and pager and exile your friends and family during your study period.

If you really are bothered by silence, try background music. Light classical music at a low volume has been shown to aid in concentration over other types. Music that evokes pleasant emotions without lyrics is highly suggested. Try just about anything by Mozart. It relaxes you.

7. <u>**Use arrows not highlighters**</u>. At best, it's difficult to read a page full of yellow, pink, blue, and green streaks. Try staring at a neon sign for a while and you'll soon see that the horde of colors obscure the message.

A quick note, a brief dash of color, an underline, and an arrow pointing to a particular passage is much clearer than a horde of highlighted words.

8. <u>**Budget your study time**</u>. Although you shouldn't ignore any of the material, *allocate your available study time in the same ratio that topics may appear on the test.*

Testing Tips:

1. Get smart, play dumb. Don't read anything into the question. Don't make an assumption that the test writer is looking for something else than what is asked. Stick to the question as written and don't read extra things into it.

2. Read the question and all the choices *twice* before answering the question. You may miss something by not carefully reading, and then re-reading both the question and the answers.

If you really don't have a clue as to the right answer, leave it blank on the first time through. Go on to the other questions, as they may provide a clue as to how to answer the skipped questions.

If later on, you still can't answer the skipped ones . . . ***Guess.*** The only penalty for guessing is that you *might* get it wrong. Only one thing is certain; if you don't put anything down, you will get it wrong!

3. Turn the question into a statement. Look at the way the questions are worded. The syntax of the question usually provides a clue. Does it seem more familiar as a statement rather than as a question? Does it sound strange?

By turning a question into a statement, you may be able to spot if an answer sounds right, and it may also trigger memories of material you have read.

4. Look for hidden clues. It's actually very difficult to compose multiple-foil (choice) questions without giving away part of the answer in the options presented.

In most multiple-choice questions you can often readily eliminate one or two of the potential answers. This leaves you with only two real possibilities and automatically your odds go to Fifty-Fifty for very little work.

5. Trust your instincts. For every fact that you have read, you subconsciously retain something of that knowledge. On questions that you aren't really certain about, go with your basic instincts. **Your first impression on how to answer a question is usually correct.**

6. Mark your answers directly on the test booklet. Don't bother trying to fill in the optical scan sheet on the first pass through the test.

Just be very careful not to miss-mark your answers when you eventually transcribe them to the scan sheet.

7. Watch the clock! You have a set amount of time to answer the questions. Don't get bogged down trying to answer a single question at the expense of 10 questions you can more readily answer.

THIS PAGE BLANK

DOMAIN I.   READING

COMPETENCY 1.0   UNDERSTAND THE READING PROCESS

Skill 1.1   Understand reading as a process of constructing meaning through dynamic interaction among the reader, the text, and the context of the reading situation

Understanding that print carries meaning is demonstrated every day in the elementary classroom as the teacher holds up a selected book to read it aloud to the class. The teachers explicitly and deliberately think aloud about how to hold the book, how to focus the class on looking at its cover, where to start reading, and in what direction to begin.

Even in writing the morning message on the board, the teacher targets the children on the placement of the message and its proper place at the top of the board to be followed by additional activities and a schedule for the rest of the day.

When the teacher challenges children to make letter posters of a single letter and the items in the classroom, their home, or their knowledge base which start with that letter, the children are making concrete the understanding that print carries meaning.

Teachers need to look for five basic behaviors in students:
- Do students know how to hold the book?
- Can students match speech to print?
- Do students know the difference between letters and words?
- Do students know that print conveys meaning?
- Can students track print from left to right?

In order for students to understand concepts of print, they must be able to recognize text and understand the various mechanics text contains. This includes:

- All text contains a message
- The English language has a specific structure
- In order to decode words and read text, students must be able to understand that structure.

The structure of the English language consists of rules of grammar, capitalization and punctuation. For younger children, this means being able to recognize letters and form words. For older children, it means being able to recognize different types of text, such as lists, stories and signs, and knowing the purpose of each one.

When reading to children, teachers point to words as they read them. Illustrations and pictures also contribute to being able to understand the meaning of the text. Therefore, teachers should also discuss illustrations related to the text.

When reading to students, teachers also discuss the common characteristics of books (author, title page, table of contents, etc). Asking students to predict what the story might be about is a good strategy to employ to help teach students about the cover and its importance to the story. Pocket charts, big books and song charts provide ample opportunity for teachers to point to words as they read.

Instructional Strategies:

1.   **Using big books in the classroom**

Gather the children around you in a group with the big book placed on a stand. This allows all children to see the words and pictures. As you read, point to each word. It is best to use a pointer so you are not covering any other words or part of the page. When students read from the big book on their own, have them also use the pointer for each word.

When students begin reading from smaller books, have them transfer what they have learned about pointing to the words by using their finger to track the reading.

Observation is a key point in assessing students' ability to track words and speech.

2.   *A classroom rich in print*

Having words from a familiar rhyme or poem in a pocket chart lends itself to an activity where the students arrange the words in the correct order and then read the rhyme. This is an instructional strategy that reinforces directionality of print. It also reinforces punctuation, capitalization and matching print to speech.

Using highlighters or sticky tabs to locate upper and lower case letters or specific words can help students isolate words and learn about the structure of language for reading.

There should be plenty of books in the classroom for children to read on their own or in small groups. As you observe each of these groups, take note of how the child holds the book in addition to how he/she tracks and reads the words.

3. Word Wall

The use of a word wall is a great teaching tool for words in isolation and with writing. Each of the letters of the alphabet is displayed with words under each one that begin with that letter. Students are able to find the letter on the wall and read the words under each one.

4. Sounds of the letters

In addition to teaching the letter names, students should learn the corresponding sound of each letter. This is a key feature of decoding when beginning to read. The use of rhyming words is an effective way to teach letter sounds so that children have a solid background.

Students should be exposed to daily opportunities for viewing and reading texts. Teachers can do this by engaging the students in discussions about books during shared, guided and independent reading times. The teacher should draw the students' attention to the conventions of print and discuss with them the reasons for choosing different books. For example, teachers should let the students know that it is perfectly acceptable to return a book and select another if they think it is too hard for them.

Predictable books help engage the students in reading. Once the students realize what words are repeated in the text, they will eagerly chime in to repeat the words at the appropriate time during the reading. Rereading of texts helps the students learn the words and helps them to read these lines fluently.

Some things for teachers to observe during reading:

- Students' responses during reading conferences, such as pointing to letters or words.
- Ask students where they should begin reading and how they know to stop or pause depending on the punctuation.
- Student behavior when holding a book (e.g., holding the book right side up or upside down, reading from left to right, stopping to look at the pictures to confirm meaning)

Skill 1.2   Understand factors that affect reading (e.g., cultural, social, linguistic, developmental, environmental)

Oftentimes, students absorb the culture and social environment around them without deciphering contextual meaning of the experiences. When provided with a diversity of cultural contexts, students are able to adapt and incorporate multiple meanings from cultural cues vastly different from their own socioeconomic backgrounds. Socio-cultural factors provide a definitive impact on a students' psychological, emotional, affective, and physiological development, along with a students' academic learning and future opportunities.

The educational experience for most students is a complicated and complex experience with a diversity of interlocking meanings and inferences. If one aspect of the complexity is altered, it affects other aspects, which may impact how a student or teacher views an instructional or learning experience. With the current demographic profile of today's school communities, the complexity of understanding, interpreting, synthesizing the nuances from the diversity of cultural lineages can provide many communication and learning blockages that could impede the acquisition of learning for students.

Teachers must create personalized learning communities where every student is a valued member and contributor of the classroom experiences. In classrooms where socio-cultural attributes of the student population are incorporated into the fabric of the learning process, dynamic interrelationships are created that enhance the learning experience and the personalization of learning. When students are provided with numerous academic and social opportunities to share cultural incorporations into the learning, everyone in the classroom benefits from bonding through shared experiences and having an expanded viewpoint of a world experience and culture that vastly differs from their own.

Researchers continue to show that personalized learning environments increase the learning affect for students; decrease drop-out rates among marginalized students; and decrease unproductive student behavior which can result from constant cultural misunderstandings or miscues between students. Promoting diversity of learning and cultural competency in the classroom for students and teachers creates a world of multicultural opportunities and learning. When students are able to step outside their comfort zones and share the world of a homeless student or empathize with an English Language Learner (ELL) student who has just immigrated to the United States and is learning English for the first time and is still trying to keep up with the academic learning in an unfamiliar language; then students grow exponentially in social understanding and cultural connectedness.

Personalized learning communities provide supportive learning environments that address the academic and emotional needs of students. As socio-cultural knowledge is conveyed continuously in the interrelated experiences shared cooperatively and collaboratively in student groupings and individualized learning, the current and future benefits will continue to present the case and importance of understanding the "whole" child, inclusive of the social and the cultural context.

Skill 1.3   Understand the oral language foundation of reading and the interrelatedness of reading, writing, listening, and speaking

When students practice fluency, they practice reading connected pieces of text. In other words, instead of looking at a word as just a word, they might read a sentence straight through. The point of this is that in order for the student to comprehend what she is reading, she would need to be able to "fluently" piece together words in a sentence quickly. If a student is NOT fluent in reading, he or she would sound out each letter or word slowly and pay more attention to the phonics of each word. A fluent reader, on the other hand, might read a sentence aloud using appropriate intonations. The best way to test for fluency, in fact, is to have a student read something aloud, preferably a few sentences in a row—or more. Sure, most students just learning to read will probably not be very fluent right away; but with practice, they will increase their fluency. Even though fluency is not the same as comprehension, it is said that fluency is a good predictor of comprehension. Think about it: If you're focusing too much on sounding out each word, you're not going to be paying attention to the meaning.

During the preschool years, children acquire cognitive skills in oral language that they apply to reading comprehension later. Reading aloud to young children is one of the most important things an adult can do because they are teaching children how to monitor, question, predict, and confirm what they hear in the stories. Reid(1988, p. 165) described four meta-linguistic abilities that young children acquire through early involvement in reading activities:

1. *Word consciousness.* Children who have access to books first can tell the story through the pictures. Gradually they begin to realize the connection between the spoken words and the printed words. The beginning of letter and word discrimination begins in the early years.

2. *Language and conventions of print.* During this stage children learn how to hold a book, where to begin to read, the left to right motion, and how to continue from one line to the next.

3. *Functions of print.* Children discover that print can be used for a variety of purposes and functions, including entertainment and information.

The typical variation in literacy backgrounds children bring to reading can make teaching more difficult. Often a teacher must choose between focusing on the learning needs of a few students at the expense of the group or focusing on the group at the risk of leaving some students behind academically. This situation is particularly critical for children with gaps in their literacy knowledge who may be at risk in subsequent grades for becoming "diverse learners."

Areas of Emerging Evidence

1. Experiences with print (through reading and writing) help preschool children develop an understanding of the conventions, purpose, and functions of print. Children learn about print from a variety of sources and in the process come to realize that print carries the story. They also learn how text is structured visually (i.e., text begins at the top of the page, moves from left to right, and carries over to the next page when it is turned). While knowledge about the conventions of print enables children to understand the physical structure of language, the conceptual knowledge that printed words convey a message also helps children bridge the gap between oral and written language.

2. Phonological awareness and letter recognition contribute to initial reading acquisition by helping children develop efficient word recognition strategies (e.g., detecting pronunciations and storing associations in memory.) Phonological awareness and knowledge of print-speech relations play an important role in facilitating reading acquisition. Therefore, phonological awareness instruction should be an integral component of early reading programs. Within the emergent literacy research, viewpoints diverged on whether acquisition of phonological awareness and letter recognition are preconditions of literacy acquisition or whether they develop interdependently with literacy activities such as story reading and writing.

Storybook reading affects children's knowledge about, strategies for, and attitudes towards reading. Of all the strategies intended to promote growth in literacy acquisition, none is as commonly practiced, nor as strongly supported across the emergent literacy literature, as storybook reading. Children in different social and cultural groups have differing degrees of access to storybook reading. For example, it is not unusual for a teacher to have students who have experienced thousands of hours of story reading time, along with other students who have had little or no such exposure.

Learning approach

Early theories of language development were formulated from learning theory research. The assumption was that language development evolved from learning the rules of language structures and applying them through imitation and reinforcement. This approach also assumed that language, cognitive, and social developments were independent of each other. Thus, children were expected to learn language from patterning after adults who spoke and wrote Standard English. No allowance was made for communication through child jargon, idiomatic expressions, or grammatical and mechanical errors resulting from too-strict adherence to the rules of inflection (*childs* instead of *children*) or conjugation (*runned* instead of *ran*). No association was made between physical and operational development and language mastery.

Linguistic approach

Studies spearheaded by Noam Chomsky in the 1950s formulated the theory that language ability is innate and develops through natural human maturation as environmental stimuli trigger acquisition of syntactical structures appropriate to each exposure level. The assumption of a hierarchy of syntax downplayed the significance of semantics. Because of the complexity of syntax and the relative speed with which children acquire language, linguists attributed language development to biological rather than cognitive or social influences.

Cognitive approach

Researchers in the 1970s proposed that language knowledge derives from both syntactic and semantic structures. Drawing on the studies of Piaget and other cognitive learning theorists, supporters of the cognitive approach maintained that children acquire knowledge of linguistic structures after they have acquired the cognitive structures necessary to process language. For example, joining words for specific meaning necessitates sensory motor intelligence. The child must be able to coordinate movement and recognize objects before she can identify words to name the objects or word groups to describe the actions performed with those objects. Children must have developed the mental abilities for organizing concepts as well as concrete operations, predicting outcomes, and theorizing before they can assimilate and verbalize complex sentence structures, choose vocabulary for particular nuances of meaning, and examine semantic structures for tone and manipulative effect.

Socio-cognitive approach

Other theorists in the 1970s proposed that language development results from sociolinguistic competence. Language, cognition, and social knowledge are interactive elements of total human development. Emphasis on verbal communication as the medium for language expression resulted in the inclusion of speech activities in most language arts curricula.

Unlike previous approaches, the socio-cognitive allowed that determining the appropriateness of language in given situations for specific listeners is as important as understanding semantic and syntactic structures. By engaging in conversation, children at all stages of development have opportunities to test their language skills, receive feedback, and make modifications. As a social activity, conversation is as structured by social order as grammar is structured by the rules of syntax. Conversation satisfies the learner's need to be heard and understood and to influence others. Thus, his choices of vocabulary, tone, and content are dictated by his ability to assess the language knowledge of his listeners. He is constantly applying his cognitive skills to using language in a social interaction. If the capacity to acquire language is inborn, without an environment in which to practice language, a child would not pass beyond grunts and gestures as did primitive man.

Of course, the varying degrees of environmental stimuli to which children are exposed at all age levels create a slower or faster development of language. Some children are prepared to articulate concepts and recognize symbolism by the time they enter fifth grade because they have been exposed to challenging reading and conversations with well-spoken adults at home or in their social groups. Others are still trying to master the sight recognition skills and are not yet ready to combine words in complex patterns.

COMPETENCY 2.0   UNDERSTAND PHONOLOGICAL SKILLS AND STRATEGIES RELATED TO READING

Skill 2.1   Understand how to foster students' phonemic awareness (i.e., ability to perceive and discriminate the sounds of the English language) through rhyming, blending, and segmenting sounds in words

Phonological Awareness

Phonological awareness is the ability of the reader to recognize the sound of spoken language. This recognition includes how these sounds can be blended together, segmented (divided up), and manipulated (switched around). This awareness then leads to phonics, a method for teaching children to read. It helps them "sound out words."

Development of phonological skills may begin during pre-K years. Indeed, by the age of 5, a child who has been exposed to rhyme can recognize a rhyme. Such a child can demonstrate phonological awareness by filling in the missing rhyming word in a familiar rhyme or rhymed picture book.

You teach children phonological awareness when you teach them the sounds made by the letters, the sounds made by various combinations of letters and how to recognize individual sounds in words.

Phonological Awareness Skills include:

1. Rhyming and syllabification
2. Blending sounds into words—such as pic-tur-bo-k
3. Identifying the beginning or starting sounds of words and the ending or closing sounds of words
4. Breaking words down into sounds -- also called "segmenting" words
5. Recognizing other smaller words in the big word, by removing starting sounds, "hear" to ear

Phonemic Awareness

Phonemic awareness is the idea that words are comprised of sounds. To be phonemically aware, means the reader and listener can recognize and manipulate specific sounds in spoken words.

Phonemic awareness deals with sounds in words that are spoken. The majority of phonemic awareness tasks, activities, and exercises are ORAL. Theorist Marilyn Jager Adams, who researches early reading, has outlined five basic types of phonemic awareness tasks.

Task 1- Ability to hear rhymes and alliteration.
For example, the children would listen to a poem, rhyming picture book or song and identify the rhyming words heard which the teacher might then record or list on an experiential chart.

Task 2- Ability to do oddity tasks (recognize the member of a set that is different [odd]) among the group.
For example, the children would look at the pictures of a blade of grass, a garden and a rose—which starts with a different sound?

Task 3 –The ability to orally blend words and split syllables.
For example, the children can say the first sound of a word and then the rest of the word and put it together as a single word.

Task 4 –The ability to orally segment words.
For example, the ability to count sounds. The children would be asked as a group to count the sounds in "hamburger."

Task 5- The ability to do phonics manipulation tasks.
For example, replace the "r" sound in rose with a "p" sound.

Since the ability to distinguish between individual sounds, or phonemes, within words is a prerequisite to association of sounds with letters and manipulating sounds to blend words—a fancy way of saying "reading," the teaching of phonemic awareness is crucial to emergent literacy (early childhood K-2 reading instruction). Children need a strong background in phonemic awareness in order for phonics instruction (sound –spelling relationship-printed materials) to be effective.

Instructional methods effective for teaching phonemic awareness can include:
- Clapping syllables in words
- Distinguishing between a word and a sound
- Using visual cues and movements to help children understand when the speaker goes from one sound to another
- Incorporating oral segmentation activities which focus on easily distinguished syllables rather than sounds
- Singing familiar songs (e.g. Happy Birthday, Knick Knack Paddy Wack) and replacing key words in it with words with a different ending or middle sound (oral segmentation)
- Dealing children a deck of picture cards and having them sound out the words for the pictures on their cards or calling for a picture by asking for its first and second sound.

Skill 2.2   Demonstrate knowledge of instruction in letter-sound correspondences and systematic, explicit phonics

The Alphabetic Principle is sometimes called Graphophonemic Awareness. This multi-syllabic technical reading foundation term recognizes that written words are composed of patterns of letters which represent the sounds of spoken words.

There are basically two parts to the alphabetic principle:

1. An understanding that words are made up of letters and that each of these letters has a specific sound.
2. The correspondence between sounds and letters leads to phonological reading. This consists of reading regular and irregular words and doing advanced analysis of words.

Since the English language is dependant on the alphabet, being able to recognize and sound out letters is the first step for beginning readers. Relying simply on memorization for recognition of words is just not feasible as a way for children to learn to recognize words. Therefore decoding is essential. The most important goal of beginning reading teachers is to teach students to decode text so they can read fluently and with understanding.

There are four basic features of the alphabetic principle:

1. Students need to be able to take spoken words apart and blend different sounds together to make new words.
2. Students need to apply letter sounds to all their reading.
3. Teachers need to use a systematic effective program in order to teach children to read.
4. The teaching of the alphabetic principle usually begins in Kindergarten.

It is important to keep in mind that some children already know the letters and sounds before they come to school. Others may catch on to this quite quickly and still others need to have one-on-one instruction in order to learn to read.

Critical skills students need to learn are:
- Letter-sound correspondence
- How to sound out words
- How to decode text to make meaning

Skill 2.3   Understand strategies to promote students' rapid, automatic decoding through the application of phonics skills

The Structure of Language

Morphology is the study of word structure. When readers develop morphemic skills, they are developing an understanding of patterns they see in words. For example, English speakers realize that cat, cats, and caterpillar share some similarities in structure. This understanding helps readers to recognize words at a faster and easier rate, since each word doesn't need individual decoding.

Syntax refers to the rules or patterned relationships that correctly create phrases and sentences from words. When readers develop an understanding of syntax, they begin to understand the structure of how sentences are built, and eventually the beginning of grammar.

Example:
    "I am going to the movies"

This statement is syntactically and grammatically correct

Example:
    "They am going to the movies:

This statement is syntactically correct since all the words are in their correct place, but it is grammatically incorrect due to use of the word "They" rather than "I."

Semantics refers to the meaning expressed when words are arranged in a specific way. This is where connotation and denotation of words eventually will have a role with readers.

All of these skill sets are important to eventually developing effective word recognition skills, which help emerging readers develop fluency.

Phonics

As opposed to phonemic awareness, the study of phonics must be done with the eyes open. It's the connection between the sounds and letters on a page. In other words, students learning phonics might see the word "bad" and sound each letter out slowly until they recognize that they just said the word.

Phonological awareness is the ability of the reader to recognize the sound of spoken language. This recognition includes how these sounds can be blended together, segmented (divided up), and manipulated (switched around). This awareness then leads to phonics, a method for teaching children to read. It helps them "sound out words."

Development of phonological skills may begin during pre-K years. Indeed by the age of 5, a child who has been exposed to rhyme can recognize a rhyme. Such a child can demonstrate phonological awareness by filling in the missing rhyming word in a familiar rhyme or rhymed picture book.

You teach children phonological awareness when you teach them the sounds made by the letters, the sounds made by various combinations of letters and how to recognize individual sounds in words.

Phonological awareness skills include:

- Rhyming and syllabification
- Blending sounds into words—such as pic-tur-bo-k
- Identifying the beginning or starting sounds of words and the ending or closing sounds of words
- Breaking words down into sounds-also called "segmenting" words
- Recognizing other smaller words in the big word, by removing starting sounds, "hear" to ear

COMPETENCY 3.0   UNDERSTAND SKILLS AND STRATEGIES RELATED TO WORD IDENTIFICATION AND VOCABULARY DEVELOPMENT

Skill 3.1   Apply knowledge of word identification strategies (e.g., decoding, recognizing affixes, using context clues)

The Structure of Language

Morphology is the study of word structure. When readers develop morphemic skills, they are developing an understanding of patterns they see in words. For example, English speakers realize that cat, cats, and caterpillar share some similarities in structure. This understanding helps readers to recognize words at a faster and easier rate, since each word doesn't need individual decoding.

Syntax refers to the rules or patterned relationships that correctly create phrases and sentences from words. When readers develop an understanding of syntax, they begin to understand the structure of how sentences are built, and eventually the beginning of grammar.

Example:
    "I am going to the movies"

This statement is syntactically and grammatically correct

Example:
    "They am going to the movies:

This statement is syntactically correct since all the words are in their correct place, but it is grammatically incorrect due to use of the word "They" rather than "I."

Semantics refers to the meaning expressed when words are arranged in a specific way. This is where connotation and denotation of words eventually will have a role with readers.

All of these skill sets are important to eventually developing effective word recognition skills, which help emerging readers develop fluency.

Phonics

As opposed to phonemic awareness, the study of phonics must be done with the eyes open. It's the connection between the sounds and letters on a page. In other words, students learning phonics might see the word "bad" and sound each letter out slowly until they recognize that they just said the word.

Phonological awareness is the ability of the reader to recognize the sound of spoken language. This recognition includes how these sounds can be blended together, segmented (divided up), and manipulated (switched around). This awareness then leads to phonics, a method for teaching children to read. It helps them "sound out words."

Development of phonological skills may begin during pre-K years. Indeed by the age of 5, a child who has been exposed to rhyme can recognize a rhyme. Such a child can demonstrate phonological awareness by filling in the missing rhyming word in a familiar rhyme or rhymed picture book.

You teach children phonological awareness when you teach them the sounds made by the letters, the sounds made by various combinations of letters and to recognize individual sounds in words.

Phonological awareness skills include:

- Rhyming and syllabification
- Blending sounds into words—such as pic-tur-bo-k
- Identifying the beginning or starting sounds of words and the ending or closing sounds of words
- Breaking words down into sounds-also called "segmenting" words
- Recognizing other smaller words in the big word, by removing starting sounds, "hear" to ear

Decoding, Word Recognition, & Spelling

Word analysis (a.k.a. phonics or decoding) is the process readers use to figure out unfamiliar words based on written patterns. Word recognition is the process of automatically determining the pronunciation and some degree of the meaning of an unknown word. In other words, fluent readers recognize most written words easily and correctly, without consciously decoding or breaking them down. These elements of literacy are skills readers need for word recognition.

To decode means to change communication signals into messages. Reading comprehension requires that the reader learn the code within which a message is written and be able to decode it to get the message. Encoding involves changing a message into symbols. For example to encode oral language into writing (spelling) or to encode an idea into words or to encode a mathematical or physical idea into appropriate mathematical symbols.

Although effective reading comprehension requires identifying words automatically (Adams, 1990, Perfetti, 1985), children do not have to be able to identify every single word or know the exact meaning of every word in a text to understand it. Indeed, Nagy (1988) says children can read a work with a high level of comprehension even if they do not fully know as many as 15 percent of the words within a given text. Children develop the ability to decode and recognize words automatically. They then can extend their ability to decode to multi-syllabic words.

Skill 3.2 Understand ways to help students master common irregular sight words

Common irregular sight words are words that are irregular enough not to be considered sight words children can memorize easily, or begin to pick up through context. Additionally, they cannot be decoded easily because they have irregular spellings. Students cannot be expected to memorize these as quickly as other, more regularized words. Over time, however, students should be able to identify, write, and spell these words. Examples include "design" and "thought."

Regardless of the irregularity of these words, students still should be taught to tackle these words, letter-by-letter, sometimes chunking groups of letters if necessary. Students then need to be made aware that other words, for example, have similar spelling structures. For example, the "g" in design is silent, like the "b" in comb. Reminding students periodically for a longer period of time, is a good method for dealing with the specific words that may cause them problems.

Memorizing hundreds of irregular words is NOT effective because most children will not remember most of them. It simply takes reinforcement, practice, and repeated exposure.

Skill 3.3 Understand strategies for increasing students' vocabulary knowledge and their ability to apply vocabulary knowledge in new contexts

CONTEXTUAL REDEFINITION

This strategy encourages children to use context more effectively by presenting them with sufficient context BEFORE they begin reading. It models for the children the use of contextual clues to make informed guesses about word meanings.

To apply this strategy, the teacher should first select unfamiliar words for teaching. No more than two or three words should be selected for direct teaching. The teacher should then write a sentence in which there are sufficient clues supplied for the child to successfully figure out the meaning. Among the types of context clues the teacher can use are: compare/contrast, synonyms, and direct definition.

Then the teacher should present the words only on the experiential chart or as letter cards. Have the children pronounce the words. As they pronounce them, challenge them to come up with a definition for each word. After more than one definition is offered, encourage the children to decide as a group what the definition is. Write down their agreed upon definition with no comment as to its true meaning.

Then share with the children the contexts (sentences the teacher wrote with the words and explicit context clues). Ask the children to read the sentences aloud. Then have them derive a definition for each word. Make certain that as they present their definitions, the teacher does not comment. Ask them to justify their definitions by making specific references to the context clues in the sentences. As the discussion continues direct the children's attention to their previously-agreed-upon definition of the word. Facilitate them in discussing the differences between their guesses about the word when they saw only the word itself and their guesses about the word when they read it in contexts. Finally have the children check their use of context skills to correctly define the word by using a dictionary.

This type of direct teaching of word definitions is useful when the children have dictionary skills and the teacher is aware of the fact that there are not sufficient clues about the words in the context to help the students define it. In addition, struggling readers and students from ELL backgrounds may benefit tremendously from being walked through this process that highly proficient and successful readers apply automatically.

By using this strategy, the teacher can also "kid watch" and note the students' prior knowledge as they guess the word in isolation. The teacher can also actually witness and hear how various students use context skills.

Through their involvement in this strategy, struggling readers gain a feeling of community as they experience how their struggles and guesses resonate in other peers' responses to the text. They are also getting a chance to be 'walked through" this maze of meaning and learning how to use context clues in order to navigate it themselves.

Use of Semantic and Syntactic Cues

Semantic Cues

The teacher can use prompts which will alert the children to semantic cues, including:

- You said (the child's statement and incorrect attempt). Does that make sense to you?
- If someone said (repeat the child's attempt), would you know what he or she meant?
- You said (child's incorrect attempt). Would you write that?

Children need to use meaning to predict what the text says so the relevant information can prompt the correct words to surface as they identify the words. If children come to a word they can't immediately recognize, they need to try to figure it out using their past reading (or being read to) experiences background knowledge, and what they can deduce so far from the text itself.

Syntactic Cues

- You said (child's incorrect attempt). Does that sound right?
- You said (child's incorrect attempt). Can we say it like that?

Phonics terminology-
    Morpheme, Base word, root, inflection and/or any other affix.

"It is the good reader that makes the good book."
Ralph Waldo Emerson

Development of Word Analysis Skills and Strategies

Strategy (A Balanced Literacy Approach detailed in Sharon Taberski's On Solid Ground (2000)): Word Study Group-

This involves the teacher taking time to meet with children from grades 3-6 in a small group of no more than 6 children for a word study session. Taberski suggests that this meeting take place next to the Word Wall (see Spelling Wall on p 20). The children selected for this group are those who need to focus more on the relationship between spelling patterns and their consonant sounds.

It is important that this not be a formalized traditional reading group that meets at a set time each week or biweekly. Rather the group should be spontaneously formed by the teacher based on the teacher's quick inventory of the selected children's needs at the start of the week. Taberski has templates in her book of *Guided Reading Planning Sheets.* These sheets are essentially targeted word and other skills sheets with her written dated observations of children who are in need of support to develop a given skill (kid watching-see Dictionary).

The teacher should try to meet with this group for at least two consecutive twenty-minute-per-day periods. Over those two meetings, the teacher can model a Making Words Activity. Once the teacher has modeled making words the first day, the children would then make their own words. On the second day, the children would "sort" their words.

Other topics for a word study group within the framework of the Balanced Literacy Approach that Taberski advocates are: inflectional endings, prefixes and suffixes, and/or common spelling patterns.

It should be noted that this activity would be classified by theorists as a structural analysis activity because the structural components (i.e. prefixes, suffixes, and spelling patterns) of the words are being studied.

COMPETENCY 4.0   UNDERSTAND SKILLS AND STRATEGIES INVOLVED IN READING COMPREHENSION

Skill 4.1   Understand factors affecting reading comprehension (e.g., reading rate and fluency, prior knowledge, vocabulary knowledge)

If there were two words synonymous with reading comprehension as far as the balanced literacy approach is concerned, they would be "Constructing Meaning."

Cooper, Taberski, Strickland, and other key theorists and classroom teachers, conceptualize the reader as designating a specific meaning to the text using both clues in the text and his/her own prior knowledge. Comprehension for the balanced literacy theorists is a strategic process.

The reader interacts with the text and brings his/her prior knowledge and experience to it or LACK of prior knowledge and experience to it. Writing is interlaced with reading and is a mutually integrative and supportive parallel process. Hence the division of literacy learning by the balanced literacy folks into reading workshop and writing workshop, with the same anchor "readings" or books being used for both.

Consider the sentence,
"The test booklet was white with black print, but very scary looking."

According to the idea of constructing meaning as the reader read this sentence, the schemata (generic information stored in the mind) of tests he or she was personally activated by the author's ideas that tests are scary. Therefore the ultimate meaning the reader derives from the page is from the reader's own responses and experiences with the ideas the author presents. The reader constructs a meaning that reflects the author's intent and also the reader's response to that intent.

It is also to be remembered that generally readings are fairly lengthy passages, comprised of paragraphs which in turn are comprised of more than one sentence. With each successive sentence, and every new paragraph, the reader refocuses. The schemata are reconsidered, and a new meaning is constructed.

The purpose of reading is to convert visual images (the letters and words) into a message. Pronouncing the words is not enough; the reader must be able to extract the meaning of the text. When people read, they utilize four sources of background information to comprehend the meaning behind the literal text (Reid, pp.166-171).

1. *Word Knowledge:* Information about words and letters. One's knowledge about word meanings is *lexical knowledge*—a sort of dictionary. Knowledge about spelling patterns and pronunciations is *orthographic knowledge.* Poor readers do not develop the level of automatically in using orthographic knowledge to identify words and decode unfamiliar words.

2. *Syntax and Contextual Information.* When children encounter unknown words in a sentence, they rely on their background knowledge to choose a word that makes sense. Errors of younger children therefore are often substitutions of words in the same syntactic class. Poor readers often fail to make use of context clues to help them identify words or activate the background knowledge that would help them with comprehension. Poor readers also process sentences word by word, instead of "chunking" phrases and clauses, resulting in a slow pace that focuses on the decoding rather than comprehension. They also have problems answering wh- (Who, what, where, when, why) questions as a result of these problems with syntax.

3. *Semantic Knowledge:* This includes the reader's background knowledge about a topic, which is combined with the text information as the reader tries to comprehend the material. New information is compared to the background information and incorporated into the reader's schema. Poor readers have problems with using their background knowledge, especially with passages that require inference or cause-and-effect.

3. *Text Organization:* Good readers are able to differentiate types of text structure, e.g., story narrative, exposition, compare-contrast, or time sequence. They use knowledge of text to build expectations and construct a framework of ideas on which to build meaning. Poor readers may not be able to differentiate types of text and miss important ideas. They may also miss important ideas and details by concentrating on lesser or irrelevant details.

Research on reading development has yielded information on the behaviors and habits of good readers vs. poor readers. Some of the characteristics of good readers are:

- They think about the information they will read in the text, formulate questions they predict will be answered in the text, and confirm those predictions from the information in the text.
- When faced with unfamiliar words, they attempt to pronounce them using analogies to familiar words.
- Before reading, good readers establish a purpose for reading, select possible text structure, choose a reading strategy, and make predictions about what will be in the reading.
- As they read, good readers continually test and confirm their predictions, go back when something does not make sense, and make new predictions.

Skill 4.2   Demonstrate knowledge of literal, inferential, and evaluative comprehension skills

Fact and Opinion

Facts are verifiable statements. Opinions are statements that must be supported in order to be accepted. Facts are used to support opinions. For example, "Jane is a bad girl" is an opinion. However, "Jane hit her sister with a baseball bat" is a *fact* upon which the opinion is based. Judgments are opinions—decisions or declarations based on observation or reasoning that express approval or disapproval. Facts report what has happened or exists and come from observation, measurement, or calculation. Facts can be tested and verified whereas opinions and judgments cannot. They can only be supported with facts.

Most statements cannot be so clearly distinguished. "I believe that Jane is a bad girl" is a fact. The speaker knows what he/she believes. However, it obviously includes a judgment that could be disputed by another person who might believe otherwise. Judgments are not usually so firm. They are, rather, plausible opinions that provoke thought or lead to factual development.

Author's Purpose

An author may have more than one purpose in writing.   An **author's purpose** may be to entertain, to persuade, to inform, to describe, or to narrate.

There are no tricks or rules to follow in attempting to determine an author's purpose. It is up to the reader to use his or her judgment.

Read the following paragraph.

> Charles Lindbergh had no intention of becoming a pilot. He was enrolled in the University of Wisconsin until a flying lesson changed the entire course of his life. He began his career as a pilot by performing daredevil stunts at fairs.

The author wrote this paragraph primarily to:

(A) Describe
(B) Inform
(C) Entertain
(D) Narrate

Since the author is simply telling us or informing us about the life of Charles Lindbergh, the correct answer is (B).

Author's Tone and Point of View

The **author's tone** is his or her attitude as reflected in the statement or passage. His or her choice of words will help the reader determine the overall tone of a statement or passage.

Read the following paragraph.

> I was shocked by your article, which said that sitting down to breakfast was a thing of the past. Many families consider breakfast time, family time. Children need to realize the importance of having a good breakfast. It is imperative that they be taught this at a young age. I cannot believe that a writer with your reputation has difficulty comprehending this.

The author's tone in this passage is one of

(A) concern
(B) anger
(C) excitement
(D) disbelief

Since the author directly states that he "cannot believe" the writer feels this way, the answer is (D) disbelief.

Valid and Invalid Arguments

An argument is a generalization that is proven or supported with facts. If the facts are not accurate, the generalization remains unproven. Using inaccurate "facts" to support an argument is called a *fallacy* in reasoning. Some factors to consider in judging whether the facts used to support an argument are accurate are as follows:

1. Are the facts current or are they out of date? For example, if the proposition "birth defects in babies born to drug-using mothers are increasing," then the data must include the latest that is available.
2. Another important factor to consider in judging the accuracy of a fact is its source. Where were the data obtained, and is that source reliable?
3. The calculations on which the facts are based may be unreliable. It's a good idea to run one's own calculations before using a piece of derived information.

Even facts that are true and have a sharp impact on the argument may not be relevant to the case at hand.

1. Health statistics from an entire state may have no relevance, or little relevance, to a particular county or zip code. Statistics from an entire country cannot be used to prove very much about a particular state or county.
2. An analogy can be useful in making a point, but the comparison must match up in all characteristics or it will not be relevant. Analogy should be used very carefully. It is often just as likely to destroy an argument as it is to strengthen it.

The importance or significance of a fact may not be sufficient to strengthen an argument. For example, of the millions of immigrants in the U.S., using a single family to support a solution to the immigration problem will not make much difference overall even though those single-example arguments are often used to support one approach or another. They may achieve a positive reaction, but they will not prove that one solution is better than another. If enough cases were cited from a variety of geographical locations, the information might be significant.

How much is enough? Generally speaking, three strong supporting facts are sufficient to establish the thesis of an argument. For example:

Conclusion: All green apples are sour.

- When I was a child, I bit into a green apple from my grandfather's orchard, and it was sour.
- I once bought green apples from a roadside vendor, and when I bit into one, it was sour.
- My grocery store had a sale on green Granny Smith apples last week, and I bought several only to find that they were sour when I bit into one.

The fallacy in the above argument is that the sample was insufficient. A more exhaustive search of literature, etc., will probably turn up some green apples that are not sour.

Sometimes more than three arguments are too many. On the other hand, it's not unusual to hear public speakers, particularly politicians, cite a long litany of facts to support their positions.

A very good example of the omission of facts in an argument is the résumé of an applicant for a job. The applicant is arguing that he/she should be chosen to be awarded a particular job. The application form will ask for information about past employment, and unfavorable dismissals from jobs in the past may just be omitted. Employers are usually suspicious of periods of time when the applicant has not listed an employer.

A writer makes choices about which facts will be used and which will be discarded in developing an argument. Those choices may exclude anything that is not supportive of the point of view the arguer is taking. It's always a good idea for the reader to do some research to spot the omissions and to ask whether they have impact on acceptance of the point of view presented in the argument.

No judgment is either black or white. If the argument seems too neat or too compelling, there are probably facts that might be relevant that have not been included.

Skill 4.3   Identify strategies to facilitate comprehension before, during, and after reading (e.g., predicting, self-monitoring, questioning, rereading)

Comprehension simply means that the reader can ascribe meaning to text. Even though students may be good with phonics and even know what many words on a page mean, some of them are not good with comprehension because they do not know the strategies that would help them to comprehend. For example, students should know that stories often have structures (beginning, middle, and end). They should also know that when they are reading something and it does not make sense, they will need to employ "fix-up" strategies where they go back into the text they just read and look for clues. Teachers can use many strategies to teach comprehension, including questioning, asking students to paraphrase or summarize, utilizing graphic organizers, and focusing on mental images.

The point of comprehension instruction is not necessarily to focus just on the text(s) students are using at the very moment of instruction, but rather to help them learn the strategies they can use independently with any other text.

Some of the most common methods of instruction are:

- **Summarization:** This is where, either in writing or verbally, students go over the main point of the text, along with strategically chosen details that highlight the main point. This is not the same as paraphrasing, which is saying the same thing in different words. Teaching students how to summarize is very important as it will help them look for the most critical areas in a text, and in non-fiction. For example, it will help them distinguish between main arguments and examples. In fiction, it helps students learn how to focus on the main characters and events and distinguish those from lesser characters and events.
- **Question answering:** While this tends to be over-used in many classrooms, it is still a valid method of teaching students to comprehend. As the name implies, students answer questions regarding a text, either out loud, in small groups, or individually on paper. The best questions are those that cause students to think about the text (rather than just find an answer within the text).

- **Question generating:** This is the opposite of question answering, although students can then be asked to answer their own questions or the questions of peer students. In general, we want students to constantly question texts as they read. This is important because it causes students to become more critical readers. To teach students to generate questions helps them to learn the types of questions they can ask, and it gets them thinking about how best to be critical of texts.

- **Graphic organizers:** Graphic organizers are graphical representations of content within a text. For example, Venn Diagrams can be used to highlight the difference between two characters in a novel or two similar political concepts in a Social Studies textbook. Or, a teacher can use flow-charts with students to talk about the steps in a process (for example, the steps of setting up a science experiment or the chronological events of a story). Semantic organizers are similar in that they graphically display information. The difference, usually, is that semantic organizers focus on words or concepts. For example, a word web can help students make sense of a word by mapping from the central word all the similar and related concepts to that word.

- **Text structure:** Often in non-fiction, particularly in textbooks, and sometimes in fiction, text structures will give important clues to readers about what to look for. Often, students do not know how to make sense of all the types of headings in a textbook and do not realize that, for example, the side-bar story about a character in history is not the main text on a particular page in the history textbook. Teaching students how to interpret text structures gives them tools with which to tackle other similar texts.

- **Monitoring comprehension:** Students need to be aware of their comprehension, or lack of it, in particular texts. So, it is important to teach students what to do when suddenly text stops making sense. For example, students can go back and re-read the description of a character. Or, they can go back to the table of contents or the first paragraph of a chapter to see where they are headed.

- **Textual marking:** This is where students interact with the text as they read. For example, armed with Post-it Notes, students can insert questions or comments regarding specific sentences or paragraphs within the text. This enables students to focus on the importance of the small things, particularly when they are reading larger works (such as novels in high school). It also gives students a reference point at which to go back into the text when they need to review something.

- **Discussion:** Small group or whole-class discussion stimulates thoughts about texts and gives students a larger picture of the impact of those texts. For example, teachers can strategically encourage students to discuss concepts related to the text. This helps students learn to consider texts within larger societal and social concepts; or teachers can encourage students to provide personal opinions in discussion. By listening to various students' opinions, all students in a class will be able to see the wide range of possible interpretations and thoughts regarding one text.

Many people mistakenly believe the terms "research-based" or "research-validated" or "evidence-based" relate mainly to specific programs, such as early reading textbook programs. While research does validate that some of these programs are effective, much research has been conducted regarding the effectiveness of particular instructional strategies. In reading, many of these strategies have been documented in the report from the National Reading Panel (2000). However, just because a strategy has not been validated as effective by research does not necessarily mean that it is not effective with certain students in certain situations. The number of strategies out there far outweighs researchers' ability to test their effectiveness. Some of the strategies listed above have been validated by rigorous research, while others have been shown consistently to help improve students' reading abilities in localized situations. There simply is not enough space to list all the strategies out there that have been proven effective; just know that the above strategies are very commonly cited ones that work in a variety of situations.

Making Predictions

One theory or approach to the teaching of reading that gained currency in the late sixties and the early seventies was the importance of asking inferential and critical thinking questions of the reader which would challenge and engage the children in the text. This approach to reading went beyond the literal level of what was stated in the text to an inferential level of using text clues to make predictions and to a critical level of involving the child in evaluating the text. While asking engaging and thought-provoking questions is still viewed as part of the teaching of reading, it is only viewed currently as a component of the teaching of reading.

Prior Knowledge

Prior knowledge can be defined as all of an individual's prior experiences, learning, and development which precede his/her entering a specific learning situation or attempting to comprehend a specific text. Sometimes prior knowledge can be erroneous or incomplete. Obviously, if there are misconceptions in a child's prior knowledge, these must be corrected so the child's overall comprehension skills can continue to progress. Prior knowledge, of even kindergarteners, includes their accumulated positive and negative experiences both in and out of school.

These might range from wonderful family travels, watching television, visiting museums and libraries, to visiting hospitals or prisons and surviving poverty. Whatever the prior knowledge the child brings to the school setting, the independent reading and writing the child does in school immeasurably expands his/her prior knowledge and hence broadens his/her reading comprehension capabilities.

Literary response skills are dependent on prior knowledge, schemata and background. Schemata (the plural of schema) are those structures which represent generic concepts stored in our memory. Effective comprehension of text, whether by adults or children, uses both their schemata and prior knowledge PLUS the ideas from the printed text for reading comprehension, and graphic organizers help organize this information.

Graphic Organizers

Graphic organizers solidify in a chart format a visual relationship among various reading and writing ideas including: sequence, timelines, character traits, fact and opinion, main idea and details, differences and likenesses (generally done using a VENN DIAGRAM of interlocking circles, KWL Chart, etc). These charts and formats are essential for providing scaffolding for instruction through activating pertinent prior knowledge.

KWL charts are exceptionally useful for reading comprehension by outlining what they KNOW, what they WANT to know, and what they've LEARNED after reading. Students are asked to activate prior knowledge about a topic and further develop their knowledge about a topic using this organizer. Teachers often opt to display and maintain KWL charts throughout a text to continually record pertinent information about students' reading.

When the teacher first introduces the K-W-L strategy, the children should be allowed sufficient time to brainstorm in response to the first question, what all of them in the class or small group actually know about the topic. The children should have a three-columned K-W-L worksheet template for their journals and there should be a chart to record the responses from class or group discussion. The children can write under each column in their own journal, and should also help the teacher with notations on the chart. This strategy involves the children actually gaining experience in note taking and having a concrete record of new data and information they have gleaned from the passage about the topic.

Depending on the grade level of the participating children, the teacher may also want to channel them into considering categories of information they hope to find out from the expository passage. For instance, they may be reading a book on animals to find out more about the animal's habitats during the winter or about the animal's mating habits.

When children are working on the middle -- What I want to know section of their K-W-L strategy sheet -- the teacher may want to give them a chance to share what they would like to learn further about the topic and help them to express it in question format.

K-W-L is useful and can even be introduced as early as grade 2 with extensive teacher discussion support. It not only serves to support the child's comprehension of a particular expository text, but also models for children a format for note taking. Beyond note taking, when the teacher wants to introduce report writing, the K-W-L format provides excellent outlines and question introductions for at least three paragraphs of a report.

Cooper (2004) recommends this strategy for use with thematic units and with reading chapters in required science, social studies, or health text books. In addition to its usefulness with thematic unit study, K-W-L is wonderful for providing the teacher with a concrete format to assess how well children have absorbed pertinent new knowledge within the passage (by looking at the third L section). Ultimately it is hoped that students will learn to use this strategy, not only under explicit teacher direction with templates of K-W-L sheets, but also on their own by informally writing questions they want to find out about in their journals and then going back to their own questions and answering them after the reading.

COMPETENCY 5.0 UNDERSTAND READING INSTRUCTION AND STUDY SKILLS IN THE CONTENT AREAS

Skill 5.1 Apply knowledge of reading strategies to promote learning in the content areas (e.g., activating and developing prior knowledge)

First, teachers should realize that historically, there are two broad sides regarding the construction of meaning, the application of strategies, etc. One is behavioral learning. Behavioral learning theory suggests that people learn socially or through some sort of stimulation or repetition. For example, when we touch a hot stove, we learn not to do that again. Or, when we make a social error, and are made fun of for it, we learn proper social conventions. Or, we learn to produce something by watching someone do the same thing.

The other broad theory is cognitive. Cognitive learning theories suggest that learning takes place in the mind, and that the mind processes ideas through brain mapping and connections with other material and experiences. In other words, with behaviorism, learning is somewhat external. We see something, for example, and then we copy it. With cognitive theories, learning is internal. For example, we see something, analyze it in our minds, and make sense of it for ourselves. Then, if we choose to copy it, we do, but we do so having internalized (or thought about) the process.

Today, even though behavioral theories exist, most educators believe children learn cognitively. So, for example, when teachers introduce new topics by relating those topics to information students are already familiar with or exposed to, they are expecting that students will be able to better integrate new information into their memories by attaching it to something that is already there. Or, when teachers apply new learning to real-world situations, they are expecting that the information will make more sense when it is applied to a real situation. In all of the examples given in this standard, the importance is the application of new learning to something concrete. In essence, what is going on with these examples is that the teacher is slowly building on knowledge or adding knowledge to what students already know. Cognitively, this makes a great deal of sense. Think of a file cabinet. When we already have files for certain things, it's easy for us to find a file and throw new information into it. When we're given something that doesn't fit into one of the pre-existing files, we struggle to know what to do with it. The same is true with human minds.

Skill 5.2 Understand strategies for reading for different purposes

One of the common fallacies students have about reading comes from the ways in which students are taught to read. Sure, as students are being taught to read, they must learn the strategies of careful reading, which includes sounding out words, focusing on fluency, obtaining meaning, etc. However, at points in the learning-to-read process, teachers can help students learn that there are various reasons why people read. Sometimes people read for pleasure, in which case they can decide whether to skim through quickly for the content or read slowly to savor ideas and language. Other times, people simply want to find information fast, in which case they will skim or scan. In some texts, re-reading is necessary to fully comprehend information.

Skimming is when readers read quickly while paying little attention to specific words. This is often done when readers want a full picture of a text, but do not want to focus on the details. Skimming can be done as a preview or a review purpose. When done as a preview, often readers will look to see what it is they can expect from the text. When done as a review, readers will hope to be reminded of the main points through the skim.

Scanning is a bit different from skimming. In skimming, readers read connected text quickly. In scanning, readers go straight to specific ideas, words, sections, or examples. They pick and choose what they will read within a text. This is done when the reader does not need to know everything from a text.

In-depth reading is the reading most people think is the only legitimate type of reading. Strangely, though, all types of reading are done by all types of people— all the time! In-depth reading is done when readers want to enjoy a text or learn from it thoroughly. For the most part, in this type of reading, readers will move forward quickly and not stop to focus on a specific word or idea, although sometimes this is necessary. The main idea of this type of reading, though, is that readers not skip over or read fast to get information. They read everything carefully and thoroughly.

The final type of reading is re-reading. This comes in many forms. Sometimes, whole texts must be re-read for the concepts. This is usually the case when the text is difficult. Re-reading can also be done as someone is doing regular in-depth reading. For example, a word, concept, or a few ideas may need to be reviewed before the reader can go on. Another method of re-reading is re-reading a whole text months or years after reading it the first time. This is done when readers realize that through their life experiences since the first reading, they will view the text in a different light.

All these methods are acceptable forms of reading, however, all must be done with specific purposes in mind. Generally, it is not a good idea to skim or scan a class novel; however, skimming and scanning through a textbook may be acceptable if only a few ideas are crucial.

Skill 5.3 **Apply knowledge of study skills in the content areas (e.g., note-taking skills, interpretation of graphs, use of reference materials)**

Most libraries will only allow the downloading and printing of 75 pages of information during any given month. The point is to provide the user with hardcopy of specific information in a limited and environmentally friendly manner. Libraries limit the number of pages that could be wasted during a singular download which limits the number of trees needed to conduct Internet research and subsequent printing. Once the information is collected and categorized according to the research design and outline, the user can begin to take notes on the gathered information to create a cut and paste format for the final report.

Being effective note takers requires consistent technique whether the mode of note taking is on 5X7 note cards, lined notebook pages, or on a computer. Organizing all collected information according to a research outline will allow the user to take notes on each section and begin the writing process. If the computer is used, then the actual format of the report can be word-processed and information input to speed up the writing process of the final research report. Creating a title page and the bibliography page will allow each downloaded report to have its resources cited immediately in that section.

Note taking involves identification of specific resources that include the author's or organization's name, year of publication, title, publisher location and publisher. When taking notes, whether on the computer or using note cards, use the author's last name and page number on cited information. In citing information for major categories and subcategories on the computer, create a file for notes that includes summaries of information and direct quotes. When direct quotes are put into a word file, the cut and paste process for incorporation into the report is quick and easy.

In outline information, it is crucial to identify the headings and subheadings for the topic being researched. When researching information, it is easier to cut and paste information under the indicated headings in creating a visual flow of information for the report. In the actual drafting of the report, the writer is able to lift direct quotations and citations from the posted information to incorporate in the writing.

COMPETENCY 6.0   **UNDERSTAND CHARACTERISTIC FEATURES OF CHILDREN'S LITERATURE AND STRATEGIES TO PROMOTE STUDENTS' LITERARY RESPONSE AND ANALYSIS**

Skill 6.1   **Demonstrate knowledge of major works, authors, and genres of children's literature**

The social changes of post-World War II significantly affected adolescent literature. The Civil Rights movement, feminism, the protest of the Vietnam Conflict, and issues surrounding homelessness, neglect, teen pregnancy, drugs, and violence bred a new vein of contemporary fiction that helps adolescents understand and cope with the world they live in.

Popular books for preadolescents deal more with establishing relationships with members of the opposite sex (Sweet Valley High series) and learning to cope with their changing bodies, personalities, or life situations, as in Judy Blume's *Are You There, God? It's Me, Margaret*. Adolescents are still interested in the fantasy and science fiction genres as well as popular juvenile fiction. Middle school students still read the Little House on the Prairie series and the mysteries of the Hardy boys and Nancy Drew. Teens value the works of Emily and Charlotte Bronte, Willa Cather, Jack London, William Shakespeare, and Mark Twain as much as those of Piers Anthony, S.E. Hinton, Madeleine L'Engle, Stephen King, and J.R.R. Tolkein, because they're fun to read, whatever their underlying worth may be.

Older adolescents enjoy the writers in these genres.

- Fantasy: Piers Anthony, Ursula LeGuin, Ann McCaffrey
- Horror: V.C. Andrews, Stephen King
- Juvenile fiction: Judy Blume, Robert Cormier, Rosa Guy, Virginia Hamilton, S.E. Hinton, M.E. Kerr, Harry Mazer, Norma Fox Mazer, Richard Newton Peck, Cynthia Voight, and Paul Zindel.
- Science fiction: Isaac Asimov, Ray Bradbury, Arthur C. Clarke, Frank Herbert, Larry Niven, H.G. Wells.

These classic and contemporary works combine the characteristics of multiple theories. Functioning at the concrete operations stage (Piaget), being of the "good person" orientation (Kohlberg), still highly dependent on external rewards (Bandura), and exhibiting all five needs previously discussed from Maslow's hierarchy, these eleven to twelve year olds should appreciate the following titles, grouped by reading level. These titles are also cited for interest at that grade level and do not reflect high-interest titles for older readers who do not read at grade level. Some high interest titles will be cited later.

Reading level 6.0 to 6.9

- Barrett, William. *Lilies of the Field*
- Cormier, Robert. *Other Bells for Us to Ring*
- Dahl, Roald. *Danny, Champion of the World; Charlie and the Chocolate*
- *Factory*
- Lindgren, Astrid. *Pippi Longstocking*
- Lindbergh, Anne. *Three Lives to Live*
- Lowry, Lois. *Rabble Starkey*
- Naylor, Phyllis. *The Year of the Gopher, Reluctantly Alice*
- Peck, Robert Newton. *Arly*
- Speare, Elizabeth. *The Witch of Blackbird Pond*
- Sleator, William. *The Boy Who Reversed Himself*

For seventh and eighth grades

Most seventh and eighth grade students, according to learning theory, are still functioning cognitively, psychologically, and morally as sixth graders. As these are not inflexible standards, there are some twelve and thirteen year olds who are much more mature socially, intellectually, and physically than the younger children who share the same school. They are becoming concerned with establishing individual and peer group identities, which presents conflicts with breaking from authority and the rigidity of rules. Some at this age are still tied firmly to the family and its expectations while others identify more with those their own age or older. Enrichment reading for this group must help them cope with life's rapid changes or provide escape and thus must be either realistic or fantastic depending on the child's needs. Adventures and mysteries (the Hardy Boys and Nancy Drew series) are still popular today. These preteens also become more interested in biographies of contemporary figures rather than legendary figures of the past.

Reading level 7.0 to 7.9

- Armstrong, William. *Sounder*
- Bagnold, Enid. *National Velvet*
- Barrie, James. *Peter Pan*
- London, Jack. *White Fang, Call of the Wild*
- Lowry, Lois. *Taking Care of Terrific*
- McCaffrey, Anne. The *Dragonsinger* series
- Montgomery, L. M. *Anne of Green Gables* and sequels
- Steinbeck, John. *The Pearl*
- Tolkien, J. R. R. *The Hobbit*
- Zindel, Paul. *The Pigman*

Reading level 8.0 to 8.9

- Cormier, Robert. *I Am the Cheese*
- McCullers, Carson. *The Member of the Wedding*
- North, Sterling. *Rascal*
- Twain, Mark. *The Adventures of Tom Sawyer*
- Zindel, Paul. *My Darling , My Hamburger*

Skill 6.2   Understand strategies to develop students' responses to literature (e.g., guided reading, reading logs, discussions about literature)

As with any learning experience, it is important for students to connect learning with real world experiences. Therefore with reading, students should be given opportunities to experience reading outside the classroom or traditional classroom methods.

Literature Circles involve a group discussion involving no more than six children, but usually fewer than four, who have read the same work of literature (narrative or expository text). They talk about key parts of the work, relate it to their own experience, listen to the responses of others, and discuss how parts of the text relate to the whole. Literature circles are excellent for the classroom setting because they mimic book clubs while providing a format for the discussion meeting for students who are learning to discuss literature.

Book clubs are another excellent opportunity for students to discuss reading in an open setting. Whether it is at a local library, school library group, recess group, or parent-child evening reading program, book clubs promote reading in an enjoyable setting unattached from traditional homework assignments and book reports.

Skill 6.3   Analyze the use of children's literature to promote respect for and appreciation of diversity

When a writer contextualizes a work of fiction or nonfiction in the cultural realm, there are inherent lessons and cultural issues that advance the plot and theme of the work. Cultural values and ideas are actually point of view works that focus on a particular cultural theme or resolve.

The characters and protagonist generally reflect the culture of the writing or create a plot that is dynamic in the oppositional position of the point of view. Understanding the audience targeted for the writing is important if the writer wants to target a specific age group or gender. Creating a work for a high school audience is quite different from creating a similar theme targeting early readers who may not have the maturity to understand the response elicited from them.

The point of many cultural pieces is to immerse the reader into a world different from their own worldview. The thought is that if the reader is able to empathize with someone or some issues culturally different, his/her world is broadened and expanded from a cultural perspective.

Skill 6.4 Understand elements of literary analysis and criticism (e.g., analyzing story elements, recognizing features of different genres, interpreting figurative language)

The major literary genres include allegory, ballad, drama, epic, epistle, essay, fable, novel, poem, romance, and the short story.

Allegory: A story in verse or prose with characters representing virtues and vices. There are two meanings, symbolic and literal. John Bunyan's The Pilgrim's Progress is the most renowned of this genre.

Ballad: An *in medias res* story told or sung, usually in verse and accompanied by music. Literary devices found in ballads include the refrain, or repeated section, and incremental repetition, or anaphora, for effect. Earliest forms were anonymous folk ballads. Later forms include Coleridge's Romantic masterpiece, "The Rime of the Ancient Mariner."

Drama: Plays – comedy, modern, or tragedy - typically in five acts. Traditionalists and neoclassicists adhere to Aristotle's unities of time, place and action. Plot development is advanced via dialogue. Literary devices include asides, soliloquies and the chorus representing public opinion. Greatest of all dramatists/playwrights is William Shakespeare. Other dramaturges include Ibsen, Williams, Miller, Shaw, Stoppard, Racine, Moliére, Sophocles, Aeschylus, Euripides, and Aristophanes.

Epic: A long poem, usually of book length, reflecting values inherent in the generative society. Epic devices include an invocation to a Muse for inspiration, purpose for writing, universal setting, protagonist and antagonist who possess supernatural strength and acumen, and interventions of a God or the gods. Understandably, there are very few epics: Homer's Iliad and Odyssey, Virgil's Aeneid, Milton's Paradise Lost, Spenser's The Fairie Queene, Barrett Browning's Aurora Leigh, and Pope's mock-epic, The Rape of the Lock.

Epistle: A letter that is not always originally intended for public distribution, but due to the fame of the sender and/or recipient, becomes public domain. An epistle treats broad themes and does not address or respond to a specific situation.

Essay: Typically a limited-length prose work focusing on a topic and propounding a definite point of view and authoritative tone. Great essayists include Carlyle, Lamb, DeQuincy, Emerson and Montaigne, who is credited with defining this genre.

Fable: A terse tale offering up a moral or exemplum. Chaucer's "The Nun's Priest's Tale" is a fine example of a *bete fabliau* or beast fable in which animals speak and act in ways characteristically human, illustrating human foibles.

Legend: A traditional narrative or collection of related narratives, popularly regarded as historically factual but actually a mixture of fact and fiction.

Myth: Stories that are more or less universally shared within a culture to explain its history and traditions and origins.

Novel: The longest form of fictional prose containing a variety of characterizations, settings, local color and regionalism. Most have complex plots, expanded description, and attention to detail. Some of the great novelists include Austin, the Brontes, Twain, Tolstoy, Hugo, Hardy, Dickens, Hawthorne, Forster, and Flaubert.

Poem: The only requirement is rhythm. Sub-genres include fixed types of literature such as the sonnet, elegy, ode, pastoral, and villanelle. Unfixed types of literature include blank verse and dramatic monologue.

Romance: A highly imaginative tale set in a fantastical realm dealing with the conflicts between heroes, villains and/or monsters. "The Knight's Tale" from Chaucer's Canterbury Tales, Sir Gawain and the Green Knight and Keats' "The Eve of St. Agnes" are prime representatives.

Short Story: Typically a terse narrative, with less developmental background about characters. It may include description, author's point of view, and tone. Poe emphasized that a successful short story should create one focused impact. Considered great short story writers are Hemingway, Faulkner, Twain, Joyce, Shirley Jackson, Flannery O'Connor, de Maupassant, Saki, Edgar Allen Poe, and Pushkin.

Children's literature is a genre of its own and emerged as a distinct and independent form in the second half of the 18th century. *The Visible World in Pictures* by John Amos Comenius, a Czech educator, was one of the first printed works and the first picture book. For the first time, educators acknowledged that children are different from adults in many respects. Modern educators acknowledge that introducing elementary students to a wide range of reading experiences plays an important role in their mental/social/psychological development. Some of the most common forms of literature specifically for children follow:

Traditional Literature: Traditional literature opens up a world where right wins out over wrong, where hard work and perseverance are rewarded, and where helpless victims find vindication—all worthwhile values that children identify with even as early as kindergarten. In traditional literature, children will be introduced to fanciful beings, humans with exaggerated powers, talking animals, and heroes that will inspire them. For younger elementary children, these stories in Big Book format are ideal for providing predictable and repetitive elements that can be grasped by these children.

Folktales/Fairy Tales: Some examples: The Three Bears, Little Red Riding Hood, Snow White, Sleeping Beauty, Puss-in-Boots, Rapunzel and Rumpelstiltskin. Adventures of animals or humans and the supernatural characterize these stories. The hero is usually on a quest and is aided by other-worldly helpers. More often than not, the story focuses on good and evil and reward and punishment.

Fables: Animals that act like humans are featured in these stories and usually reveal human foibles or sometimes teach a lesson. Example: Aesop's Fables.

Myths: These stories about events from the earliest times, such as the origin of the world, are considered true in their own societies.

Legends: These are similar to myths except that they tend to deal with events that happened more recently. Example: Arthurian legends.

Tall tales: Examples: Paul Bunyan, John Henry, and Pecos Bill. These are purposely exaggerated accounts of individuals with superhuman strength.

Modern Fantasy: Many of the themes found in these stories are similar to those in traditional literature. The stories start out based in reality, which makes it easier for the reader to suspend disbelief and enter worlds of unreality. Little people live in the walls in *The Borrowers* and time travel is possible in *The Trolley to Yesterday*. Including some fantasy tales in the curriculum helps elementary-grade children develop their senses of imagination. These often appeal to ideals of justice and issues having to do with good and evil; and because children tend to identify with the characters, the message is more likely to be retained.

Science Fiction: Robots, spacecraft, mystery, and civilizations from other ages often appear in these stories. Most presume advances in science on other planets or in a future time. Most children like these stories because of their interest in space and the "what if" aspect of the stories. Examples: *Outer Space and All That Junk* and *A Wrinkle in Time*.

Modern Realistic Fiction: These stories are about real problems that real children face. By finding that their hopes and fears are shared by others, young children can find insight into their own problems. Young readers also tend to experience a broadening of interests as the result of this kind of reading. It's good for them to know that a child can be brave and intelligent and can solve difficult problems.

Historical Fiction: *Rifles for Watie* is an example of this kind of story. Presented in a historically-accurate setting, it's about a young boy (16 years) who serves in the Union army. He experiences great hardship but discovers that his enemy is an admirable human being. It provides a good opportunity to introduce younger children to history in a beneficial way.

Biography: Reading about inventors, explorers, scientists, political and religious leaders, social reformers, artists, sports figures, doctors, teachers, writers, and war heroes help children to see that one person can make a difference. They also open new vistas for children to think about when they choose an occupation to fantasize about.

Informational Books: These are ways to learn more about something you are interested in or something that you know nothing about. Encyclopedias are good resources, of course, but a book like *Polar Wildlife* by Kamini Khanduri shows pictures and facts that will capture the imaginations of young children.

Story Elements

Most works of fiction contain a common set of elements that make them come alive to readers. In a way, even though writers do not consciously think about each of these elements as story elements when they sit down to write, all stories essentially contain these "markers" that make them the stories that they are. But, even though all stories have these elements, they are a lot like fingerprints: Each story's story elements are just a bit different.

Let's look at a few of the most commonly discussed elements. The most commonly discussed story element in fiction is plot. Plot is the series of events in a story. Typically, but not always, plot moves in a predictable fashion:

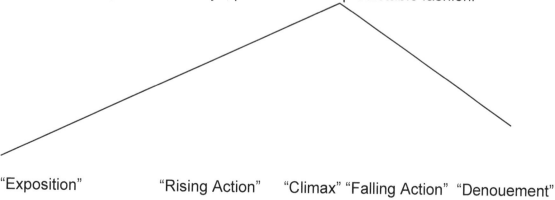

"Exposition"   "Rising Action"   "Climax" "Falling Action" "Denouement"

Exposition is where characters and their situations are introduced. *Rising action* is the point at which conflict starts to occur. *Climax* is the highest point of conflict, often a turning point. *Falling action* is the result of the climax. *Denouement* is the final resolution of the plot.

Character is another commonly studied story element. We will often find in stories heroes, villains, comedic characters, dark characters, etc. When we examine the characters of a story, we look to see who they are and how their traits contribute to the story. Often, because of their characteristics, plot elements become more interesting. For example, authors will pair unlikely characters together in a way that, in turn, creates specific conflict.

The setting of a story is the place or location where it occurs. Often, the specific place is not as important as some of the specifics about the setting. For example, the setting of *The Great Gatsby*, New York, is not as significant as the fact that it takes place amongst incredible wealth. Conversely, *The Grapes of Wrath*, although taking place in Oklahoma and California, has a more significant setting of poverty. In fact, as the story takes place *around* other migrant workers, the setting is even more significant. In a way, the setting serves as a reason for various conflicts to occur.

Themes of stories are the underlying messages, above and beyond all plot elements, that writers want to convey. Very rarely will one find that good literature is without a theme—or a lesson, message, or ideal. The best writers in the English language all seem to want to convey something about human nature or the world, and they turn to literature in order to do that. Common themes in literature are jealousy, money, love, human against corporation or government, etc. These themes are never explicitly stated; rather, they are the result of the portrayal of characters, settings, and plots. Readers get the message even if the theme is not directly mentioned.

Finally, the mood of a story is the atmosphere or attitude the writer conveys through descriptive language. Often, mood fits in nicely with theme and setting. For example, in Edgar Allen Poe's stories, we often find a mood of horror and darkness. We get that from the descriptions of characters and the setting, as well as from specific plot elements. Mood simply helps us better understand the writer's theme and intentions through descriptive, stylistic language.

Figurative Language

Figurative language is present in both fiction and non-fiction. Figurative language is language, usually in fiction or nonfiction prose, that utilizes creative or poetic methods to convey points. Figurative language is used for effect, as well as to make a point stand out. The most common examples of figurative language include hyperbole, metaphor, personification, simile, and idiom. Each is explained below:

Hyperbole: The term, hyperbole, is the literary version of exaggeration. When authors exaggerate in their text, they are using hyperbole. Often, hyperbole is used as irony, often to over-emphasize a point.

Metaphor: A metaphor is any time one thing is used in place of something else in text, signifying some sort of resemblance. For example, we might say that "it is raining cats and dogs." We use this to signify heavy rain. Authors use metaphor for emphasis, creativity, and often clarity. Sometimes, metaphors provide a better picture than accurate language.

Personification: Whenever an author gives life to an inanimate item, personification is used. For example, we might say that the wind is whistling. Authors use personification to provide a more poetic look at common events.

Simile: Similes are comparisons between two objects (or between a person and an object, for example). Similes are like metaphors; however, they typically use "like" or "as" to identify the similarities. For example, love is like a rose.

Idiom: Idioms are locally-flavored phrases or words. For example, a common American idiom, found anywhere in the country, is "break a leg," which is a wish for good luck. However, each region of the country has its own, distinctive idioms, as well. Idioms are used in writing generally to spice the language with local flavor. Often, idioms are used to make characters seem more real--or even to indicate where in the country the action is taking place.

COMPETENCY 7.0 **UNDERSTAND SKILLS AND STRATEGIES INVOLVED IN WRITING FOR VARIOUS PURPOSES**

Skill 7.1 **Analyze factors a writer should consider when writing for a variety of audiences and purposes (e.g., expressive, informative, persuasive), including factors related to selection of topic and mode of written expression**

In the past, teachers have assigned reports, paragraphs and essays that focused on the teacher as the audience with the purpose of explaining information. However, for students to be meaningfully engaged in their writing, they must write for a variety of reasons. Writing for different audiences and aims allows students to be more involved in their writing. If they write for the same audience and purpose, they will continue to see writing as just another assignment. Listed below are suggestions that give students an opportunity to write in more creative and critical ways:

- Write letters to the editor, to a college, to a friend, to another student that would be sent to the intended audience.
- Write stories that would be read aloud to a group (the class, another group of students, to a group of elementary school students) or published in a literary magazine or class anthology.
- Write plays that would be performed.
- Have students discuss the parallels between the different speech styles we use and writing styles for different readers or audiences.
- Allow students to write a particular piece for different audiences.
- Expose students to writing that is on the same topic but with a different audience and have them identify the variations in sentence structure and style.
- As part of the prewriting, have students identify the audience. Make sure students consider the following when analyzing the needs of their audience.
  1. Why is the audience reading my writing? Do they expect to be informed, amused or persuaded?
  2. What does my audience already know about my topic?
  3. What does the audience want or need to know? What will interest them?
  4. What type of language suits my readers?

Remind your students that it is not necessary to identify all the specifics of the audience in the initial stage of the writing process but that at some point they must make some determinations about audience.

- **See also** Skill 7.4

Skill 7.2 **Understand steps and procedures associated with given components of the writing process (e.g., prewriting, gathering and synthesizing information, writing a first draft, revising, proofreading)**

Students gather ideas before writing. Prewriting may include clustering, listing, brainstorming, mapping, free writing, and charting. Providing many ways for a student to develop ideas on a topic will increase his/her chances for success.

Remind students that as they pre-write they need to consider their audience. Prewriting strategies assist students in a variety of ways. Listed below are the most common prewriting strategies students can use to explore, plan and write on a topic. It is important to remember when teaching these strategies that not all prewriting must eventually produce a finished piece of writing. In fact, in the initial lesson of teaching prewriting strategies, it might be more effective to have students practice prewriting strategies without the pressure of having to write a finished product.

- Keep an idea book so they can jot down ideas that come to mind
- Write in a daily journal
- Write down whatever comes to mind; this is called free writing. Students do not stop to make corrections or interrupt the flow of ideas.

A variation of this technique is focused free writing - writing on a specific topic - to prepare for an essay.

- Make a list of all ideas connected with their topic; this is called brainstorming
- Make sure students know that this technique works best when they let their mind work freely. After completing the list, students should analyze the list to see if a pattern or way to group the ideas
- Ask the questions Who? What? When? Where? When? and How? Help the writer approach a topic from several perspectives
- Create a visual map on paper to gather ideas. Cluster circles and lines to show connections between ideas. Students should try to identify the relationship between their ideas. If they cannot see the relationships, have them pair up, exchange papers and have their partners look for some related ideas
- Observe details of sight, hearing, taste, touch, and sound
- Visualize by making mental images of something and write down the details in a list

After they have practiced with each of these prewriting strategies, ask them to pick out the ones they prefer and ask them to discuss how they might use the techniques to help them with future writing assignments. It is important to remember that they can use more than one prewriting strategy at a time. Also they may find that different writing situations suggest certain techniques.

Skill 7.3   Understand developmental stages of a writer, including the use of pictures and developmental spelling

Writing is a recursive process. As students engage in the various stages of writing, they develop and improve not only their writing skills, but their thinking skills as well. Students must understand that writing is a process and typically involves many steps when writing quality work. No matter the level of writer, students should be experienced in the following stages of the writing process. The stages of the writing process are as follows:

Prewriting
Students gather ideas before writing. Prewriting may include clustering, listing, brainstorming, mapping, free writing, and charting. Providing many ways for a student to develop ideas on a topic will increase his/her chances for success. Remind students that as they pre-write they need to consider their audience.

Drafting
Students compose the first draft. Students should follow their notes/writing plan from the prewriting stage.

Revision and Editing
Revise comes from the Latin word *revidere*, meaning, "to see again." Revision is probably the most important step for the writer in the writing process. Here, students examine their work and make changes in wording, details and ideas. Many times, students write a draft and then feel they're done. On the contrary – students must be encouraged to develop, change, and enhance their writing as they go, as well as once they've completed a draft.

As you discuss revision, you begin with discussing the definition of revise. Also, state that all writing must be revised to improve it. After students have revised their writing, it is time for the final editing and proofreading.

Proofreading

Students proofread the draft for punctuation and mechanical errors. There are a few key points to remember when helping students learn to edit and proofread their work.

- It is crucial that students are not taught grammar in isolation, but in context of the writing process
- Ask students to read their writing and check for specific errors like using a subordinate clause as a sentence
- Provide students with a proofreading checklist to guide them as they edit their work

Publishing

Students may have their work displayed on a bulletin board, read aloud in class, or printed in a literary magazine or school anthology.

It is important to realize that these steps are recursive; as a student engages in each aspect of the writing process, he or she may begin with prewriting, write, revise, write, revise, edit, and publish. They do not engage in this process in a lockstep manner; it is more circular.

Developmental Spelling

Spelling instruction should include words misspelled in daily writing, generalizing spelling knowledge, and mastering objectives in progressive phases of development. Developmental stages of spelling:

1) *Pre-phonemic spelling*—Children know that letters stand for a message, but they do not know the relationship between spelling and pronunciation.

2) *Early phonemic spelling*—Children are beginning to understand spelling. They usually write the beginning letter correctly, with the rest consonants or long vowels.

3) *Letter-name spelling*—Some words are consistently spelled correctly. The student is developing a sight vocabulary and a stable understanding of letters as representing sounds. Long vowels are usually used accurately, but silent vowels are omitted. Unknown words are spelled by the child attempting to match the name of the letter to the sound.

4) *Transitional spelling*—This phase is typically entered in late elementary school. Short vowel sounds are mastered and some spelling rules known. They are developing a sense of which spellings are correct and which are not.

5) *Derivational spelling*—This is usually reached from high school to adulthood. This is the stage where spelling rules are being mastered.

How Words Are Built

Knowledge of how words are build can help students with basic and more advanced decoding. A *root word* is the primary base of a word. A *prefix* is the affix (a morpheme that attaches to a base word) that is placed at the start of a root word, but can't make a word on its own. Examples of prefixes include re-, pre-, and un-. A *suffix* follows the root word to which it attaches and appears at the end of the word. Examples of suffixes include –s, -es, -ed, -ly, and –tion. In the word unlikely, "un" is a prefix, "like" is the root work, and "ly" is a suffix.

Skill 7.4   **Compare characteristic features and requirements associated with written materials in various formats (e.g., letter, essay) and modes (e.g., narrative, descriptive, evaluative)**

Discourse, whether in speaking or writing, falls naturally into four different forms: narrative, descriptive, expository, and persuasive. The first question to be asked when reading a written piece, listening to a presentation, or writing is "What's the point?" This is usually called the thesis. If you are reading an essay, when you've finished, you want to be able to say, "The point of this piece is that the foster-care system in America is a disaster." If it's a play, you should also be able to say, "The point of that play is that good overcomes evil." The same is true of any written document or performance. If it doesn't make a point, the reader/listener/viewer is confused or feels that it's not worth the effort. Knowing this is very helpful when you are sitting down to write your own document, be it essay, poem, or speech. What point do you want to make? We make these points in the forms that have been the structure of western thinking since the Greek Rhetoricians.

Persuasion is a piece of writing, a poem, a play, a speech whose purpose is to change the minds of the audience members or to get them to do something. This is achieved in many ways:

1. The credibility of the writer/speaker might lead the listeners/readers to a change of mind or a recommended action.
2. Reasoning is important in persuasive discourse. No one wants to believe that he accepts a new viewpoint or goes out and takes action just because he likes and trusts the person who recommended it. Logic comes into play in reasoning that is persuasive.
3. The third and most powerful force that leads to acceptance or action is emotional appeal. Even if a person has been persuaded logically, reasonably, that he should believe in a different way, he is unlikely to act on it unless he is moved emotionally. A man with resources might be convinced that people suffered in New Orleans after Katrina, but he will not be likely to do anything about it until he is moved emotionally, until he can see dead bodies floating in the dirty water or elderly people stranded on houses. Sermons are good examples of persuasive discourse.

Exposition is discourse whose only purpose is to inform. Expository writing is not interested in changing anyone's mind or getting anyone to take a certain action. It exists to give information. Some examples are driving directions to a particular place or the directions for putting together a toy that arrives unassembled. The writer doesn't care whether you do or don't follow the directions. She only wants to be sure you have the information in case you do decide to use them.

Narration is discourse that is arranged chronologically—something happened, and then something else happened, and then something else happened. It is also called a story. News reports are often narrative in nature as are records of trips, etc.

Description is discourse whose purpose is to make an experience available through one of the five senses—seeing, smelling, hearing, feeling (as with the fingers), and tasting. Descriptive words are used to make it possible for the reader to "see" with her own mind's eye, hear through her own mind's ear, smell through her own mind's nose, taste with her mind's tongue, and feel with her mind's fingers. This is how language moves people. Only by experiencing an event can the emotions become involved. Poets are experts in descriptive language.

Persuasive writing often uses all forms of discourse. The introduction may be a history or background of the idea being presented—exposition. Details supporting some of the points may be stories—narrations. Descriptive writing will be used to make sure the point is established emotionally.

Paraphrase is the rewording of a piece of writing. The result will not necessarily be shorter than the original. It will use different vocabulary and possibly different arrangement of details. Paraphrases are sometimes written to clarify a complex piece of writing. Sometimes material is paraphrased because it cannot be borrowed due to copyright restraints.

Summary is a distilling of the elements of a piece of writing or speech. It will be much shorter than the original. To write a good summary, the writer must determine what the "bones" of the original piece are. What is its structure? What is the thesis and what are the sub-points? A summary does not make judgments about the original; it simply reports the original in condensed form.

Letters are often expository in nature—their purpose is to give information. However, letters are also often persuasive—the writer wants to persuade or get the recipient to do something. They are also sometimes descriptive or narrative—the writer will share an experience or tell about an event.

Research reports are a special kind of expository writing. A topic is researched—explored by some appropriate means such as searching literature, interviewing experts, or even conducting experiments, and the findings will be written up in such a way that a particular audience may know what was discovered. They can be very simple such as delving into the history of an event or very complex such as a report on a scientific phenomenon that requires complicated testing and reasoning to explain. A research reports often reports possible conclusions but puts forth one as the best answer to the question that inspired the research in the first place, which will become the thesis of the report.

COMPETENCY 8.0   ANALYZE WRITTEN WORK IN RELATION TO ITS STATED PURPOSE; EVALUATE AREAS IN NEED OF IMPROVEMENT; AND REVISE WRITTEN TEXTS FOR STYLE, CLARITY, AND ORGANIZATION

Skill 8.1   Evaluate revision strategies for improving the effectiveness of written material in relation to a given purpose (e.g., expressive, informative, persuasive)

Both teachers and students should be aware of the difference between these two writing processes. Revising typically entails substantial changes to a written draft, and it is during this process that the look, idea and feel of a draft may be altered, sometimes significantly. Like revising, editing continues to make changes to a draft; however the changes made during the editing process do more to enhance the ideas in the draft, rather than change or alter them. Finally, proofreading is the stage where grammatical and technical errors are addressed.

Effective teachers realize that revision and editing go hand-in-hand and students often move back and forth between these stages during the course of one written work. Also, these stages must be practiced in small groups, pairs and/or individually. Students must learn to analyze and improve their own work as well as the works of their peers. Some methods to use include:

- Students, working in pairs, analyze sentences for variety.
- Students work in pairs or groups to ask questions about unclear areas in the writing or to help students add details, information, etc.
- Students perform final edit.

To help students revise, provide students with a series of questions that will assist them in revising their writing

- Do the details give a clear picture? Add details that appeal to more than just the sense of sight.
- How effectively are the details organized? Reorder the details if it is needed.
- Are the thoughts and feelings of the writer included? Add personal thoughts and feelings about the subject.

Gone are the days when students engage in skill practice with grammar worksheets. Grammar needs to be taught in the context of the students' own work. Listed below is a series of classroom practices that encourage meaningful context-based grammar instruction, combined with occasional mini-lessons and other language strategies that can be used on a daily basis.

- Connect grammar with the student's own writing while emphasizing grammar as a significant aspect of effective writing.
- Emphasize the importance of editing and proofreading as an essential part of classroom activities.
- Provide students with an opportunity to practice editing and proofreading cooperatively.
- Give instruction in the form of 15-20 minute mini-lessons.
- Emphasize the sound of punctuation by connecting it to pitch, stress, and pause.
- Involve students in all facets of language learning including reading, writing, listening, speaking and thinking. Good use of language comes from exploring all forms of it on a regular basis.

There are a number of approaches that involve grammar instruction in the context of the writing.

Sentence Combining—try to use the student's own writing as much as possible. The theory behind combining ideas and the correct punctuation should be emphasized.

1. Sentence and paragraph modeling—provide students with the opportunity to practice imitating the style and syntax of professional writers.

2. Sentence transforming—give students an opportunity to change sentences from one form to another, i.e. from passive to active, inverting the sentence order, change forms of the words used.

3. Daily Language Practice—introduce or clarify common errors using daily language activities. Use actual student examples whenever possible. Correct and discuss the problems with grammar and usage.

Skill 8.2   Analyze given texts in terms of unity and organization, and make appropriate revisions (e.g., adding topic sentences, reordering sentences or paragraphs, using transitional words and phrases, deleting distracting details)

Effective teachers realize that revision and editing go hand-in-hand and which students often move back and forth between these stages during the course of one written work. Also, these stages must be practiced in small groups, pairs and/or individually. Students must learn to analyze and improve their own work as well as the works of their peers. Some methods to use include:

1. Students, working in pairs, analyze sentences for variety.
2. Students work in pairs or groups to ask questions about unclear areas in the writing or to help students add details, information, etc.
3. Students perform final edit.

Many teachers introduce Writer's Workshop to their students to maximize learning about the writing process. Writer's Workshops vary across classrooms, but the main idea is for students to become comfortable with the writing process to produce written work. A basic Writer's Workshop will include a block of classroom time committed to writing various projects (i.e., narratives, memoirs, book summaries, fiction, book reports, etc). Students use this time to write, meet with others to review/edit writing, make comments on writing, revise their own work, proofread, meet with the teacher, and publish their work.

Teachers who facilitate effective Writer's Workshops are able to meet with students one at a time and can guide each student in their individual writing needs. This approach allows the teacher to differentiate instruction for each student's writing level.

Students need to be trained to become effective at proofreading, revising and editing strategies. Begin by training them using both desk-side and scheduled conferences. Listed below are some strategies to use to guide students through the final stages of the writing process (and these can easily be incorporated into Writer's Workshop).

- Provide some guide sheets or forms for students to use during peer responses
- Allow students to work in pairs and limit the agenda
- Model the use of the guide sheet or form for the entire class
- Give students a time limit or number of written pieces to be completed in a specific amount of time
- Have the students read their partners' papers and ask at least three who, what, when, why, how questions. The students answer the questions and use them as a place to begin discussing the piece
- At this point in the writing process a mini-lesson that focuses on some of the problems your students are having would be appropriate

To help students revise, provide students with a series of questions that will assist them in revising their writing:

1. Do the details give a clear picture? Add details that appeal to more than just the sense of sight.

2. How effectively are the details organized? Reorder the details if it is needed.

3. Are the thoughts and feelings of the writer included? Add personal thoughts and feelings about the subject.

As you discuss revision, you begin with discussing the definition of revise. Also, state that all writing must be revised to improve it. After students have revised their writing, it is time for the final editing and proofreading.

Writing Introductions

It's important to remember that in the writing process, the introduction should be written last. Until the body of the paper has been determined—thesis, development—it's difficult to make strategic decisions regarding the introduction. The Greek rhetoricians called this part of a discourse *exordium*, a "leading into." The basic purpose of the introduction, then, is to lead the audience into the discourse. It can let the reader know what the purpose of the discourse is and it can condition the audience to be receptive to what the writer wants to say. It can be very brief or it can take up a large percentage of the total word count. Aristotle said the introduction could be compared to the flourishes flute players make before their performance—an overture in which the musicians display what they can play best in order to gain the favor and attention of the audience for the main performance.

In order to do this, we must first of all know what we are going to say; who the readership is likely to be; what the social, political, economic, etc., climate is; what preconceived notions the audience is likely to have regarding the subject; and how long the discourse is going to be.

There are many ways to do this:
- Show that the subject is important.
- Show that although the points we are presenting may seem improbable, they are true.
- Show that the subject has been neglected, misunderstood, or misrepresented.
- Explain an unusual mode of development.
- Forestall any misconception of the purpose.
- Apologize for a deficiency.
- Arouse interest in the subject with an anecdotal lead-in.
- Ingratiate oneself with the readership.
- Establish one's own credibility.

The introduction often ends with the thesis, the point or purpose of the paper. However, this is not set in stone. The thesis may open the body of the discussion, or it may conclude the discourse. The most important thing to remember is that the purpose and structure of the introduction should be deliberate if it is to serve the purpose of "leading the reader into the discussion."

Writing Conclusions

It's easier to write a conclusion after the decisions regarding the introduction have been made. Aristotle taught that the conclusion should strive to do five things:

1. Inspire the reader with a favorable opinion of the writer.
2. Amplify the force of the points made in the body of the paper.
3. Reinforce the points made in the body.
4. Rouse appropriate emotions in the reader.
5. Restate in a summary way what has been said.

The conclusion may be short or it may be long depending on its purpose in the paper. Recapitulation, a brief restatement of the main points or certainly of the thesis is the most common form of effective conclusions. A good example is the closing argument in a court trial.

Text Organization

In studies of professional writers and how they produce their successful works, it has been revealed that writing is a process that can be clearly defined although in practice it must have enough flexibility to allow for creativity. The teacher must be able to define the various stages that a successful writer goes through in order to make a statement that has value. There must be a discovery stage when ideas, materials, supporting details, etc., are deliberately collected. These may come from many possible sources: the writer's own experience and observations, deliberate research of written sources, interviews of live persons, television presentations, or the internet.

The next stage is organization where the purpose, thesis, and supporting points are determined. Most writers will put forth more than one possible thesis and in the next stage, the writing of the paper, settle on one as the result of trial and error. Once the paper is written, the editing stage is necessary and is probably the most important stage. This is not just the polishing stage. At this point, decisions must be made regarding whether the reasoning is cohesive—does it hold together? Is the arrangement the best possible one or should the points be rearranged? Are there holes that need to be filled in? What form will the introduction take? Does the conclusion lead the reader out of the discourse or is it inadequate or too abrupt, etc.

It's important to remember that the best writers engage in all of these stages recursively. They may go back to discovery at any point in the process. They may go back and rethink the organization, etc. To help students become effective writers, the teacher needs to give them adequate practice in the various stages and encourage them to engage deliberately in the creative thinking that makes writers successful.

Skill 8.3   Improve the clarity, precision, and effectiveness of given texts through changes in word choice

Most students want to write one draft of their writing and then be finished with it. It takes years of practice to reinforce the idea that they need to revise the writing by elaborating on the words to bring clarity to the topic. Elaboration is the detail or description that brings the characters, places and events in the writing to life. Students need instruction and modeling on how they can add words, reorder sentences or phrases, make good transitions from one paragraph to the next and to take out unnecessary information.

One of the best ways to model this craft of good writing is to read from descriptive books and point out how the author uses words that help the readers see what the author wants them to see. Students also need examples of good writing for comparison with their own writing. This gives them models to go by as they craft their own pieces.

Transition words and phrases help deliver clear connections between the sentences so the writing flows smoothly. Teachers can introduce this in a mini-lesson and then follow up by working with small groups of students who need extra help. A poster displaying a list of transition words in the classroom gives the students a reference they can use when revising their writing. Common transition words and phrases include:

-   Besides
-   Furthermore
-   Therefore
-   In addition to
-   As a result
-   First
-   Next
-   Moreover
-   In order to
-   However
-   Although
-   Meanwhile

Early writers often overuse the word "then" and use it to start every paragraph. Another problem early writers have is that they connect every sentence with the word "and" so that each paragraph consists of one long sentence. Teachers should use models of poor writing to demonstrate how students can improve their writing.

A list of ways students can include elaboration in their writing is:

- Add details about a person, place or event
- Use vocabulary to paint a picture
- Tell how something feels, tastes, smells, sounds or looks
- Make a comparison between two things
- Use the exact words of a character

Writers need to see the difference between vague and specific writing. A good way of describing vague writing is comparing it to the bones of a skeleton. When writers add details or specific word choices, then they add meat to the bones. By reading two separate pieces of writing to students- one that is vague and one that is specific – students can determine which piece was best. The teacher can then dissect each one to show how the revision helped improve the writing.

COMPETENCY 9.0 APPLY KNOWLEDGE OF ENGLISH GRAMMAR AND MECHANICS IN REVISING TEXTS

Skill 9.1 **Evaluate given texts in terms of sentence construction, and make appropriate revisions (e.g., revising run-on sentences, misplaced or dangling modifiers, lack of parallel structure)**

Revise misplaced or dangling modifiers

Particular phrases that are not placed near the one word they modify often result in misplaced modifiers. Particular phrases that do not relate to the subject being modified result in dangling modifiers.

Error:

Weighing the options carefully, a decision was made regarding the punishment of the convicted murderer.

Problem:

Who is weighing the options? No one capable of weighing is named in the sentence; thus, the participle phrase weighing the options carefully dangles. This problem can be corrected by adding a subject of the sentence capable of doing the action.

Correction:

Weighing the options carefully, the judge made a decision regarding the punishment of the convicted murderer.

Sentence completeness

Avoid fragments and run-on sentences. Recognition of sentence elements necessary to make a complete thought, proper use of independent and dependent clauses (see *Use correct coordination and subordination*), and proper punctuation will correct such errors.

Recognize simple, compound, complex, and compound-complex sentences. Use dependent (subordinate) and independent clauses correctly to create these sentence structures.

Simple	Joyce wrote a letter.
Compound	Joyce wrote a letter, and Dot drew a picture.
Complex	While Joyce wrote a letter, Dot drew a picture.
Compound/Complex	When Mother asked the girls to demonstrate their new-found skills, Joyce wrote a letter, and Dot drew a picture.

Note: Do **not** confuse compound sentence elements with compound sentences.

Simple sentence with compound subject
> <u>Joyce</u> and <u>Dot</u> wrote letters.
> The <u>girl</u> in row three and the <u>boy</u> next to her were passing notes across the aisle.

Simple sentence with compound predicate
> Joyce <u>wrote letters</u> and <u>drew pictures</u>.
> The captain of the high school debate team <u>graduated with honors</u> and <u>studied broadcast journalism in college</u>.

Skill 9.2   Revise texts for subject-verb agreement and pronoun-antecedent agreement

Subject-verb agreement

A verb agrees in number with its subject. Making them agree relies on the ability to properly identify the subject.

> One of the boys *was playing* too rough.
> <u>No one</u> in the class, not the teacher nor the students, <u>was</u>
> <u>listening</u> to the message from the intercom.
> The <u>candidates,</u> including a grandmother and a teenager, <u>are debating</u> some controversial issues.

If two singular subjects are connected by *and* the verb must be plural.

> A *man* and his *dog* were jogging on the beach.

If two singular subjects are connected by *or* or *nor,* a singular verb is required.

> Neither Dot nor <u>Joyce</u> has missed a day of school this year.
> Either Fran or Paul is missing.

If one singular subject and one plural subject are connected by *or* or *nor,* the verb agrees with the subject nearest to the verb.

> Neither the coach nor the <u>players</u> were able to sleep on the bus.

If the subject is a collective noun, its sense of number in the sentence determines the verb: singular if the noun represents a group or unit and plural if the noun represents individuals.

> The House of Representatives has adjourned for the holidays.
> The House of Representatives have failed to reach agreement on the subject of adjournment.

Pronoun-Antecedent Agreement

A noun is any word that names a person, place, thing, idea, animal, quality, or activity. A pronoun is a word that is used in place of a noun or more pronouns. The word or word group that a pronoun stands for (or refers to) is called its antecedent.

We use pronouns in many of the sentences that we write. Pronouns add variety to our writing by enabling us to avoid monotonous repetition of nouns. They also help us maintain coherence within and among sentences. Pronouns must agree with their antecedents in number and person. Therefore, if the antecedent is plural, use a plural pronoun; if the antecedent is feminine, use a feminine pronoun. They must show a clear reference to their antecedents as well.

The following are nine different types of pronouns: *personal, possessive, indefinite, reflexive, reciprocal, intensive, interrogative, relative, and demonstrative*.

In order to aid students in revising their texts to correct errors, have them complete the following steps:

- Read focusing only on pronouns.
- Circle each pronoun and draw an arrow to its antecedent.
- Replace the pronoun with a noun to eliminate a vague pronoun reference.
- Supply missing antecedents where needed.
- Place the pronoun so that the nearest noun is its antecedent.

Once the student focuses on pronoun antecedent agreement a few times, they will progress from correcting errors to avoiding errors. The only way to develop a student's skill with pronoun reference, however, is to focus clear attention on pronouns until it becomes a habit of their writing.

Skill 9.3   Use standard verb forms, pronouns, adverbs, adjectives, and plural and possessive forms of nouns in context

Use of verbs (tense)

Present tense is used to express what is currently happening or is always true.
- Randy is playing the piano.
- Randy plays the piano like a pro.

Past tense is used to express action that occurred in a past time.
- Randy learned to play the piano when he was six years old.

Future tense is used to express action or a condition of future time.
- Randy will probably earn a music scholarship.

Present perfect tense is used to express action or a condition that started in the past and is continued to or completed in the present.
- Randy has practiced piano every day for the last ten years. Randy has never been bored with practice.

Past perfect tense expresses action or a condition that occurred as a precedent to some other action or condition.
- Randy had considered playing clarinet before he discovered the piano.

Future perfect tense expresses action that started in the past or the present and will conclude at some time in the future.
- By the time he goes to college, Randy will have been an accomplished pianist for more than half of his life.

Use of verbs (mood)
Indicative mood is used to make unconditional statements; subjunctive mood is used for conditional clauses or wish statements that pose conditions that are untrue. Verbs in subjunctive mood are plural with both singular and plural subjects.

- If I were a bird, I would fly.
- I wish I were as rich as Donald Trump.

Verb conjugation
The conjugation of verbs follows the patterns used in the discussion of tense above. However, the most frequent problems in verb use stem from the improper formation of past and past participial forms.

- Regular verb: believe, believed, (have) believed
- Irregular verbs: run, ran, run; sit, sat, sat; teach, taught, taught

Other problems stem from the use of verbs that are the same in some tenses but have different forms and different meanings in other tenses.

- I lie on the ground. I lay on the ground yesterday. I have lain down.
- I lay the blanket on the bed. I laid the blanket there yesterday. I have laid the blanket every night.
- The sun rises. The sun rose. The sun has risen.
- He raises the flag. He raised the flag. He had raised the flag.
- I sit on the porch. I sat on the porch. I have sat in the porch swing.
- I set the plate on the table. I set the plate there yesterday. I had set the table before dinner.

Two other verb problems stem from misusing the preposition *of* for the verb auxiliary *have* and misusing the verb *ought* (now rare).

Incorrect:	I should of gone to bed.
Correct:	I should have gone to bed.

Incorrect:	He hadn't ought to get so angry.
Correct:	He ought not to get so angry.

Use of pronouns

A pronoun used as a subject of predicate nominative is in nominative case.
- She was the drum majorette.
- The lead trombonists were Joe and he.
- The band director accepted whoever could march in step.

A pronoun used as a direct object, indirect object or object of a preposition is in objective case.
- The teacher praised him.
- She gave him an A on the test.
- Her praise of him was appreciated.
- The students whom she did not praise will work harder next time.

Common pronoun errors occur from misuse of reflexive pronouns: Singular: *myself, yourself, herself, himself, itself* Plural: *ourselves, yourselves, themselves.*

- Incorrect: Jack cut hisself shaving.
- Correct: Jack cut himself shaving.

- Incorrect: They backed theirselves into a corner.
- Correct: They backed themselves into a corner.

Use of adjectives

An adjective should agree with its antecedent in number.

- Those apples are rotten.
- This one is ripe.
- These peaches are hard.

Comparative adjectives end in -er and superlatives in -est, with some exceptions like *worse* and *worst*. Some adjectives that cannot easily make comparative inflections are preceded by *more* and *most*.

- Mrs. Carmichael is the better of the two basketball coaches.
- That is the hastiest excuse you have ever contrived.

Avoid double comparisons.

Incorrect:
> This is the worstest headache I ever had.

Correct:
> This is the worst headache I ever had.

When comparing one thing to others in a group, exclude the thing under comparison from the rest of the group.

Incorrect:
> Joey is larger than any baby I have ever seen. (Since you have seen him, he cannot be larger than himself.)

Correct:
> Joey is larger than any other baby I have ever seen.

Include all necessary words to make a comparison clear in meaning.
> I am as tall as my mother. I am as tall as she (is).
> My cats are better behaved than those of my neighbor.

Plurals

The multiplicity and complexity of spelling rules based on phonics, letter doubling, and exceptions to rules - not mastered by adulthood - should be replaced by a good dictionary. As spelling mastery is also difficult for adolescents, our recommendation is the same. Learning the use of a dictionary and thesaurus will be a more rewarding use of time.

Most plurals of nouns that end in hard consonants or hard consonant sounds followed by a silent *e* are made by adding *s*. Some words ending in vowels only add *s*.

fingers, numerals, banks, bugs, riots, homes, gates, radios, bananas

Nouns that end in soft consonant sounds *s, j, x, z, ch,* and *sh,* add *es*. Some nouns ending in *o* add es.

dresses, waxes, churches, brushes, tomatoes

Nouns ending in *y* preceded by a vowel just add *s*.

boys, alleys

Nouns ending in *y* preceded by a consonant change the *y* to *i* and add *es*.

babies, corollaries, frugalities, poppies

Some nouns' plurals are formed irregularly or remain the same.

sheep, deer, children, leaves, oxen

Some nouns derived from foreign words, especially Latin, may make their plurals in two different ways - one of them Anglicized. Sometimes, the meanings are the same; other times, the two plurals are used in slightly different contexts. It is always wise to consult the dictionary.

appendices, appendixes   criterion, criteria
indexes, indices   crisis, crises

Make the plurals of closed (solid) compound words in the usual way except for words ending in *ful* which make their plurals on the root word.

timelines, hairpins, cupsful

Make the plurals of open or hyphenated compounds by adding the change in inflection to the word that changes in number.

fathers-in-law, courts-martial, masters of art, doctors of medicine

Make the plurals of letters, numbers, and abbreviations by adding *s*.

fives and tens, IBMs, 1990s, *p*s and *q*s (Note that letters are italicized.)

Possessives

Make the possessives of singular nouns by adding an apostrophe followed by the letter s ('s).

> baby's bottle, father's job, elephant's eye, teacher's desk, sympathizer's protests, week's postponement

Make the possessive of singular nouns ending in s by adding either an apostrophe or an ('s) depending upon common usage or sound. When making the possessive causes difficulty, use a prepositional phrase instead. Even with the sibilant ending, with a few exceptions, it is advisable to use the ('s) construction.

> dress's color, species' characteristics or characteristics of the species, James' hat or James's hat, Delores's shirt.

Make the possessive of plural nouns ending in s by adding the apostrophe after the s.

> horses' coats, jockeys' times, four days' time

Make possessives of plural nouns that do not end in s the same as singular nouns by adding 's.

> children's shoes, deer's antlers, cattle's horns

Make possessives of compound nouns by adding the inflection at the end of the word or phrase.

> the mayor of Los Angeles' campaign, the mailman's new truck, the mailmen's new trucks, my father-in-law's first wife, the keepsakes' values, several daughters-in-law's husbands

Note: Because a gerund functions as a noun, any noun preceding it and operating as a possessive adjective must reflect the necessary inflection. However, if the gerundive following the noun is a participle, no inflection is added.

> The general was perturbed by the private's sleeping on duty.

(The word *sleeping* is a gerund, the object of the preposition *by*.

> *but*
> The general was perturbed to see the private sleeping on duty.

(The word *sleeping* is a participle modifying private.)

Skill 9.4 **Make appropriate revisions involving punctuation and capitalization in a given text**

Capitalization

Capitalize all proper names of persons (including specific organizations or agencies of government); places (countries, states, cities, parks, and specific geographical areas); and things (political parties, structures, historical and cultural terms, and calendar and time designations); and religious terms (any deity, revered person or group, sacred writings).

> Percy Bysshe Shelley, Argentina, Mount Rainier National Park, Grand Canyon, League of Nations, the Sears Tower, Birmingham, Lyric Theater, Americans, Midwesterners, Democrats, Renaissance, Boy Scouts of America, Easter, God, Bible, Dead Sea Scrolls, Koran

Capitalize proper adjectives and titles used with proper names.

> California gold rush, President John Adams, French fries, Homeric epic, Romanesque architecture, Senator John Glenn

Note: Some words that represent titles and offices are not capitalized unless used with a proper name.

Capitalized	Not Capitalized
Congressman McKay	the congressman from Florida
Commander Alger	commander of the Pacific Fleet
Queen Elizabeth	the queen of England

Capitalize all main words in titles of works of literature, art, and music. The candidate should be cognizant of proper rules and conventions of punctuation, capitalization, and spelling. Competency exams will generally test the ability to apply the more advanced skills; thus, a limited number of more frustrating rules is presented here. Rules should be applied according to the American style of English, i.e. spelling *theater* instead of *theatre* and placing terminal marks of punctuation almost exclusively within other marks of punctuation.

Punctuation

Quotation marks

In a quoted statement that is either declarative or imperative, place the period inside the closing quotation marks.

> "The airplane crashed on the runway during takeoff."

If the quotation is followed by other words in the sentence, place a comma inside the closing quotation marks and a period at the end of the sentence.

> "The airplane crashed on the runway during takeoff," said the announcer.

In most instances in which a quoted title or expression occurs at the end of a sentence, the period is placed before either the single or double quotation marks.

- The middle school readers were unprepared to understand Bryant's poem 'Thanatopsis.'"
- Early book-length adventure stories like *Don Quixote* and *The Three Musketeers* were known as "picaresque novels."

In sentences that are interrogatory or exclamatory, the question mark or exclamation point should be positioned outside the closing quotation marks if the quote itself is a statement or command or cited title.

- Who decided to lead us in the recitation of the "Pledge of Allegiance"?
- Why was Tillie shaking as she began her recitation, "Once upon a midnight dreary..."?
- I was embarrassed when Mrs. White said, "Your slip is showing"!

In sentences that are declarative but the quotation is a question or an exclamation, place the question mark or exclamation point inside the quotation marks.

- The hall monitor yelled, "Fire! Fire!"
- Cory shrieked, "Is there a mouse in the room?"

(In this instance, the question supersedes the exclamation.)

Using periods with parentheses

Place the period inside the parentheses or brackets if they enclose a complete sentence that is independent of the other sentences around it.

- Stephen Crane was a confirmed alcohol and drug addict. (He admitted as much to other journalists in Cuba.)

If the parenthetical expression is a statement inserted within another statement, the period in the enclosure is omitted.

- Mark Twain used the character Indian Joe (he also appeared in *The Adventures of Tom Sawyer*) as a foil for Jim in *The Adventures of Huckleberry Finn*.

Commas

Separate two or more coordinate adjectives modifying the same word and three or more nouns, phrases, or clauses in a list.

- Maggie's hair was dull, dirty, and lice-ridden.
- Dickens portrayed the Artful Dodger as a skillful pickpocket, loyal follower of Fagin, and defendant of Oliver Twist.
- Ellen daydreamed about getting out of the rain, taking a shower, and eating a hot dinner.
- In Elizabethan England, Ben Johnson wrote comedy, Christopher Marlowe wrote tragedies, and William Shakespeare composed both.

Use commas to separate antithetical or complimentary expressions from the rest of the sentence.

- The veterinarian, not his assistant, would perform the delicate surgery.
- The more he knew about her, the less he wished he had known.
- Randy hopes to, and probably will, get an appointment to the Naval Academy.
- His thorough, though esoteric, scientific research could not easily be understood by high school students.

Semicolons

Use semicolons to separate independent clauses when the second clause is introduced by a transitional adverb. (These clauses may also be written as separate sentences, preferably by placing the adverb within the second sentence.)

- The Elizabethans modified the rhyme scheme of the sonnet; thus, it
- was called the English sonnet.

  or

- The Elizabethans modified the rhyme scheme of the sonnet. It thus was called the English sonnet.

Use semicolons to separate items in a series that are long and complex or have internal punctuation.

- The Italian Renaissance produced masters in the fine arts: Dante Alighieri, author of the *Divine Comedy;* Leonardo da Vinci, painter of *The Last Supper;* and Donatello, sculptor of the *Quattro Coronati*, the four saints.
- The leading scorers in the WNBA were Haizhaw Zheng, averaging 23.9 points per game; Lisa Leslie, 22; and Cynthia Cooper, 19.5.

Colons

Place a colon at the beginning of a list of items. (Note its use in the sentence about Renaissance Italians on the previous page.)

- The teacher directed us to compare Faulkner's three symbolic novels: *Absalom, Absalom; As I Lay Dying;* and *Light in August*.

Do **not** use a comma if the list is preceded by a verb.

- Three of Faulkner's symbolic novels are *Absalom, Absalom; As I Lay Dying,* and *Light in August*.

Dashes

Place dashes to denote sudden breaks in thought.

- Some periods in literature - the Romantic Age, for example - spanned different time periods in different countries.

Use dashes instead of commas if commas are already used elsewhere in the sentence for amplification or explanation.

- The Fireside Poets included three Brahmans - James Russell Lowell, Henry David Wadsworth, Oliver Wendell Holmes - and John Greenleaf Whittier.

Use italics to punctuate the titles of long works of literature, names of periodical publications, musical scores, works of art and motion picture television, and radio programs. (When unable to write in italics, students should be instructed to underline in their own writing where italics would be appropriate.)

The Idylls of the King	*Hiawatha*	*The Sound and the Fury*
Mary Poppins	*Newsweek*	*The Nutcracker Suite*

COMPETENCY 10.0   UNDERSTAND SKILLS AND STRATEGIES INVOLVED IN LISTENING FOR VARIOUS PURPOSES

Skill 10.1   Compare listening strategies in terms of their appropriateness for given contexts and purposes (e.g., acquiring information, appreciating literature read aloud, interpreting and evaluating information)

Listening is not a skill that is talked about much, except when someone clearly does not listen. Listening is, however, a very specific skill for very specific circumstances. There are two aspects of listening that warrant attention. The first is comprehension. This is, simply, understanding what someone says, the purposes behind the message, and the contexts in which it is said. The second is purpose. While someone may completely understand a message, what is the listener supposed to do with it? Just nod and smile? Go out and take action? While listening comprehension is indeed a significant skill in itself that deserves a lot of focus in the classroom (much in the same way that reading comprehension does), we will focus on purpose here. Often, when we understand the purpose of listening in various contexts, comprehension will be much easier. Furthermore, when we know the purpose of listening, we can better adjust our comprehension strategies.

First, when complex or new information is provided to us orally, we must analyze and interpret that information. What is the author's most important point? How do the figures of speech impact meaning? How are conclusions reached? Often, making sense of this information can be difficult when presented orally—first, because we have no place to go back and review material already stated; second, because oral language is so much less predictable than written language. However, when we focus on extracting the meaning, message, and speaker's purpose, rather than just "listen" and wait for things to make sense for us—in other words, when we are more "active" in our listening—we have greater success in interpreting speech.

Second, listening is often done for the purpose of enjoyment. We like to listen to stories; we enjoy poetry; we like radio dramas and theater. Listening to literature can also be a great pleasure. The problem today is that students have not learned out to extract great pleasure on a wide scale from listening to literature, poetry, or language read aloud. Perhaps this is because we have not done a good enough job of showing students how listening to literature, for example, can indeed be more interesting than television or video games. In the classrooms of exceptional teachers, we will often find that students are captivated by the reading-aloud of good literature. It is refreshing and enjoyable to just sit and soak in the language, story, and poetry of literature being read aloud. Therefore, we must teach students *how* to listen and enjoy such work. We do this by making it fun and giving many possibilities and alternatives to capture the wide array of interests in each classroom.

Finally, we will discuss listening in large and small group conversation. The difference here is that conversation requires more than just listening: It involves feedback and active involvement. This can be particularly challenging because in our culture we are trained to move conversations along, to discourage silence in a conversation, and to always get in the last word. This poses significant problems for the art of listening. In a discussion, for example, when we are preparing our next response—rather than listening to what others are saying—we do a large disservice to the entire discussion. Students need to learn how listening carefully to others in discussions actually promotes better responses on the part of subsequent speakers. One way teachers can encourage this in both large and small group discussions is to expect students to respond *directly* to the previous student's comments before moving ahead with their new comments. This will encourage them to pose their new comments in light of the comments that came just before them.

Skill 10.2   Analyze barriers to effective listening and strategies for active listening

Oral speech can be very difficult to follow. First, we have no written record in which to "re-read" things we didn't hear or understand. Second, oral speech can be much less structured and even than written language. Yet, aside from re-reading, many of the skills and strategies that help us in reading comprehension can help us in listening comprehension. For example, as soon as we start listening to something new, we should tap into our prior knowledge in order to attach new information to what we already know. This will not only help us understand the new information more quickly, it will also assist us in remembering the material.

We can also look for transitions between ideas. Sometimes, in oral speech, this is pretty simple when voice tone or body language changes. Of course, we don't have the luxury of looking at paragraphs in oral language, but we do have the animation that comes along with live speech. Human beings have to try very hard to be completely non-expressive in their speech. Listeners should take advantage of this and notice how the speaker changes character and voice in order to signal a transition of ideas.

Speaking of animation of voice and body language, listeners can also better comprehend the underlying intent of authors when they notice nonverbal cues. Simply looking to see expression on the face of a speaker can do more to signal irony, for example, than trying to extract irony from actual words. And often in oral speech, unlike written text, elements like irony are not indicated by the actual words, but rather by the tone and nonverbal cues.

One good way to follow oral speech is to take notes and outline major points. Because oral speech can be more circular (as opposed to linear) than written text, it can be of great assistance to keep track of an author's message. Students can learn this strategy in many ways in the classroom: by taking notes of the teacher's oral messages, as well as other students' presentations and speeches.

Other classroom methods can help students learn good listening skills. For example, teachers can have students practice following complex directions. They can also have students orally retell stories—or retell (in writing or in oral speech) oral presentations of stories or other materials. These activities give students direct practice in the very important skills of listening. They provide students with outlets in which they can slowly improve their abilities to comprehend oral language and take decisive action based on oral speech.

Skill 10.3 **Apply knowledge of factors affecting the ability to listen effectively and construct meaning from oral messages in various listening situations (e.g., ability to recognize nonverbal cues, to use prior knowledge, to distinguish fact from opinion, to recognize transitions, to identify faulty reasoning)**

Teachers should relate to students the specific purpose of their reading assignment. This will help them to:

- ASSOCIATE: Relate ideas to each other.
- VISUALIZE: Try to see pictures in your mind as you read.
- CONCENTRATE: Have a specific purpose for reading.
- REPEAT: Keep telling yourself important points and associate details to these points.

Oral language (listening and speaking) involves receiving and understanding messages sent by other people and also expressing our own feelings and ideas. Students must learn that listening is a communication process; in order to be successful must be an active process. In other words, they must be an active participant in this communication process. In active listening, meaning and evaluation of a message must occur before a student can respond to the teacher.

Evaluating messages

Analyzing the speech of others is an excellent technique to help students improve their own public speaking abilities. Because in most circumstances students cannot view themselves as they give speeches and presentations, when they get the opportunity to critique, question, and analyze others' speeches, they begin to learn what works and what doesn't work in effective public speaking. However, a very important word of warning: DO NOT have students critique each others' public speaking skills. It could be very damaging to a student to have his or her peers point out what did not work in a speech. Instead, video is a great tool teachers can use. Any appropriate source of public speaking can be used in the classroom for students to analyze and critique.

Some of the things students can pay attention to include the following:

- Volume: A speaker should use an appropriate volume—not too loud to be annoying, but not too soft to be inaudible.
- Pace: The rate at which words are spoken should be appropriate—not too fast to prohibit understanding, but not too slow so as to put listeners to sleep.
- Pronunciation: A speaker should make sure words are spoken clearly. Listeners do not have a text to go back and re-read things they didn't catch.
- Body language: While animated body language can help a speech, too much of it can be distracting. Body language should help convey the message, not detract from it.
- Word choice: The words speakers choose should be consistent with their intended purpose and the audience.
- Visual aids: Visual aids, like body language, should enhance a message. Many visual aids can detract from the message.

Overall, instead of telling students to keep these factors in mind when presenting information orally, having them view speakers who these things well and poorly will help them know and remember the next time they give a speech.

Voice: Many people fall into one of two traps when speaking: using a monotone, or talking too fast. These are both caused by anxiety. A monotone restricts your natural inflection, but can be remedied by releasing tension in upper and lower body muscles. Talking too fast on the other hand, is not necessarily a bad thing if the speaker is exceptionally articulate. If not though, or if the speaker is talking about very technical things, it becomes far too easy for the audience to become lost. When you talk too fast and begin tripping over your words, consciously pause after every sentence you say. Don't be afraid of brief silences. The audience needs time to absorb what you are saying.

Volume: Problems with volume, whether too soft or too loud, can usually be combated with practice. If you tend to speak too softly, have someone stand in the back of the room and give you a signal when your volume is strong enough. If possible, have someone in the front of the room as well to make sure you're not overcompensating with excessive volume. Conversely, if you have a problem with speaking too loud, have the person in the front of the room signal you when your voice is soft enough and check with the person in the back to make sure it is still loud enough to be heard. In both cases, note your volume level for future reference. Don't be shy about asking your audience, "Can you hear me in the back?" Suitable volume is beneficial for both you and the audience.

Pitch: Pitch refers to the length, tension and thickness of a person's vocal bands. As your voice gets higher, the pitch gets higher. In oral performance, pitch reflects upon the emotional arousal level. More variation in pitch typically corresponds to more emotional arousal, but can also be used to convey sarcasm or highlight specific words.

Posture: Maintain a straight, but not stiff posture. Instead of shifting weight from hip to hip, point your feet directly at the audience and distribute your weight evenly. Keep shoulders orientated towards the audience. If you have to turn your body to use a visual aid, turn 45 degrees and continue speaking towards the audience.

Movement: Instead of staying glued to one spot or pacing back and forth, stay within four to eight feet of the front row of your audience, and take maybe a step or half-step to the side every once in a while. If you are using a lectern, feel free to move to the front or side of it to engage your audience more. Avoid distancing yourself from the audience, you want them to feel involved and connected.

Gestures: Gestures are a great way to keep a natural atmosphere when speaking publicly. Use them just as you would when speaking to a friend. They shouldn't be exaggerated, but they should be utilized for added emphasis. Avoid keeping your hands in your pockets or locked behind your back, wringing your hands and fidgeting nervously, or keeping your arms crossed.

Eye Contact: Many people are intimidated by using eye contact when speaking to large groups. Interestingly, eye contact usually helps the speaker overcome speech anxiety by connecting with their attentive audience and easing feelings of isolation. Instead of looking at a spot on the back wall or at your notes, scan the room and make eye contact for one to three seconds per person.

Responding to messages

How students respond to messages is more than communication going from one person's mouth to the teacher's ear. In addition to the words, messages are transferred by eye contact, physical closeness, the tone of voice, visual cues, and overall body language. Language employs symbols— gestures, visual clues, or spoken sounds—to represent communication between the teacher and the student. Children first learn to respond to messages by listening to and understanding what they hear (supported by overall body language); next, they experiment with expressing themselves through speaking.

As children become proficient in language, they expect straight messages from the teacher. A straight message is one in which words, vocal expression, and body movements are all congruent. Students need to feel secure and safe. If the message is not straight; if the words say one thing but the tone and facial expression say another, the child is confused. When students are confused, they often feel threatened in the school environment.

Remembering message content

Reading is more than pronouncing the words correctly; the reader has to gain meaning from the words. A competent reader can pronounce the words on a page; remember what they mean, and learn information from them.

The processes that increase the student's ability to remember.

- ASSOCIATION: When you associate, you make the things you want to remember relate to each other in some way.
- VISUALIZATION: Visualization helps you to create a strong, vivid memory. Try to picture in your mind what you wish to remember.
- CONCENTRATION: Concentration can be defined as focusing attention on one thing and to one thing only. How can you learn to concentrate better? Visualizing will help because it forces attention to one thing only. If you try to see specific pictures as you read, it will help you to concentrate. Making sure of your purpose is a third way to force concentration. When you read for a particular purpose, you will concentrate on what you read.
- REPETITION: When you have difficulty remembering textbook information, you should repeat the procedures for associating, visualizing, and concentration. The repetition will help retain the information in your memory.

COMPETENCY 11.0 UNDERSTAND SKILLS AND STRATEGIES INVOLVED IN SPEAKING FOR VARIOUS PURPOSES

Skill 11.1 Analyze ways in which features of oral language (e.g., choice of language, rate, pitch, tone, volume) and nonverbal cues (e.g., body language, visual aids) affect communication in given situations

Analyzing the speech of others is a very good technique for helping students to improve their own public speaking abilities. Because in most circumstances, students cannot view themselves as they give speeches and presentations, when they get the opportunity to critique, question, and analyze others' speeches, they begin to learn what works and what doesn't work in effective public speaking. However, a very important word of warning: DO NOT have students critique each others' public speaking skills. It could be very damaging to a student to have his or her peers point out what did not work in a speech. Instead, video is a great tool teachers can use. Any appropriate source of public speaking can be used in the classroom for students to analyze and critique.

Some of the things students can pay attention to include the following:

- Volume: A speaker should use an appropriate volume—not too loud to be annoying, but not too soft to be inaudible.
- Pace: The rate at which words are spoken should be appropriate—not too fast to make the speech non-understandable, but not too slow so as to put listeners to sleep.
- Pronunciation: A speaker should make sure words are spoken clearly. Listeners do not have a text to go back and re-read things they didn't catch.
- Body language: While animated body language can help a speech, too much of it can be distracting. Body language should help convey the message, not detract from it.
- Word choice: The words speakers choose should be consistent with their intended purpose and the audience.
- Visual aids: Visual aids, like body language, should enhance a message. Many visual aids can be distracting, and that detracts from the message.

Overall, instead of telling students to keep these factors in mind when presenting information orally, having them view speakers who do these things well and poorly will help them know and remember the next time they give a speech.

Voice: Many people fall into one of two traps when speaking: using a monotone or talking too fast. These are both caused by anxiety. A monotone restricts your natural inflection, but can be remedied by releasing tension in upper and lower body muscles. Talking too fast on the other hand, is not necessarily a bad thing if the speaker is exceptionally articulate. If not though, or if the speaker is talking about very technical things, it becomes far too easy for the audience to become lost. When you talk too fast and begin tripping over your words, consciously pause after every sentence you say. Don't be afraid of brief silences. The audience needs time to absorb what you are saying.

Volume: Problems with volume, whether too soft or too loud, can usually be overcome with practice. If you tend to speak too softly, have someone stand in the back of the room and give you a signal when your volume is strong enough. If possible, have someone in the front of the room as well to make sure you're not overcompensating with excessive volume. Conversely, if you have a problem with speaking too loud, have the person in the front of the room signal you when your voice is soft enough and check with the person in the back to make sure it is still loud enough to be heard. In both cases, note your volume level for future reference. Don't be shy about asking your audience, "Can you hear me in the back?" Suitable volume is beneficial for both you and the audience.

Pitch: Pitch refers to the length, tension and thickness of a person's vocal bands. As your voice gets higher, the pitch gets higher. In oral performance, pitch reflects upon the emotional arousal level. More variation in pitch typically corresponds to more emotional arousal, but can also be used to convey sarcasm or highlight specific words.

Posture: Maintain a straight, but not stiff, posture. Instead of shifting weight from hip to hip, point your feet directly at the audience and distribute your weight evenly. Keep shoulders orientated towards the audience. If you have to turn your body to use a visual aid, turn 45 degrees and continue speaking towards the audience.

Movement: Instead of staying glued to one spot or pacing back and forth, stay within four to eight feet of the front row of your audience, and take maybe a step or half-step to the side every once in a while. If you are using a lectern, feel free to move to the front or side of it to engage your audience more. Avoid distancing yourself from the audience, you want them to feel involved and connected.

Gestures: Gestures are a great way to keep a natural atmosphere when speaking publicly. Use them just as you would when speaking to a friend. They shouldn't be exaggerated, but they should be utilized for added emphasis. Avoid keeping your hands in your pockets or locked behind your back, wringing your hands and fidgeting nervously, or keeping your arms crossed.

Eye Contact: Many people are intimidated by using eye contact when speaking to large groups. Interestingly, eye contact usually *helps* the speaker overcome speech anxiety by connecting with their attentive audience and easing feelings of isolation. Instead of looking at a spot on the back wall or at your notes, scan the room and make eye contact for one to three seconds per person.

Skill 11.2   Evaluate various methods of organizing and presenting thoughts, feelings, ideas, and information for different audiences and purposes (e.g., giving instructions, participating in group discussions, persuading an audience, entertaining)

In public speaking, not all speeches deserve the same type of speaking style. For example, when providing a humorous speech, it is important to utilize body language in order to accent humorous moments. However, when giving instructions, it is extremely important to speak clearly and slowly, carefully noting the mood of the audience, so that if there is general confusion on peoples' faces, the speaker can go back and review something. In group discussions, it is important for speakers to ensure that they are listening to other speakers carefully and tailoring their messages so that the messages fit into the general mood and location of the discussion at hand. When giving an oral presentation, the mood should be both serious and friendly. The speaker should focus on ensuring that the content is covered, while also relating to audience members as much as possible.

As students practice these skills, they can receive guidance and modeling from video of various types of speeches appropriate to the types they are giving. Also, the various attributes of each type of oral speaking strategy should be covered with students so they clearly hear the differences.

Skill 11.3   Recognize factors affecting oral communication and nonverbal cues in different situations

It used to be that we thought of speaking and communication only in terms of effective and non-effective. Today, we realize that there is more to communication than just good and bad. We must take into consideration that we must adjust our communication styles for various audiences. While we should not stereotype audiences, we can still recognize that certain methods of communication are more appropriate with certain people than with others. Age is an easy one to consider: Adults know that when they talk to children, they should come across pleasant and non-threatening, and they should use vocabulary that is simple for children to understand. On the other hand, teenagers realize that they should not speak to their grandmothers they way the speak with their peers. When dealing with communications between cultures and genders, people must be sensitive, considerate, and appropriate.

How do teachers help students understand these "unspoken" rules of communication? Well, these rules are not easy to communicate in regular classroom lessons. Instead, teachers must model these behaviors, and they must have high expectations for students (clearly communicated, of course) inside and outside the classroom walls.

Teachers must also consider these aspects as they deal with colleagues, parents, community members, and even students. They must realize that all communication should be tailored so that it conveys appropriate messages and tones to listeners.

Skill 11.4 Apply knowledge of language conventions appropriate to a variety of social situations (e.g., informal conversations, job interviews)

Informal and formal language is a distinction made on the basis of the occasion as well as the audience. At a "formal" occasion, for example, a meeting of executives or of government officials, even conversational exchanges are likely to be more formal. A cocktail party or a golf game is an example where the language is likely to be informal. Formal language uses fewer or no contractions, less slang, longer sentences, and more organization in longer segments.

Speeches delivered to executives, college professors, government officials, etc., is likely to be formal. Speeches made to fellow employees are likely to be informal. Sermons tend to be formal; Bible lessons will tend to be informal.

Different from the basic writing forms of discourse is the art of debating, discussion, and conversation. The ability to use language and logic to convince the audience to accept your reasoning and to side with you is an art. This form of writing/speaking is extremely confined/structured, logically sequenced, with supporting reasons and evidence. At its best, it is the highest form of propaganda. A position statement, evidence, reason, evaluation and refutation are integral parts of this writing schema.

Interviewing provides opportunities for students to apply expository and informative communication. It teaches them how to structure questions to evoke fact-filled responses. Compiling the information from an interview into a biographical essay or speech helps students to list, sort, and arrange details in an orderly fashion.

Speeches that encourage them to describe persons, places, or events in their own lives or oral interpretations of literature help them sense the creativity and effort used by professional writers.

COMPETENCY 12.0   UNDERSTAND MAJOR IDEAS, ERAS, THEMES, DEVELOPMENTS, AND TURNING POINTS IN THE HISTORY OF OKLAHOMA, THE UNITED STATES, AND THE WORLD; AND ANALYZE THEIR SIGNIFICANCE FROM MULTIPLE PERSPECTIVES

Skill 12.1   Analyze the societal effects of major developments in world history (e.g., the agricultural revolution, the scientific revolution, the industrial revolution, the information revolution)

The **Scientific Revolution** was characterized by a shift in scientific approach and ideas. Near the end of the sixteenth century Galileo Galilei introduced a radical approach to the study of motion. He moved from attempts to explain why objects move the way they do and began to use experiments to describe precisely how they move. He also used experimentation to describe how forces affect non-moving objects. Other scientists continued in the same approach. Outstanding scientists of the period included Johannes Kepler, Evangelista Torricelli, Blaise Pascal, Isaac Newton and Leibniz. This was the period when experiments dominated scientific study. This method was particularly applied to the study of physics.

The **Agricultural Revolution** occurred first in England. It was marked by experimentation that resulted in increased production of crops from the land and a new and more technical approach to the management of agriculture. The revolution in agricultural management and production was hugely enhanced by the industrial revolution and the invention of the steam engine. The introduction of steam-powered tractors greatly increased crop production and significantly decreased labor costs. Developments in Agriculture were also enhanced by the scientific revolution and the learning from experimentation that led to philosophies of crop rotation and soil enrichment. Improved systems of irrigation and harvesting also contributed to the growth of agricultural production.

The **Industrial Revolution**, which began in Great Britain and spread elsewhere, was the development of power-driven machinery (fueled by coal and steam) leading to the accelerated growth of industry with large factories replacing homes and small workshops as work centers. The lives of people changed drastically, and a largely agricultural society changed to an industrial one. In Western Europe, the period of empire and colonialism began. The industrialized nations seized and claimed parts of Africa and Asia in an effort to control and provide the raw materials needed to feed the industries and machines in the "mother country". Later developments included power based on electricity and internal combustion, replacing coal and steam.

The Information Revolution refers to the sweeping changes during the latter half of the twentieth century as a result of technological advances and a new respect for the knowledge or information provided by trained, skilled and experienced professionals in a variety of fields. This approach to understanding a number of social and economic changes in global society arose from the ability to make computer technology both accessible and affordable. In particular, the development of the computer chip has led to such technological advances as the Internet, the cell phone, Cybernetics, wireless communication, and the related ability to disseminate and access a massive amount of information quite readily.

In terms of economic theory and segmentation, it is now the norm to think of three basic economic sectors: agriculture and mining, manufacturing, and "services." Indeed, labor is now often divided between manual labor and informational labor. The fact that businesses are involved in the production and distribution, processing and transmission of information has, according to some, created a new business sector.

Skill 12.2   **Understand the principal political, social, economic, and geographic characteristics of ancient civilizations and the connections and interactions among these civilizations**

Prehistory is defined as the period of man's achievements before the development of writing. In Stone Age cultures, there were three different periods. They are the **Lower Paleolithic Period** with the use of crude tools. The **Upper Paleolithic Period** exhibiting a greater variety of better-made tools and implements, the wearing of clothing, highly organized group life, and skills in art. And finally the **Neolithic Period** which was marked by domesticated animals, food production, the arts of knitting, spinning and weaving cloth, starting fires through friction, building houses rather than living in caves, the development of institutions including the family, religion, and a form of government or the origin of the state.

Ancient civilizations were those cultures which developed to a greater degree and were considered advanced. These included the following eleven with their major accomplishments.

Egypt made numerous significant contributions including construction of the great pyramids; development of hieroglyphic writing; preservation of bodies after death; making paper from papyrus; contributing to developments in arithmetic and geometry; the invention of the method of counting in groups of 1-10 (the decimal system); completion of a solar calendar; and laying the foundation for science and astronomy.

The ancient civilization of the **Sumerians** invented the wheel; developed irrigation through use of canals, dikes, and devices for raising water; devised the system of cuneiform writing; learned to divide time; and built large boats for trade. The Babylonians devised the famous **Code of Hammurabi**, a code of laws.

The ancient **Assyrians** were warlike and aggressive due to a highly organized military and used horse-drawn chariots.

The **Hebrews**, also known as the ancient Israelites instituted "monotheism," which is the worship of one God, Yahweh.

The **Minoans** had a system of writing using symbols to represent syllables in words. They built palaces with multiple levels containing many rooms, water and sewage systems with flush toilets, bathtubs, hot and cold running water, and bright paintings on the walls.

The **Mycenaeans** changed the Minoan writing system to aid their own language and used symbols to represent syllables.

The **Phoenicians** were sea traders well known for their manufacturing skills in glass and metals and the development of their famous purple dye. They became so proficient in navigation that they were able to sail by the stars at night. Further, they devised an alphabet using symbols to represent single sounds, which was an improved extension of the Egyptian writing system.

In **India**, the caste system was developed, the principle of zero in mathematics was discovered, and the major religion of Hinduism was begun. In **India**, Hinduism was a continuing influence along with the rise of Buddhism. Industry and commerce developed along with extensive trading with the Near East. Outstanding advances in the fields of science and medicine were made along with being among the first to be active in navigation and maritime enterprises during this time.

China began building the Great Wall; practiced crop rotation and terrace farming; increased the importance of the silk industry, and developed caravan routes across Central Asia for extensive trade. Also, they increased proficiency in rice cultivation and developed a written language based on drawings or pictographs (no alphabet symbolizing sounds as each word or character had a form different from all others). China is considered by some historians to be the oldest, uninterrupted civilization in the world and was in existence around the same time as the ancient civilizations founded in **Egypt**, **Mesopotamia**, and the **Indus Valley**. The Chinese studied nature and weather; stressed the importance of education, family, and a strong central government; followed the religions of Buddhism, Confucianism, and Taoism; and invented such things as gunpowder, paper, printing, and the magnetic compass.

The ancient **Persians** developed an alphabet; contributed the religions/philosophies of **Zoroastrianism**, **Mithraism**, and **Gnosticism**; and allowed conquered peoples to retain their own customs, laws, and religions.

The classical civilization of **Greece** reached the highest levels in man's achievements based on the foundations already laid by such ancient groups as the Egyptians, Phoenicians, Minoans, and Mycenaeans.

Among the more important contributions of Greece were the Greek alphabet derived from the Phoenician letters, which formed the basis for the Roman alphabet and our present-day alphabet. Extensive trading and colonization resulted in the spread of the Greek civilization. The love of sports, with emphasis on a sound body, led to the tradition of the Olympic Games. Greece was responsible for the rise of independent, strong city-states. Note the complete contrast between independent, freedom-loving Athens with its practice of pure democracy, i.e. direct, personal, active participation in government by qualified citizens, and the rigid, totalitarian, militaristic Sparta. Other important areas that the Greeks are credited with influencing include drama, epic and lyric poetry, fables, myths centered on the many gods and goddesses, science, astronomy, medicine, mathematics, philosophy, art, architecture, and recording historical events. The conquests of Alexander the Great spread Greek ideas to the areas he conquered and brought to the Greek world many ideas from Asia including the value of ideas, wisdom, curiosity, and the desire to learn as much about the world as possible.

A most interesting and significant characteristic of the Greek, Hellenistic, and Roman civilizations was "secularism" where emphasis shifted away from religion to the state. Men were not absorbed in or dominated by religion as had been the case in Egypt and the nations located in Mesopotamia. Religion and its leaders did not dominate the state and its authority was greatly diminished.

The civilization in **Japan** appeared during this time, having borrowed much of their culture from China. It was the last of these classical civilizations to develop. Although they used, accepted, and copied Chinese art, law, architecture, dress, and writing, the Japanese refined these into their own unique way of life, including incorporating the religion of Buddhism into their culture.

The civilizations in **Africa** south of the Sahara were developing the refining and use of iron, especially for farm implements and later for weapons. Trading was overland using camels and at important seaports. The Arab influence was extremely important, as was their later contact with Indians, Christian Nubians, and Persians. In fact, their trading activities were probably the most important factor in the spread of and assimilation of different ideas and stimulation of cultural growth.

The **Vikings** had a lot of influence at this time, with spreading their ideas and knowledge of trade routes and sailing, accomplished first through their conquests and later through trade.

In other parts of the world were the **Byzantine** and **Saracenic** (or Islamic) civilizations, both dominated by religion. The major contributions of the Saracens were in the areas of science and philosophy. Included were accomplishments in astronomy, mathematics, physics, chemistry, medicine, literature, art, trade and manufacturing, agriculture, and a marked influence on the Renaissance period of history. The **Byzantines** (Christians) made important contributions in art and the preservation of Greek and Roman achievements including architecture (especially in Eastern Europe and Russia), the Code of Justinian and Roman law.

The ancient empire of **Ghana** occupied an area that is now known as Northern Senegal and Southern Mauritania. There is no absolute certainty regarding the origin of this empire. Oral history dates the rise of the empire to the seventh century BCE. Most believe, however, that the date should be placed much later. Many believe the nomads who were herding animals on the fringes of the desert posed a threat to the early Soninke people, who were an agricultural community. In times of drought, it is believed the nomads raided the agricultural villages for water and places to pasture their herds. It is believed that these farming communities formed a loose confederation for protection that eventually became the empire of ancient Ghana.

The empire's economic vitality was determined by geographical location. It was situated midway between the desert, which was the major source of salt and the gold fields. This location along the trade routes of the camel caravans provided exceptional opportunity for economic development. The caravans brought copper, salt, dried fruit, clothing, manufactured goods, etc. For these goods, the people of Ghana traded kola nuts, leather goods, gold, hides, ivory and slaves. In addition, the empire collected taxes on every trade item that entered the boundaries of the empire. With the revenue from the trade goods tax, the empire supported a government, an army that protected the trade routes and the borders, the maintenance of the capital, and primary market centers. But it was control of the gold fields that gave the empire political power and economic prosperity. The location of the gold fields was a carefully guarded secret. By the tenth century, Ghana was very rich and controlled an area about the size of the state of Texas. Demand for this gold sharply increased in the ninth and tenth centuries as the Islamic states of Northern Africa began to mint coins. As the gold trade expanded, so did the empire. The availability of local iron ore enabled the early people of the Ghana kingdom to make more efficient farm implements and effective weapons.

The **Tang Dynasty** extended from 618 to 907. Its capital was the most heavily populated of any city in the world at the time. Buddhism was adopted by the imperial family (Li) and became an integral part of Chinese culture. The emperor, however, feared the monasteries and began to take action against them in the 10th century. Confucianism experienced a rebirth during the time of this dynasty as an instrument of state administration. Following a civil war, the central government lost control of local areas. Warlords arose in 907, and China was divided into north and south. These areas came to be ruled by short-lived minor dynasties. A major political accomplishment of this period was the creation of a class of career government officials, who functioned between the populace and the government. This class of "scholar-officials" continued to fulfill this function in government and society until 1911.

The period of the Tang Dynasty is generally considered a pinnacle of Chinese civilization. Through contact with the Middle East and India, the period of the Tang Dynasty was marked by great creativity in many areas. Block printing was invented, and made much information and literature available to wide audiences. In science, astronomers calculated the paths of the sun and the moon and the movements of the constellations. This facilitated the development of the calendar. In agriculture, such technologies as cultivating the land by setting it on fire, the curved-shaft plow, separate cultivation of seedlings, and sophisticated irrigation systems increased productivity. Hybrid breeds of horses and mules were created to strengthen the labor supply. In medicine, there were achievements like the understanding of the circulatory system and the digestive system and great advances in pharmacology. Ceramics was another area in which great advances were made. A new type of glazing was invented that gave Tang Dynasty porcelain and earthenware its unique appearance through three-colored glazing.

In literature, the poetry of the period is generally considered the best in the entire history of Chinese literature. The rebirth of Confucianism led to the publication of many commentaries on the classical writings. Encyclopedias on several subjects were produced, as well as histories and philosophical works.

Skill 12.3   Understand the history of interactions among American Indian peoples and European Americans in Oklahoma and the western United States

Archaeologists have discovered evidence of the presence of Native peoples, near present-day Anadarko, of the Clovis culture that dates to about 9000 BCE. From 500 to 1300 CE, a group called "Mound Builders" lived near the Arkansas/Oklahoma border. Artifacts indicate that these people were skilled artisans with an advanced economy. The culture was extinct by the time explorers discovered the mounds in the seventeenth and eighteenth centuries. The region was claimed by the **Quapaw** and **Osage** tribes.

The Osage Indians settled in northeastern Oklahoma around 1796. This area soon became part of the United States in the Louisiana Purchase. A group of Cherokees settled near the Osage after migrating from the East Coast, which resulted in a struggle for territory between the two tribes, with white settlers caught in the middle. The government was able to achieve a truce with the Osage Chief Clermont that included the tribe ceding seven million acres of land to the government. Members of the tribe continued to attack and in 1825 were forced to turn over all of their land to the government. The Osage moved to the Kansas territory until it was opened to white settlers. In 1870, the government sold the remainder of the Osage lands, gave the money to the tribe, and opened a reservation for them. When oil was discovered on this reservation land, the Osage people became the wealthiest in the nation.

The Quapaw sold 45 million acres of land to the U.S. government before 1820 (for $18,000). In 1824 the tribal chiefs were induced with $500 each and alcohol to give up the rest of their property to the government. The Quapaw then settled near the Red River on land given to them by another tribe. The tribe was dramatically thinned during the following years by crop failures. The survivors scattered. They did not reorganize until 1890 when they were granted a very small piece of land in Indian Territory. The discovery of zinc and lead on this land has brought royalties that have supported the tribe.

The lands taken from the Quapaw and the Osage became Indian Territory. This became the home of the "Five Civilized Tribes" when they were driven out of their ancestral homes in the Southeastern part of the country, following the "Trail of Tears." These tribes were called "civilized" because they had advanced systems of government, education and law enforcement. The five tribes were: Choctaw, Chickasaw, Cherokee, Creek and Seminole. The most tragic relocation experience was that of the Cherokee. Forced to cross Missouri and Arkansas during a harsh winter, many of the tribe died and were buried along the route. This journey came to be known as **The Trail of Tears**.

By 1856 the five tribes had settled in Indian Territory and each had established a national domain (not a reservation). As they built their own cultures, forming their own constitutional governments, establishing public education, building strong economies and strong legal systems, these tribes also laid the foundation that would guide them through territorial existence and into statehood and modern society.

One of the Cherokee survivors of the Trail of Tears was **Sequoyah**. Fascinated by the ability of whites to write, he studied and experimented for 12 years and eventually created "an 86-letter syllabary" for the Cherokee language. It was easy to learn and quickly become the tribe's communication standard.

After the Civil War, the western portions of Indian Territory were confiscated by the government for the settlement of other tribes who were being relocated from the western parts of the nation because their villages stood in the way of progress. These tribes included the Cheyenne, Arapaho, Kiowa, and Comanche. Among those who were resettled at this time were **Geronimo** (the great Apache warrior) and the Cheyenne Chief **Black Kettle**.

The incursion of white settlers into the Indian lands created resentment and strengthened the determination of the Indians to maintain their territorial rights. There were numerous skirmishes between the Indians and the white settlers, some of which continued into the twentieth century. The Five Civilized Tribes tried to maintain autonomy, even attempting to organize an Indian state called Sequoyah. The idea was rejected by the U.S. government, and a plan that united the two territories into a single state prevailed in 1907. Indians and whites then united to develop the government, the economy, and the cultural assets of the new state. The **Constitution of Oklahoma** incorporates many elements of the constitutions of the governments of the Five Civilized Tribes and embraces equality in ways that established the patterns for other states.

Oklahoma has the largest Indian population of any state in the nation and is home to the tribal councils of more than 35 tribes.

Oklahoma is generally believed to have been first explored by the Spanish in the sixteenth century. Coronado crossed the western part of the state in 1541 in search of the "city of gold". It is said that a Spanish priest, Father Gilbert, led a mining expedition into the Wichita Mountains as early as 1657.

French explorers followed shortly after the settlement of Louisiana, and French trade with the Indians dates back to the early eighteenth century. The territory was included in the Louisiana Purchase, and was set apart by the United States in 1834 as an unorganized territory for the use of the Five Civilized Tribes (the Cherokees, Creeks, Seminoles, Choctaws, and Chickasaws). The tribes were forcibly removed from the southeastern states and forced to make their way to the Oklahoma Indian Territory, an event known as "The Trail of Tears."

The tribes established governments with legislative councils, governors, courts, and schools. They became very prosperous, and in the years before the Civil War, they held large numbers of slaves. At the end of the Civil War, they were forced to make new treaties with the United States. In 1866, the Creek Indians ceded part of their lands in Indian Territory to the US for $0.30 per acre, and the Seminoles sold their entire holdings at $0.15 per acre.

White men were forbidden by law to settle within the Indian lands, and a large amount of this land remained unoccupied. In 1879 systematic agitation led to the opening of these lands to white settlement. The agitators were called "boomers" (the source of the state's nickname). In 1880 it became necessary to use military troops to remove settlers who had crept into the territory. On April 22, 1889, nearly 2,000,000 acres of territory were declared open for settlement. The expectant pioneers had to be kept back by troops until the hour of the opening of the lands, and then a mad race for the best farms and town sites followed. The area acquired a population of approximately 100,000 within twenty-four hours, single towns such as Guthrie and Oklahoma City having from 10,000 to 15,000 each, during the first few days. There were, in fact, 6 land runs between 1889 and 1895. Settlers came from every part of the nation, as well as such countries as Poland, Germany, Ireland and Slavic nations.

The strip of territory known as the Panhandle originally belonged to Texas, but when Texas was admitted to the Union as a slave state it was compelled to give up that part of its territory. For a time this region was a part of no state or territory and had no established law, thus frequently called "No Man's Land." It became the haven of outlaws, and was not made a part of Oklahoma until 1890. In 1891 Oklahoma's admission as a state was defeated in the U.S. Senate. Finally, in 1906, provision was made for the admission of Oklahoma and Indian Territory as one state, if approved in each territory. The union was approved, and a constitution was drafted by delegates from both territories and adopted by the people. At this time, a governor was elected and prohibition was adopted by vote of the people.

In 1910 the "grandfather's clause" was passed, restricting the Negro vote by property and educational tests. This was declared unconstitutional by the U.S. Supreme Court in 1915.

Texas settlers were raising an abundant supply of beef, but had to move the cattle to the railroads in Kansas for shipment to the East, where there was great demand for beef. Oklahoma lay between the cattle ranches and the railroad. As cattle drives crossed the plains of Oklahoma, many of the "cowboys" recognized the advantages of building cattle ranches closer to the railroad among the grassy plains of the state.

After the cattlemen and settlers moved into Oklahoma and the Indian Territory, outlaws soon followed. By the late 1800s, law enforcement had not been firmly established and the landscape offered a number of places to hide. Among the outlaws and the lawmen who tracked them were:

- The outlaw Bill Doolin
- Marshal Heck Thomas
- Bass Reeves, believed to be the first African American deputy marshal West of the Mississippi River
- Judge Isaac C. Parker, known as "the hanging judge"
- Belle Star

As the oil business began to grow in the early twentieth century, many whites came to the state to seek their fortune. Many became quite rich. The early quarter of the century was a time of some political unrest. Many diverse groups of people had settled in the state. "Black towns" (populated by African Americans who chose to live separately) began to form throughout the state, perhaps partly in response to the tendency of the whites to abide by the Jim Crow laws which permitted separating people and carried a bias against any non-whites. One of the most deadly race riots is U.S. history occurred in 1921 in Tulsa. The Socialist Party was somewhat successful in Oklahoma during this time. Their rejection of the Jim Crow laws and their willingness to embrace African American and Native American voters, and their willingness to change some of the traditional ideology when it was in their best interest, were the primary reasons for their success. The Party was crushed in the period following WWI.

During the Great Depression, drought and poor agricultural practices combined to cause the Dust Bowl. The crop failures and losses of farms led many to leave the state. Many relocated to California, where they tended to form their own communities and came to be called "Okies". After the Great Depression, the oil boom and the post-war upswing in the economy led to the rise of tribal sovereignty as well as growth of suburban areas. In 1995 Oklahoma captured the attention of the world as the scene of one of the worst acts of terrorism in U.S. History when the **Federal Building** in Oklahoma City was bombed.

Skill 12.4   Analyze the roles and contributions of individuals and groups to U.S. social, political, economic, cultural, and religious life, including historically underrepresented groups

During the colonial period, political parties, as the term is now understood, did not exist. The issues which divided the people, were centered on the relations of the colonies to the mother country. There was initially little difference of opinion on these issues. About the middle of the eighteenth century, after England began to develop a harsher colonial policy, two factions arose in America. One favored the attitude of home government and the other declined to obey and demanded a constantly increasing level of self-government. The former came to be known as **Tories**, the latter as **Whigs**. During the course of the American Revolution a large number of Tories left the country either to return to England or move into Canada.

The first real party organization developed soon after the inauguration of Washington as President. His cabinet included people of both factions. Hamilton was the leader of the **Nationalists** – the **Federalist Party** – and Jefferson was the spokesman for the Anti-Federalists, later known as **Republicans**, **Democratic-Republicans**, and finally **Democrats**.   Several other parties formed over the years including the Anti-Masonic Party and the Free Soil Party who existed for the 1848 and 1852 elections only. They opposed slavery in the lands acquired from Mexico. The Liberty Party of this period was abolitionist. The American Party was called the "Know Nothings." They lasted from 1854 to 1858 and were opposed to Irish-Catholic immigration. The **Constitution Union Party** was formed in 1860. It was made up of entities from other extinguished political powers. They claimed to support the Constitution above all and thought this would do away with the slavery issue. The **National Union Party** of 1864 was formed only for the purpose of the Lincoln election. That was the only reason for its existence. There were many more to follow.

The election of Andrew Jackson as President signaled a swing of the political pendulum from government influence of the wealthy, aristocratic Easterners to the interests of the **Western farmers** and **pioneers** and the era of the "**common man**." Jacksonian democracy was a policy of equal political power for all. After the War of 1812, Henry Clay and supporters favored economic measures that came to be known as the American System. This involved tariffs protecting American farmers and manufacturers from having to compete with foreign products, stimulating industrial growth and employment. With more people working, more farm products would be consumed, prosperous farmers would be able to buy more manufactured goods, and the additional monies from tariffs would make it possible for the government to make the needed internal improvements. To get this going, in 1816, Congress not only passed a high tariff, but also chartered a second Bank of the United States. Upon becoming President, Jackson fought to get rid of the bank.

Many **social reform movements** began during this period, including education, women's rights, labor and working conditions, temperance, prisons and insane asylums. But the most intense and controversial was the abolitionists' efforts to end slavery, an effort alienating and splitting the country, hardening Southern defense of slavery, and leading to four years of bloody war. The abolitionist movement had political fallout, affecting admittance of states into the Union and the government's continued efforts to keep a balance between total numbers of free and slave states. Congressional legislation after 1820 reflected this.

Robert Fulton's "**Clermont**," the first commercially successful steamboat, led the way in the fastest way to ship goods, making it the most important way to do so. Later, steam-powered railroads soon became the biggest rival of the steamboat as a means of shipping, eventually being the most important transportation method opening the West. With expansion into the interior of the country, the United States became the leading agricultural nation in the world. The hardy pioneer farmers produced a vast surplus and emphasis went to producing products with a high-sale value. These implements, such as the cotton gin and reaper, improved production. Travel and shipping were greatly assisted in areas not yet touched by railroad or, by improved or new roads, such as the National Road in the East and in the West the Oregon and Santa Fe Trails.

People were exposed to works of literature, art, newspapers, drama, live entertainment, and political rallies. With better communication and travel, more information was desired about previously unknown areas of the country, especially the West. The discovery of gold and other mineral wealth resulted in a literal surge of settlers and even more interest.

Public schools were established in many of the states with more and more children being educated. With more literacy and more participation in literature and the arts, the young nation was developing its own unique culture becoming less and less influenced by and dependent on that of Europe.

More industries and factories required more and more labor. Women, children, and, at times, entire families worked the long hours and days, until the 1830s. By that time, the factories were getting even larger and employers began hiring immigrants who were coming to America in huge numbers. Before then, efforts were made to organize a labor movement to improve working conditions and increase wages. It never really caught on until after the Civil War, but the seed had been sown.

In between the growing economy, expansion westward of the population, and improvements in travel and mass communication, the federal government did face periodic financial depressions. Contributing to these downward spirals were land speculations, availability and soundness of money and currency, failed banks, failing businesses, and unemployment. Sometimes conditions outside the nation would help trigger it; at other times, domestic politics and presidential elections affected it. The growing strength and influence of two major political parties with opposing philosophies and methods of conducting government did not ease matters at times.

As 1860 began, the nation had extended its borders north, south, and west. Industry and agriculture were flourishing. Although the U.S. did not involve itself actively in European affairs, the relationship with Great Britain was much improved and it and other nations that dealt with the young nation accorded it more respect and admiration. Nevertheless, war was on the horizon. The country was deeply divided along political lines concerning slavery and the election of **Abraham Lincoln.**

Religion has always been a factor in American life. Many early settlers came to America in search of religious freedom. Religion, particularly Christianity, was an essential element of the value and belief structure shared by the Founding Fathers. Yet the Constitution prescribes a separation of Church and State.

The **First Great Awakening** was a religious movement within American Protestantism in the 1730s and 1740s. This was primarily a movement among Puritans seeking a return to strict interpretation of morality and values as well as emphasizing the importance and power of personal religious or spiritual experience. Many historians believe the First Great Awakening unified the people of the original colonies and supported the independence of the colonists.

The **Second Great Awakening** (the Great Revival) was a broad movement within American Protestantism that led to several kinds of activities that were distinguished by region and denominational tradition. In general terms, the Second Great Awakening, which began in the 1820s, was a time of recognition that "awakened religion" must weed out sin on both a personal and a social level. It inspired a wave of social activism. In New England, the Congregationalists established missionary societies to evangelize the West. Publication and education societies arose, most notably the American Bible Society. This social activism gave rise to the temperance movement, prison reform efforts, help for the handicapped and mentally ill. This period was particularly notable for the abolition movement. In the Appalachian region, the camp meeting was used to revive religion. The camp meeting became a primary method of evangelizing new territory.

The **Third Great Awakening** (the Missionary Awakening) gave rise to the Social Gospel Movement. This period (1858 to 1908) resulted in a massive growth in membership of all major Protestant denominations through their missionary activities. This movement was partly a response to claims that the Bible was fallible. Many churches attempted to reconcile or change biblical teaching to fit scientific theories and discoveries. Colleges associated with Protestant churches began to appear rapidly throughout the nation. In terms of social and political movements, the Third Great Awakening was the most expansive and profound. Coinciding with many changes in production and labor, it won battles against child labor and stopped the exploitation of women in factories. Compulsory elementary education for children came from this movement, as did the establishment of a set work day. Much was also done to protect and rescue children from abandonment and abuse, to improve the care of the sick, to prohibit the use of alcohol and tobacco, as well as numerous other "social ills."

Numerous conflicts, often called the **Indian Wars** broke out between the U.S. army and many different native tribes. Many treaties were signed with the various tribes, but most were broken by the government for a variety of reasons. Two of the most notable battles were the Battle of Little Bighorn in 1876, in which native people defeated General Custer and his forces, and the massacre of Native Americans in 1890 at Wounded Knee. In 1876, the U.S. government ordered all surviving Native Americans to move to reservations.

Nineteenth century contributors.

Following is just a partial list of well-known Americans who contributed their leadership and talents in various fields and reforms:

- **Lucretia Mott** and **Elizabeth Cady Stanton** for women's rights
- **Emma Hart Willard, Catharine Esther Beecher,** and **Mary Lyon** for education for women
- **Dr. Elizabeth Blackwell**, the first woman doctor
- **Antoinette Louisa Blackwell**, the first female minister
- **Dorothea Lynde Dix** for reforms in prisons and insane asylums
- **Elihu Burritt** and **William Ladd** for peace movements
- **Robert Owen** for a Utopian society
- **Horace Mann, Henry Barmard, Calvin E. Stowe, Caleb Mills**, and **John Swett** for public education
- **Benjamin Lundy, David Walker, William Lloyd Garrison, Isaac Hooper, Arthur and Lewis Tappan, Theodore Weld, Frederick Douglass, Harriet Tubman, James G. Birney, Henry Highland Garnet, James Forten, Robert Purvis, Harriet Beecher Stowe, Wendell Phillips, and John Brown** for abolition of slavery and the **Underground Railroad**

- **Louisa Mae Alcott, James Fenimore Cooper, Washington Irving, Walt Whitman, Henry David Thoreau, Ralph Waldo Emerson, Herman Melville, Richard Henry Dana, Nathaniel Hawthorne, Henry Wadsworth Longfellow, John Greenleaf Whittier, Edgar Allan Poe, Oliver Wendell Holmes**, famous writers
- **John C. Fremont, Zebulon Pike, Kit Carson**, explorers
- **Henry Clay, Daniel Webster, Stephen Douglas, John C. Calhoun**, American statesmen
- **Robert Fulton, Cyrus McCormick, Eli Whitney**, inventors
- **Noah Webster**, American dictionary and spellers

As African Americans left the rural South and migrated to the North in search of opportunity, many settled in Harlem in New York City. By the 1920s Harlem had become a center of life and activity for persons of color. The music, art, and literature of this community gave birth to a cultural movement known as **the Harlem Renaissance**. The artistic expressions that emerged from this community in the 1920s and 1930s celebrated the black experience, black traditions, and the voices of black America. Major writers and works of this movement included:

- Langston Hughes (*The Weary Blues),*
- Nella Larsen (*Passing),*
- Zora Neale Hurston (*Their Eyes Were Watching God),*
- Claude McKay, Countee Cullen, and Jean Toomer.

Many refer to the decade of the 1920s as **The Jazz Age**. The decade was a time of optimism and exploration of new boundaries. It was a clear movement in many ways away from conventionalism. Jazz music, uniquely American, was the country's popular music at the time. The jazz musical style perfectly typified the mood of society. Jazz is essentially free-flowing improvisation on a simple theme with a four-beat rhythm. Jazz originated in the poor districts of New Orleans as an outgrowth of the Blues. The leading jazz musicians of the time included: Buddy Bolden, Joseph "King" Oliver, Duke Ellington, Louis Armstrong, and Jelly Roll Morton.

As jazz grew in popularity and in the intricacy of the music, it gave birth to Swing and the era of Big Band Jazz by the mid 1920s. Some of the most notable musicians of the Big Band era were: Bing Crosby, Frank Sinatra, Don Redman, Fletcher Henderson, Count Basie, Benny Goodman, Billie Holiday, Ella Fitzgerald, and The Dorsey Brothers.

Hispanic Americans have contributed to American life and culture since before the Civil War. Hispanics have distinguished themselves in every area of society and culture. Mexicans taught Californians to pan for gold and introduced the technique of using mercury to separate silver from worthless ores. Six state names are of Hispanic origin.

Native Americans have made major contributions to the development of the nation and have been contributors, either directly or indirectly in every area of political and cultural life. In the early years of European settlement, Native Americans were both teachers and neighbors. Even during periods of extermination and relocation, their influence was profound.

Asian Americans, particularly in the West and in large cities have made significant contributions despite immigration bans, mistreatment, and confinement. Asians were particularly important in the construction of the trans-continental railroad, mining metals, and providing other kinds of labor and service.

COMPETENCY 13.0   UNDERSTAND GEOGRAPHIC CONCEPTS AND
PHENOMENA, AND ANALYZE THE
INTERRELATIONSHIPS OF GEOGRAPHY, SOCIETY,
AND CULTURE IN THE DEVELOPMENT OF
OKLAHOMA, THE UNITED STATES, AND THE
WORLD

Skill 13.1   Demonstrate an understanding of how the five themes of
geography—location, place, relationships within places,
movement, and regions—can be used to analyze geographic
phenomena and human cultures

The six themes of geography are:

Location - including relative and absolute location. A relative location refers to
the surrounding geography, e.g., "on the banks of the Mississippi River."
Absolute location refers to a specific point, such as 41 degrees North latitude, 90
degrees West longitude, or 123 Main Street.

Spatial organization is a description of how things are grouped in a given
space. In geographical terms, this can describe people, places, and
environments anywhere and everywhere on Earth. The most basic form of
spatial organization for people is where they live. The vast majority of people live
near other people, in villages and towns and cities and settlements. These
people live near others in order to take advantage of the goods and services that
naturally arise from cooperation. These villages and towns and cities and
settlements are, to varying degrees, near bodies of water. Water is a staple of
survival for every person on the planet and is also a good source of energy for
factories and other industries, as well as a form of transportation for people and
goods. For example, in a city, where are the factories and heavy industry
buildings? Are they near airports or train stations? Are they on the edge of town,
near major roads? What about housing developments? Are they near these
industries, or are they far away? Where are the other industry buildings? Where
are the schools and hospitals and parks? What about the police and fire
stations? How close are homes to each of these things? Towns and especially
cities are routinely organized into neighborhoods, so that each house or home is
near most things that its residents might need on a regular basis. This means
that large cities have multiple schools, hospitals, grocery stores, fire stations, etc.

Place - A place has both human and physical characteristics. Physical
characteristics include features such as mountains, rivers, deserts, etc. Human
characteristics are the features created by human interaction with their
environment such as canals and roads.

Human-Environmental Interaction - The theme of human-environmental interaction has three main concepts: humans adapt to the environment (wearing warm clothing in a cold climate, for instance,) humans modify the environment (planting trees to block a prevailing wind, for example,) and humans depend on the environment (for food, water and raw materials.)

Movement - The theme of movement covers how humans interact with one another through trade, communications, emigration and other forms of interaction.

Regions - A region is an area that has some kind of unifying characteristic, such as a common language, a common government, etc. There are three main types of regions. Formal regions are areas defined by actual political boundaries, such as a city, county, or state. Functional regions are defined by a common function, such as the area covered by a telephone service. Vernacular regions are less formally defined areas that are formed by people's perception, e.g. "the Middle East," and "the South."

Geography involves studying location and how living things and earth's features are distributed throughout the earth. It includes where animals, people, and plants live and the effects of their relationship with earth's physical features. Geographers also explore the locations of earth's features, how they got there, and why it is so important. Another way to describe where people live is by the **geography** and **topography** around them. The vast majority of people on the planet live in areas that are very hospitable. Yes, people live in the Himalayas and in the Sahara, but the populations in those areas are small indeed when compared to the plains of China, India, Europe, and the United States. People naturally want to live where they won't have to work really hard just to survive, and world population patterns reflect this.

Human communities subsisted initially as gatherers – gathering berries, leaves, etc. With the invention of tools it became possible to dig for roots, hunt small animals, and catch fish from rivers and oceans. Humans observed their environments and soon learned to plant seeds and harvest crops. As people migrated to areas in which game and fertile soil were abundant, communities began to develop. When people had the knowledge to grow crops and the skills to hunt game, they began to understand division of labor. Some of the people in the community tended to agricultural needs while others hunted game.

As habitats attracted larger numbers of people, environments became crowded and there was competition. The concept of division of labor and sharing of food soon came, in more heavily populated areas, to be managed. Groups of people focused on growing crops while others concentrated on hunting. Experience led to the development of skills and of knowledge that make the work easier. Farmers began to develop new plant species and hunters began to protect animal species from other predators for their own use. This ability to manage the environment led people to settle down, to guard their resources, and to manage them. Camps soon became villages. Villages became year-round settlements. Animals were domesticated and gathered into herds that met the needs of the village. With the settled life it was no longer necessary to "travel light." Pottery was developed for storing and cooking food.

By 8000 BCE, culture was beginning to evolve in these villages. Agriculture was developed for the production of grain crops, which led to a decreased reliance on wild plants. Domesticating animals for various purposes decreased the need to hunt wild game. Life became more settled. It was then possible to turn attention to such matters as managing water supplies, producing tools, making cloth, etc. There was both the social interaction and the opportunity to reflect upon existence. Mythologies arose and various kinds of belief systems. Rituals arose that re-enacted the mythologies that gave meaning to life.

As farming and animal husbandry skills increased, the dependence upon wild game and food gathering declined. With this change came the realization that a larger number of people could be supported on the produce of farming and animal husbandry.

Two things seem to have come together to produce **cultures and civilizations**: a society and culture based on agriculture and the development of centers of the community with literate social and religious structures. The members of these hierarchies then managed water supply and irrigation, ritual and religious life, and exerted their own right to use a portion of the goods produced by the community for their own subsistence in return for their management. Sharpened skills, development of more sophisticated tools, commerce with other communities, and increasing knowledge of their environment, the resources available to them, and responses to the needs to share good, order community life, and protect their possessions from outsiders led to further division of labor and community development.

As trade routes developed and travel between cities became easier, trade led to specialization. Trade enables a people to obtain the goods they desire in exchange for the goods they are able to produce. This, in turn, leads to increased attention to refinements of technique and the sharing of ideas. The knowledge of a new discovery or invention provides knowledge and technology that increases the ability to produce goods for trade.

Skill 13.2   Recognize the physical characteristics of the earth's surface, and analyze the continual reshaping of the surface by physical processes

The earth's physical environment is divided into three major parts: the atmosphere, the hydrosphere, and the lithosphere: The atmosphere is the layer of air that surrounds the earth. The hydrosphere is the water portion of the planet (70% of the earth is covered by water) and the lithosphere is the solid portion of the earth.

Mountains are landforms with rather steep slopes at least 2,000 feet or more above sea level. Mountains are found in groups called mountain chains or mountain ranges. At least one range can be found on six of the earth's seven continents. North America has the Appalachian and Rocky Mountains; South America the Andes; Asia the Himalayas; Australia the Great Dividing Range; Europe the Alps; and Africa the Atlas, Ahaggar, and Drakensburg Mountains. Mountains are commonly formed by volcanic activity, or when land is thrust upward where two tectonic plates collide.

Hills are elevated landforms rising to an elevation of about 500 to 2000 feet. They are found everywhere on earth including Antarctica where they are covered by ice.

Plateaus are elevated landforms usually level on top. Depending on location, they range from being an area that is very cold to one that is cool and healthful. Some plateaus are dry because they are surrounded by mountains that keep out any moisture. Some examples include the Kenya Plateau in East Africa, which is very cool. The plateau extending north from the Himalayas is extremely dry while those in Antarctica and Greenland are covered with ice and snow. Plateaus can be formed by underground volcanic activity, erosion, or colliding tectonic plates.

Plains are described as areas of flat or slightly rolling land, usually lower than the landforms next to them. Sometimes called lowlands (and sometimes located along **seacoasts)** they support the majority of the world's people. Some are found inland and many have been formed by large rivers. This resulted in extremely fertile soil for successful cultivation of crops and numerous large settlements of people. In North America, the vast plains areas extend from the Gulf of Mexico north to the Arctic Ocean and between the Appalachian and Rocky Mountains. In Europe, rich plains extend east from Great Britain into central Europe on into the Siberian region of Russia. Plains in river valleys are found in China (the Yangtze River valley), India (the Ganges River valley), and Southeast Asia (the Mekong River valley).

Valleys are land areas that are found between hills and mountains. Some have gentle slopes containing trees and plants; others have very steep walls and are referred to as canyons. One famous example is Arizona's Grand Canyon of the Colorado River, which was formed by erosion.

Deserts are large dry areas of land receiving ten inches or less of rainfall each year. Among the better known deserts are Africa's large Sahara Desert, the Arabian Desert on the Arabian Peninsula, and the desert Outback covering roughly one third of Australia. Deserts are found mainly in the tropical latitudes, and are formed when surrounding features such as mountain ranges extract most of the moisture from the prevailing winds

Deltas are areas of lowlands formed by soil and sediment deposited at the mouths of rivers. The soil is generally very fertile and most fertile river deltas are important crop-growing areas. One well-known example is the delta of Egypt's Nile River, known for its production of cotton.

Mesas are the flat tops of hills or mountains usually with steep sides. Mesas are similar to plateaus, but smaller.

Basins are considered to be low areas drained by rivers or low spots in mountains.

Foothills are generally considered a low series of hills found between a plain and a mountain range.

Marshes and swamps are wet lowlands providing growth of such plants as rushes and reeds.

Oceans are the largest bodies of water on the planet. The four oceans of the earth are the **Atlantic Ocean**, one-half the size of the Pacific and separating North and South America from Africa and Europe; the **Pacific Ocean**, covering almost one-third of the entire surface of the earth and separating North and South America from Asia and Australia; the **Indian Ocean**, touching Africa, Asia, and Australia; and the ice-filled **Arctic Ocean,** extending from North America and Europe to the North Pole. The waters of the Atlantic, Pacific, and Indian Oceans also touch the shores of Antarctica.

Seas are smaller than oceans and are surrounded by land. Some examples include the Mediterranean Sea found between Europe, Asia, and Africa; and the Caribbean Sea, touching the West Indies, South and Central America. A lake is a body of water surrounded by land. The Great Lakes in North America are a good example.

Rivers, considered a nation's lifeblood, usually begin as very small streams, formed by melting snow and rainfall, flowing from higher to lower land, emptying into a larger body of water, usually a sea or an ocean. Examples of important rivers for the people and countries affected by and/or dependent on them include the Nile, Niger, and Zaire Rivers of Africa; the Rhine, Danube, and Thames Rivers of Europe; the Yangtze, Ganges, Mekong, Hwang He, and Irrawaddy Rivers of Asia; the Murray-Darling in Australia; and the Orinoco in South America. River systems are made up of large rivers and numerous smaller rivers or tributaries flowing into them. Examples include the vast Amazon Rivers system in South America and the Mississippi River system in the United States.

Canals are man-made water passages constructed to connect two larger bodies of water. Famous examples include the **Panama Canal** across Panama's isthmus connecting the Atlantic and Pacific Oceans and the **Suez Canal** in the Middle East between Africa and the Arabian peninsulas connecting the Red and Mediterranean Seas.

World weather patterns are greatly influenced by ocean surface currents in the upper layer of the ocean. These current continuously move along the ocean surface in specific directions. Ocean currents that flow deep below the surface are called sub-surface currents. These currents are influenced by such factors as the location of landmasses in the current's path and the earth's rotation.

Surface currents are caused by winds and classified by temperature. Cold currents originate in the Polar Regions and flow through surrounding water that is measurably warmer. Those currents with a higher temperature than the surrounding water are called warm currents and can be found near the equator. These currents follow swirling routes around the ocean basins and the equator.

The Gulf Stream and the California Current are the two main surface currents that flow along the coastlines of the United States. The Gulf Stream is a warm northern part of the Atlantic Ocean. Benjamin Franklin studied and named the Gulf Stream. The California Current is a cold current that originates in the Artic regions and flows southward along the west coast of the United States.

Climate is average weather or daily weather conditions for a specific region or location over a long or extended period of time. Studying the climate of an area includes information gathered on the area's monthly and yearly temperatures and its monthly and yearly amounts of precipitation. In addition, a characteristic of an area's climate is the length of its growing season.

Natural changes can occur that alter habitats – floods, volcanoes, storms, earthquakes. These changes can affect the species that exist within the habitat, either by causing extinction or by changing the environment in a way that will no longer support the life systems. Climate changes can have similar effects. Inhabiting species can also alter habitats, particularly through migration.

Plate tectonics, is a geological theory that explains **continental drift**, which is the large movements of the solid portions of the Earth's crust floating on the molten mantle. There are ten major tectonic plates, with several smaller plates. The surface of the earth can be drastically affected at the boundaries of these plates. There are three types of plate boundaries, convergent, divergent and transform. Convergent boundaries are where plates are moving toward one another. When this happens, the two plates collide and fold up against one another, called **continental collision**, or one plate slides under the other, called **subduction**. Continental collision can create high mountain ranges, such as the Andes and Himalayas. Subduction often results in volcanic activity along the boundary, as in the "Ring of Fire" along the northern coasts of the Pacific Ocean.

Divergent boundaries occur where plates are moving away from one another, creating **rifts** in the surface. The Mid-Atlantic Ridge on the floor of the Atlantic Ocean, and the Great Rift Valley in east Africa are examples of rifts at divergent plate boundaries. Transform boundaries are where plates are moving in opposite directions along their boundary, grinding against one another. The tremendous pressures that build along these types of boundaries often lead to earthquake activity when this pressure is released. The San Andreas Fault along the West Coast of North America is an example of a transform boundary.

Erosion is the displacement of solid earth surfaces such as rock and soil. Erosion is often a result of wind, water or ice acting on surfaces with loose particles, such as sand, loose soils, or decomposing rock. Gravity can also cause erosion on loose surfaces. Factors such as slope, soil and rock composition, plant cover, and human activity all affect erosion.

Weathering is the natural decomposition of the Earth's surface from contact with the atmosphere. It is not the same as erosion, but can be a factor in erosion. Heat, water, ice and pressure are all factors that can lead to weathering. Chemicals in the atmosphere can also contribute to weathering

Transportation is the movement of eroded material from one place to another by wind, water or ice. Examples of transportation include pebbles rolling down a streambed and boulders being carried by moving glaciers.

Deposition is the result of transportation, and occurs when the material being carried settles on the surface and is deposited. Sand dunes and moraines are formed by transportation and deposition of glacial material.

Oklahoma is a vast, elevated plain, tilted toward the south and southeast and broken by low mountains. The Ozarks of Southwestern Missouri extend into the northeast section of the state and form a wooded table-land, carved by the deep valleys of streams, but having no high peaks. Along the eastern border, long, narrow, heavily timbered ridges rise from the prairies, culminating in the southeast in the low, rugged Washita Mountains, covered with forests of pine and oak. The Arbuckle Mountains rise 600 or 700 feet above the surrounding country in the south-central part of the state. Picturesque gypsum hills break the monotony of the grassy plains in the west-central section. The Wichita Mountains are a straggling range of rough granite peaks, rising abruptly from the seemingly level plain in the southwestern part of the state.

With the exception of these isolated clusters of mountains, most of the southwestern part of the state is a treeless plain. It is carved by the canyons of streams and dotted with buttes and mesas. In the north and west are broad prairies, marked by few streams and mostly bare of timber, but covered with rich buffalo grass. It is here that the great cattle ranches arose. Varying with the prairie grasses are several large salt plains coated with dazzling white salt crystals and containing many salt springs. The Panhandle is a high, rough table-land, extending nearly to the foot of the Rocky Mountains. This is the area of the state's highest elevation (3,000 to 4,700 feet). The lowest part of the state is in the Red River Valley, which is a gently rolling timber land and fertile agricultural region that is 300 to 600 feet above sea level.

Oklahoma is crossed by nine rivers and a large number of smaller streams. None is of any value for navigation. All flow in a southeasterly direction, following the slope of the land. The Red River forms the entire southern boundary, and with its tributaries, drains the entire southern portion of the state. The Arkansas River, crossing the northeastern part of the state, is the main waterway. There are no permanent lakes and only a few salty ponds, which evaporate during the dry season.

Oklahoma has the dry climate of the Western states and the warm temperature of the South. Due to higher elevation and greater distance from the Gulf coast, the western and central portions of the state are cooler and dryer than the eastern and southern sections. Rainfall varies from below twenty inches in the west to forty-five inches in the east and, except in the Panhandle, the climate supports agriculture. The state offers a variety of grasses covering large areas of grazing lands that have supported pasturage for cattle and other livestock. Agriculture has traditionally been a major basis of the state's economy. The lands of various parts of the state support a variety of crops and orchards. The Forests of the eastern part of the state provide timber, as well as fruit and nut trees. Oklahoma is rich is native minerals, including oil, coal, lead and zinc, granite, marble, gypsum, salt, copper, gold, iron and silver.

Skill 13.3   Analyze the development and interaction of social, political, cultural, and religious systems in different regions of Oklahoma, the United States, and the world

Cultural identity is the identification of individuals or groups as they are influenced by their belonging to a particular group or culture. This refers to the sense of who one is, what values are important, and what racial or ethnic characteristics are important in one's self-understanding and manner of interacting with the world and with others. In a nation with a well-deserved reputation as a "melting pot" the attachment to cultural identities can become a divisive factor in communities and societies. Cosmopolitanism, its alternative, tends to blur those cultural differences in the creation of a shared new culture.

Throughout the history of the nation, groups have defined themselves and/or assimilated into the larger population to varying degrees. In order for a society to function as a cohesive and unifying force, there must be some degree of enculturation of all groups. The alternative is a competing, and often conflicting, collection of sub-groups that are not able to cohere into a society. This failure to assimilate will often result in culture wars as values and lifestyles come into conflict.

Cross-cultural exchanges, however, can enrich every involved group of persons with the discovery of shared values and needs, as well as an appreciation for unique cultural characteristics of each. For the most part, the history of the nation has been the story of successful enculturation and cultural enrichment. The notable failures, often resulting from one sort of prejudice and intolerance or another, are well known. For example, cultural biases have led to the oppression of the Irish or the Chinese immigrants in various parts of the country. Racial biases have led to various kinds of disenfranchisement and oppression of other groups of immigrants. Perhaps most notably, the bias of the European settlers against the civilization and culture of the Native peoples of North America has caused mass extermination, relocation, and isolation.

In art, the primary expression of the first half of the twentieth century was Modernism. The avant-garde perspective encouraged all types of innovation and experimentation. Key elements of this movement have been abstraction, cubism, surrealism, realism, and abstract expressionism. Notable among the artists of this period for the birth or perfection of particular styles are Henri Matisse, Pablo Picasso, George Rouault, Gustav Klimt, George Braque, Salvador Dali, Hans Arp, Rene Magrite, and Marcel Duchamp. In the U.S. realism tended to find regional expressions including the Ashcan School and Robert Henri, Midwestern Regionalism and Grant Wood. Other particularly notable painters are Edward Hopper and Georgia O'Keeffe.

The New York School came to be known for a style known as Abstract Expressionism and included such artists as Jackson Pollock, Willem de Kooning, Larry Rivers. Other painters of the period were Mark Rothko, Clement Greenberg, Ellsworth Kelly and the Op Art Movement.

In painting and sculpture, the new direction of the decade was **realism**. In the early years of the twentieth century, American artists had developed several realist styles, some of which were influenced by modernism, others that reacted against it. Several groups of artists of this period are particularly notable.

- *The Eight or The Ash Can School* in New York developed around the work and style of Robert Henri. Their subjects were everyday urban life that was presented without adornment or glamour.
- *The American Scene Painters* produced a tight, detailed style of painting that focused on images of American life that were understandable to all. In the Midwest, a school within this group was called *regionalism*. One of the leading artists of regionalism was Grant Wood, best known for *American Gothic.*
- Other important realists of the day were Edward Hopper and Georgia O'Keeffe.

As one of the first colonized areas in the nation, New York was a major point of entry for immigrants. The melding of the Dutch, French and British settlers into a unified colony was the first step along the way to becoming the melting pot that New York has been to this day. New York's large harbor and the growing reputation of the state for business, industry, and commerce, made it a place of special opportunity for immigrants who were seeking freedom and opportunity.

The development of Ellis Island as an immigrant processing center made it the point of entry for millions who came to America in search of political or religious freedom, safe haven from political oppression, and the quest for the American dream. The French gift of the Statue of Liberty to the United States and its placement in New York harbor made New York the symbol of American opportunity and freedom.

Eight major religions practiced today are:

Judaism - the oldest of the eight and was the first to teach and practice the belief in one God, Yahweh.

Christianity - came from Judaism, grew and spread in the First Century throughout the Roman Empire, despite persecution. A later schism resulted in the Western (Roman Catholic) and Eastern (Orthodox) parts. Protestant sects developed as part of the Protestant Reformation. The name "Christian" means one who is a follower of Jesus Christ who started Christianity. Christians follow his teachings and examples, living by the laws and principles of the Bible.

Islam - founded in Arabia by Mohammed who preached about God, Allah. Islam spread through trade, travel, and conquest and followers of it fought in the Crusades. In addition, other wars against Christians and today against the Jewish nation of Israel. Followers of Islam, called Muslims, live by the teachings of the Koran, their holy book, and of their prophets.

Hinduism - began among people called Aryans around 1500 BC and spread into India. The Aryans blended their culture with the culture of the Dravidians, natives they conquered. Today it has many sects, promotes worship of hundreds of gods and goddesses and belief in reincarnation. Though forbidden today by law, a prominent feature of Hinduism in the past was a rigid adherence to and practice of the infamous caste system.

Buddhism - developed in India from the teachings of Prince Gautama and spread to most of Asia. Its beliefs opposed the worship of numerous deities, the Hindu caste system and the supernatural. Worshippers must be free of attachment to all things worldly and devote themselves to finding release from life's suffering.

Confucianism - is a Chinese religion based on the teachings of the Chinese philosopher Confucius. There is no clergy, no organization, and no belief in a deity or in life after death. It emphasizes political and moral ideas with respect for authority and ancestors. Rulers were expected to govern according to high moral standards.

Taoism - a native Chinese religion with worship of more deities than almost any other religion. It teaches all followers to make the effort to achieve the two goals of happiness and immortality. Practices and ceremonies include meditation, prayer, magic, reciting scriptures, special diets, breath control, beliefs in witchcraft, fortune telling, astrology, and communicating with the spirits of the dead.

Shinto - the native religion of Japan developed from native folk beliefs worshipping spirits and demons in animals, trees, and mountains. According to its mythology, deities created Japan and its people, which resulted in worshipping the emperor as a god. Shinto was strongly influenced by Buddhism and Confucianism but never had strong doctrines on salvation or life after death.

Skill 13.4 **Analyze the impact of human activity on the physical environment (e.g., industrial development, population growth, deforestation)**

Environmental and geographic factors have affected the pattern of urban development in Oklahoma and the rest of the US. In turn, urban infrastructure and development patterns are interrelated factors.

The growth of urban areas is often linked to the advantages provided by its geographic location. Before the advent of efficient overland routes of commerce such as railroads and highways, water provided the primary means of transportation of commercial goods. Most large American cities are situated along bodies of water. The Mississippi River in the United States has several large cities along the length of it because it flows south to the Gulf of Mexico. New York City is situated on a large harbor where two major rivers meet the Atlantic Ocean.

As **transportation** technology advanced, the supporting infrastructure was built to connect cities with one another and to connect remote areas to larger communities. The railroad, for example, allowed for the quick transport of agricultural products from rural areas to urban centers. This newfound efficiency not only further fueled the growth of urban centers, it changed the economy of rural America. Where once farmers had practiced only subsistence farming – growing enough to support one's own family – the new infrastructure meant that one could convert agricultural products into cash by selling them at market.

For urban dwellers, improvements in building technology and advances in transportation allowed for larger cities. Growth brought with it a new set of problems unique to each location. The bodies of water that had made the development of cities possible in their early days also formed natural barriers to growth. Further infrastructure in the form of bridges, tunnels and ferry routes were needed to connect central urban areas with outlying communities.

As cities grew in population, living conditions became more crowded. As roads and bridges became better, and transportation technology improved, many people began to look outside the city for living space. Along with the development of these new suburbs came the infrastructure to connect them to the city in the form of commuter railroads and highways.

The growth of suburbs had the effect in many cities of creating a type of economic segregation. Working class people who could not afford new suburban homes and perhaps an automobile to carry them to and from work were relegated to closer, more densely populated areas. Frequently, these areas had to be passed through by those on their way to the suburbs, and rail lines and freeways sometimes bisected these urban communities. Acres of farmland and forest were cleared to make way for growing suburban areas.

In the modern age, advancements in **telecommunications** infrastructure may have an impact on urban growth patterns as information can pass instantly and freely between almost any two points on the globe, allowing access to some aspects of urban life to those in remote areas.

By nature, people are essentially social creatures. They generally live in communities or settlements of some kind and of some size. Settlements are the cradles of culture, political structure, education, and the management of resources. The relative placement of these settlements or communities are shaped by the proximity to natural resources, the movement of raw materials, the production of finished products, the availability of a work force, and the delivery of finished products. Shared values, language, culture, religion, and subsistence will at least to some extent, determine the composition of communities.

Cities are the major hubs of human settlement. Almost half of the population of the world now lives in cities. These percentages are much higher in developed regions. Established cities continue to grow. The fastest growth, however, is occurring in developing areas. In some regions there are "metropolitan areas" made up of urban and sub-urban areas. In some places cities and urban areas have become interconnected into "megalopoli" (e.g., Tokyo-Kawasaki-Yokohama).

The concentrations of populations and the divisions of these areas among various groups that constitute the cities can differ significantly. North American cities are different from European cities in terms of shape, size, population density, and modes of transportation. While in North America, the wealthiest economic groups tend to live outside the cities, the opposite is true in Latin American cities.

There are significant differences among the cities of the world in terms of connectedness to other cities. While European and North American cities tend to be well linked both by transportation and communication connections, there are other places in the world in which communication between the cities of the country may be inferior to communication with the rest of the world.

Natural resources are naturally occurring substances that are considered valuable in their natural form. A commodity is generally considered a natural resource when the primary activities associated with it are extraction and purification, as opposed to creation. Thus, mining, petroleum extraction, fishing, and forestry are generally considered natural-resource industries, while agriculture is not.

Natural resources are often classified into **renewable** and **non-renewable resources**. Renewable resources are generally living resources (fish, coffee, and forests, for example), which can restock (renew) themselves if they are not over-harvested. Renewable resources can restock themselves and be used indefinitely if they are sustained. Once renewable resources are consumed at a rate that exceeds their natural rate of replacement, the standing stock will diminish and eventually run out. The rate of sustainable use of a renewable resource is determined by the replacement rate and amount of standing stock of that particular resource. Non-living renewable natural resources include soil, as well as water, wind, tides and solar radiation. Natural resources include soil, timber, oil, minerals, and other goods taken more or less as they are from the Earth.

In recent years, the depletion of natural capital and attempts to move to sustainable development has been a major focus of development agencies. **Deforestation** or clear cutting is of particular concern in rainforest regions, which hold most of the Earth's natural biodiversity - irreplaceable genetic natural capital. Conservation of natural resources is the major focus of Natural Capitalism, environmentalism, the ecology movement, and Green Parties. Some view this depletion as a major source of social unrest and conflicts in developing nations.

Environmental policy is concerned with the sustainability of the earth, the region under the administration of the governing group or individual or a local habitat. The concern of environmental policy is the preservation of the region, habitat or ecosystem.

Because humans, both individually and in community, rely upon the environment to sustain human life, social and environmental policy must be mutually supportable. Because humans, both individually and in community, live upon the earth, draw upon the natural resources of the earth, and affect the environment in many ways, environmental and social policy must be mutually supportive.

If modern societies have no understanding of the limitations upon natural resources or how their actions affect the environment, and they act without regard for the sustainability of the earth, it will become impossible for the earth to sustain human existence. At the same time, the resources of the earth are necessary to support the human welfare. Environmental policies must recognize that the planet is the home of humans and other species.

In an age of **global warming**, unprecedented demand upon natural resources, and a shrinking planet, social and environmental policies must become increasingly interdependent if the planet is to continue to support life and human civilization.

For example, between 1870 and 1916, more than 25 million immigrants came into the United States adding to the phenomenal **population growth** taking place. This tremendous growth aided business and industry in two ways: (1) The number of consumers increased creating a greater demand for products thus enlarging the markets for the products, and (2) with increased production and expanding business, more workers were available for newly created jobs. The completion of the nation's transcontinental railroad in 1869 contributed greatly to the nation's economic and industrial growth. Many wealthy industrialists and railroad owners saw tremendous profits steadily increasing due to this improved method of transportation. Yet, natural resources were required to support the growing population and its needs.

COMPETENCY 14.0 **UNDERSTAND CONCEPTS AND PHENOMENA RELATED TO HUMAN DEVELOPMENT AND INTERACTIONS (INCLUDING ANTHROPOLOGICAL, PSYCHOLOGICAL, AND SOCIOLOGICAL CONCEPTS**

Skill 14.1 **Evaluate factors that contribute to the development of personal identity (e.g., family, group affiliations, socialization processes)**

The study of social phenomena can draw on the methods and theories of several disciplines.

The field of **anthropology** is largely concerned with the institutions of a society and intercultural comparisons. Anthropologists observe people of a particular culture acting within their culture and interacting with people of other cultures, and interpret social phenomena. Anthropology relies on **qualitative** research, such as researching the types of rituals a culture has, as well as **quantitative** research, such as measuring the relative sizes of ethnic groups.

Psychology is mainly centered on the study of the individual and his behavior. Because humans are social animals, the methods of psychology can be used to study society and culture by asking questions about how individuals behave within these groups, what motivates them, and the ways they find to express themselves.

Sociology covers how humans act as a society and within a society, and examines the rules and mechanisms they follow as a society. Sociology also looks at groups within a society and how they interact. The field relies on research methods from several disciplines, including anthropology and psychology.

Causality: The reason something happens, its cause, is a basic category of human thinking. We want to know the causes of some major event in our lives. Within the study of history, causality is the analysis of the reasons for change. The question we are asking is why and how a particular society or event developed in the particular way it did given the context in which it occurred.

Conflict: Conflict within history is opposition of ideas, principles, values or claims. Conflict may take the form of internal clashes of principles or ideas or claims within a society or group or it may take the form of opposition between groups or societies.

Bias: A prejudice or a predisposition either toward or against something. In the study of history, bias can refer to the persons or groups studied, in terms of a society's bias toward a particular political system, or it can refer to the historian's predisposition to evaluate events in a particular way.

Interdependence: A condition in which two things or groups rely upon one another; as opposed to independence, in which each thing or group relies only upon itself.

Identity: The state or perception of being a particular thing or person. Identity can also refer to the understanding or self-understanding of groups, nations, etc.

Nation-state: A particular type of political entity that provides a sovereign territory for a specific nation in which other factors also unite the citizens (e.g., language, race, ancestry, etc.).

Culture: the civilization, achievements, and customs of the people of a particular time and place

Socialization is the process by which humans learn the expectations their society has for their behavior in order to successfully function within that society.

Socialization takes place primarily in children as they learn and are taught the rules and norms of their culture. Children grow up eating the common foods of a culture, and develop a "taste" for these foods, for example. By observing adults and older children, they learn about gender roles, and appropriate ways to interact. The family is the primary influence in this kind of socialization, and contributes directly to a person's sense of self-importance and personal identity.

Through socialization, a person gains a sense of belonging to a group of people with common ideals and behaviors. When a person encounters people affiliated with other groups, their own group affiliation can be reinforced in contrast, contributing to their own sense of personal identity.

Skill 14.2   Analyze the roles and functions of social groups and institutions in the United States (e.g., ethnic groups, schools, religions) and their influence on individual and group interactions

The traditions and behaviors of a culture are based on the prevailing beliefs and values of that culture. Beliefs and values are similar and interrelated systems.

Beliefs are those things that are thought to be true. Beliefs are often associated with religion, but beliefs can also be based on political or ideological philosophies. "All men are created equal," is an example of an ideological belief.

Values are what a society thinks are right and wrong, and are often based on and shaped by beliefs. The value that every member of the society has a right to participate in his government might be considered to be based on the belief that "All men are created equal," for instance.

A culture's beliefs and values are reflected in the cultural products it produces, such as literature, the arts, media and architecture. These products become part of the culture and last from generation to generation, becoming one way that culture is transmitted through time. A common language among all members of a culture makes this transmission possible.

Sociologists have identified five different types of institutions around which societies are structured: family, education, government, religion and economy. These institutions provide a framework for members of a society to learn about and participate in a society, and allow for a society to perpetuate its beliefs and values to succeeding generations.

The **family** is the primary social unit in most societies. It is through the family that children learn the most essential skills for functioning in their society such as language and appropriate forms of interaction. The family is connected to ethnicity, which is partly defined by a person's heritage.

Education is an important institution in a society, as it allows for the formal passing on of a culture's collected knowledge. The institution of education is connected to the family, as that is where a child's earliest education takes place. The United States has a public school system administered by the states that ensures a basic education and provides a common experience for most children.

A society's **governmental** institutions often embody its beliefs and values. Laws, for instance, reflect a society's values by enforcing its ideas of right and wrong. The structure of a society's government can reflect a society's ideals about the role of an individual in his society. The American form of democracy emphasizes the rights of the individual, but in return expects individuals to respect the rights of others, including those of ethnic or political minorities.

Religion is frequently the institution from which springs a society's primary beliefs and values, and can be closely related to other social institutions. Many religions have definite teachings on the structure and importance of the family, for instance. The U.S. Constitution guarantees the free practice of religion, which has led to a large number of denominations practicing in the U.S. today. Most Americans identify with Christian faiths.

A society's **economic** institutions define how an individual can contribute and receive economic reward from his society. The United States has a capitalist economy motivated by free enterprise. While this system allows for economic advancement for the individual, it can also produce areas of poverty and economic depression.

An example of an organization that promotes the rights of the individual is **The National Association for the Advancement of Colored People** (NAACP), founded in 1909 to assist African Americans. In the early years, the work of the organization focused on working through the courts to overturn "Jim Crow" statutes that legalized racial discrimination. The group organized voters to oppose Woodrow Wilson's efforts to weave racial segregation into federal government policy. Between WWI and WWII, much energy was devoted to stopping the lynching of blacks throughout the country.

Skill 14.3 **Analyze why individuals and groups hold different or competing points of view on issues, events, and historical developments**

Humans are social animals who naturally form groups based on familial, cultural, national and other lines. Conflicts and differences of opinion are just as natural between these groups.

One source of differing views among groups is ethnocentrism. **Ethnocentrism**, as the word suggests, is the belief that one's own culture is the central and usually superior culture. An ethnocentric view usually considers different practices in other cultures as inferior or even "savage."

Psychologists have suggested that ethnocentrism is a naturally occurring attitude. For the most part, people are most comfortable among other people who share their same upbringing, language and cultural background, and are likely to judge other cultural behaviors as alien or foreign.

Historical developments are likely to affect different groups in different ways, some positively and some negatively. These effects can strengthen the ties an individual feels to the group his belongs, and solidify differences between groups.

Skill 14.4   Understand the processes of social and cultural change

Innovation is the introduction of new ways of performing work or organizing societies, and can spur drastic changes in a culture. Prior to the innovation of agriculture, for instance, human cultures were largely nomadic and survived by hunting and gathering their food. Agriculture led directly to the development of permanent settlements and a radical change in social organization. Likewise, technological innovations in the Industrial Revolution of the 19th Century changed the way work was performed and transformed the economic institutions of western cultures. Recent innovations in communications are changing the way cultures interact today.

Cultural diffusion is the movement of cultural ideas or materials between populations independent of the movement of those populations. Cultural diffusion can take place when two populations are close to one another, through direct interaction, or across great distances, through mass media and other routes. American movies are popular all over the world, for instance. Within the US, hockey, traditionally a Canadian pastime, has become a popular sport. These are both examples of cultural diffusion.

Adaptation is the process that individuals and societies go through in changing their behavior and organization to cope with social, economic and environmental pressures.

Acculturation is an exchange or adoption of cultural features when two cultures come into regular direct contact. An example of acculturation is the adoption of Christianity and western dress by many Native Americans in the United States.

Assimilation is the process of a minority ethnic group largely adopting the culture of the larger group it exists within. These groups are typically immigrants moving to a new country, as with the European immigrants who traveled to the United States at the beginning of the 20th Century who assimilated to American culture.

Extinction is the complete disappearance of a culture. Extinction can occur suddenly, from disease, famine or war when the people of a culture are completely destroyed, or slowly over time as a culture adapts, acculturates or assimilates to the point where its original features are lost.

COMPETENCY 15.0   UNDERSTAND ECONOMIC AND POLITICAL PRINCIPLES, CONCEPTS, AND SYSTEMS; AND RELATE THIS KNOWLEDGE TO HISTORICAL AND CONTEMPORARY DEVELOPMENTS IN OKLAHOMA, THE UNITED STATES, AND THE WORLD

Skill 15.1   **Analyze the basic structure, fundamental ideas, accomplishments, and problems of the U.S. economic system**

The U.S. economy consists of the **household** or **consumer** sector, the **business** sector and the **government** sector. Households earn their incomes by selling their factors of production in the input market. Businesses hire their inputs in the factor market and use them to produce outputs. Households use their incomes earned in the factor market to purchase the output of businesses. Both households and businesses are active participants in both the input and output market. The function of organized labor was to help obtain a higher factor income for workers. They negotiate the work agreement, or contract, for their union members. This collective bargaining agreement states the terms and conditions of employment for the length of the contract, and is a contract between the worker and the employers. Households do not spend all of their income; they save some of it in banks. A well organized smoothly functioning banking system is required for the operation of the economy.

Macroeconomics refers to the functioning of the economy on the **national** level and the functioning of the aggregate units that comprise the national economy. Macroeconomics is concerned with a study of the economy's overall economic performance, or what is called the **Gross Domestic Product** or GDP. The GDP is a measure of the economy's output during a specified time period. Tabulating the economy's output can be measured in two ways, both of which give the same result: the expenditures approach and the incomes approach. Basically, what is spent on the national output by each sector of the economy is equal to what is earned producing the national output by each of the factors of production.

The macro economy consists of four broad sectors: **consumers, businesses, government** and the **foreign** sector. In the expenditures approach, GDP is determined by the amount of spending in each sector. GDP is equal to the consumption expenditures of consumers plus the investment expenditures of businesses plus spending of all three levels of government plus the net export spending in the foreign sector.

$$GDP = C + I + G + (X\text{-}M)$$

When the economy is functioning smoothly the amount of national output produced, or the aggregate supply, is just equal to the amount of national output purchased, or aggregate demand. Then we have an economy in a period of prosperity without economic instability. But market economies experience the fluctuations of the business cycle, the ups and downs in the level of economic activity. There are four phases: boom (period of prosperity), recession (a period of declining GDP and rising unemployment), trough (the low point of the recession), and recovery (a period of lessening unemployment and rising prices). There are no rules pertaining to the duration or severity of any of the phases.

The phases result in periods of unemployment and periods of inflation. Inflation results from too much spending in the economy. Buyers want to buy more than sellers can produce and bid up prices for the available output. Unemployment occurs when there is not enough spending in the economy. Sellers have produced more output than buyers are buying and the result is a surplus situation. Firms faced with surplus merchandise, lower their production levels and lay off workers and there is unemployment. These are situations that require government policy actions.

The U.S. economy is based on the concepts of individual freedom of choice and competition. Economic agents are free to pursue their own interests. They can choose their occupation and undertake entrepreneurial ventures. If they are successful, they gain in the form of profits. The profit incentive is very important because people and businesses are willing to take risks for the possibility of gaining profit. The U.S. economy is one of the most successful economies in the world with the highest total GDP. Like any market economy, it is subject to the business cycle, the temporary bouts of inflation and/or unemployment. When they occur, appropriate policies are implemented to counteract them.

Skill 15.2 Analyze values, principles, concepts, and key features of American constitutional democracy (e.g., individual freedom, separation of powers, due process)

The American nation was founded upon the belief that the people would have a large degree of autonomy and liberty. The famous maxim "no taxation without representation" was a rallying cry for the Revolution, not only because the people didn't want to suffer the increasingly oppressive series of taxes imposed on them by the British Parliament, but also because the people could not in any way influence the lawmakers in Parliament in regard to those taxes. No American colonist had a seat in Parliament and no American colonist could vote for members of Parliament.

One of the most famous words in the Declaration of Independence is "liberty," the pursuit of which all people should be free to enjoy. That idea, that a people should be free to pursue their own course, even to the extent of making their own mistakes, has dominated political thought in the 200-plus years of the American republic.

Representation, the idea that a people can vote—or even replace—their lawmakers was not a new idea, except in America. Residents of other British colonies did not have these rights, of course, and America was only a colony.. What the Sons of Liberty and other revolutionaries were asking for was to stand on an equal footing with the Mother Country. Along with the idea or representation comes the idea that key ideas and concepts can be deliberated and discussed, with theoretically everyone having a chance to voice their views. This applied to both lawmakers and the people who elected them. Lawmakers wouldn't just pass bills that became laws; rather, they would debate the issues and the strengths and weaknesses of proposed laws before voting on them. Members of both houses of Congress had the opportunity to speak out on the issues, as did the people at large, who could contact their lawmakers and express their views. This idea ran counter to the experience of the Founding Fathers before the Revolution—that of taxation without representation. The different branches of government were designed to serve as a mechanism of checks and balances on each other so that no one branch could exercise too much power.

Another key concept in the American ideal is **equality**, the idea that every person has the same rights and responsibilities under the law. Great Britain was a stratified society, with social classes firmly in place. Not everyone was equal under the law; and it was clear that the more money and power a person had, the easier it was for that person to avoid things like serving in the army and being charged with a crime. The goal of the Declaration of Independence and the Constitution was to provide equality for all who were governed by them.

Due process under law was also a big concern of the founders. Various amendments protect the rights of people.   Amendments five through eight protect citizens who are accused of crimes and are brought to trial. Every citizen has the right to due process of law, (the government must follow the same fair rules for everyone brought to trial) . These rules include the right to a trial by an impartial jury, the right to be defended by a lawyer, and the right to a speedy trial. The last two amendments limit the powers of the federal government to those that are expressly granted in the Constitution; any rights not expressly mentioned in the Constitution, thus, belong to the states or to the people. This feeds into the idea of **opportunity**. The "American Dream" is that every individual has an equal chance to make his or her fortune in a new land and that the United States welcomes and encourages that initiative.

Skill 15.3 **Compare different perspectives regarding economic and political issues and policies in Oklahoma and the United States (e.g., in relation to taxing and spending decisions)**

Fiscal policy refers to changes in the levels of government spending and taxation. All three levels of government engage in fiscal policy that has economic and social effects. At the state and local levels, the purpose of government spending and taxes is to run the state and local governments. When taxes are raised at the state or local level, the purpose is to provide revenues for the government to function, not to affect the level of aggregate spending in the economy. When Oklahoma imposes taxes, the purpose is to pay for the programs and services the State it provides to its population. These taxes will have economic and social effects on the local population who may have less money to spend. Local merchants may see a decrease in their revenues from less spending in addition to having to pay taxes themselves. When state and local governments spend money through programs like repairing or building roads, the effect is to inject money into the local economy even though the purpose is to promote transportation. The purpose isn't to stimulate spending in the area.

Fiscal policy at the national level differs from that at the state and local levels because the purpose of the fiscal policy is to affect the level of aggregate spending in the economy. One of the functions of the federal government is to promote economic stabilization. This means to correct for inflation and unemployment. The way they do this is through changing the level of government spending and/or the level of taxation. Inflation occurs when there is too high a level of aggregate spending. Producers can't keep up with the demand and the result is raising prices. In this situation the government implements contractionary fiscal policy which consists of a decrease in government spending and/ or an increase in taxes. The purpose is to slow down an economy that is expanding too quickly by enacting policies that result in people having less money to spend. These policies, depending on how they are implemented, will affect the components of aggregate demand – consumption, investment and government spending. Spending on imports will also decrease. The result of the contractionary fiscal policy will be to end the inflation.

Unemployment is another macro-economic problem that requires expansionary fiscal policy. Unemployment occurs due to a lack of spending in the economy. There is not enough aggregate demand in the economy to fully employ the labor force. Here the role for government is to stimulate spending. If they can increase spending, producers will increase their output and hire more resources, including labor, thus eliminating the problem of unemployment. Expansionary fiscal policy consists of increasing government spending and/or lowering taxes. The increase in government spending injects money into the economy. Government programs to build roads mean more jobs. More jobs mean more spending and a higher level of aggregate demand. As producers see an increase in the demand for their product, they increase their output levels. As they expand, they require more resources, including labor. As more of the labor force works, the level of spending increases still further, and so on. Lowering taxes affects the consumption and possibly the investment components of aggregate demand leaving consumers and businesses with more money to spend, thus leading to a higher level of spending and eliminating unemployment.

Skill 15.4   Analyze relationships between the United States and other nations (e.g., in the development of democratic principles and human rights)

Since the United States is based on the principle of freedom, it is active in trying to encourage other nations to respect the rights of their own citizens. This concern for democratic principles and human rights has involved the United States in World War II and other skirmishes. Troops were sent to Serbia to halt the genocide that was taking place and to restore a democratic government to the area. The U.S. and other nations were instrumental in bringing Serbian leaders to trial for war crimes. The same is true of the situation in Iraq, where the U.S. invasion resulted in the overthrow of Saddam Hussein and the establishment of a democratic form of government. The same thing can be said of Viet Nam and Korea, and other places in the world where people have been oppressed. Some of this is accomplished through the United Nations; some of this is accomplished outside of the United Nations.

The United States is said to be a melting pot. Its population consists of immigrants and descendants of immigrants. Many different ethnic cultures are thriving in the U.S. The U.S. respects the different ethnicities and cultures of other people and those that choose to settle in the U.S. America is affected by the politics of other nations, just as every nation is. Our politics exist the way they are because of our beliefs in freedom.

COMPETENCY 16.0   **UNDERSTAND THE ROLES, RIGHTS, AND RESPONSIBILITIES OF CITIZENSHIP IN THE UNITED STATES AND THE SKILLS, KNOWLEDGE, AND ATTITUDES NECESSARY FOR SUCCESSFUL PARTICIPATION IN CIVIC LIFE**

Skill 16.1   **Analyze the personal and political rights guaranteed in the Declaration of Independence, the U.S. Constitution, the constitution of the state of Oklahoma, and major civil rights legislation**

The three most basic rights guaranteed by the Declaration of Independence are "life, liberty, and the pursuit of happiness." The first is self-explanatory: Americans are guaranteed the right to live their lives in America. The second one is basic as well: Americans are guaranteed the right to live their lives *free* in America. The last basic right is more esoteric but no less important: Americans are guaranteed the right to pursue a happy life. First and foremost, they are allowed the ability to make a life for themselves in America. That happiness also extends to the pursuit of life free from oppression or discrimination.

The **Declaration of Independence** is an outgrowth of both ancient Greek ideas of democracy and individual rights and the ideas of the European Enlightenment and the Renaissance, especially the ideology of the political thinker **John Locke**. Thomas Jefferson (1743-1826) the principle author of the Declaration borrowed much from Locke's theories and writings. John Locke was one of the most influential political writers of the seventeenth century who put great emphasis on human rights and put forth the belief that when governments violate those rights people should rebel. He wrote the book "*Two Treatises of Government*" in 1690, which had tremendous influence on political thought in the American colonies and helped to shape the U.S. Constitution and Declaration of Independence.

The Declaration of Independence was the founding document of the United States of America. The Articles of Confederation were the first attempt of the newly independent states to reach a new understanding amongst their selves. The Declaration was intended to demonstrate the reasons the colonies were seeking separation from Great Britain. Conceived by and written for the most part by **Thomas Jefferson,** it is not only important for what it says, but also for how it says it. The Declaration is in many respects a poetic document. Instead of a simple recitation of the colonists' grievances, it set out clearly the reasons why the colonists were seeking their freedom from Great Britain. They had tried all means to resolve the dispute peacefully. It was the right of a people, when all other methods of addressing their grievances have been tried and failed, to separate themselves from that power that was keeping them from fully expressing their rights to **"life, liberty, and the pursuit of happiness"**.

A convention met under the presidency of George Washington, with fifty-five of the sixty-five appointed members present. A constitution was written in four months. The Constitution of the United States is the fundamental law of the republic. It is a precise, formal, written document of the *extraordinary*, or *supreme*, type of constitution. The founders of the Union established it as the highest governmental authority. There is no national power superior to it. The foundations were so broadly laid as to provide for the expansion of national life and to make it an instrument which would last for all time. To maintain its stability, the framers created a difficult process for making any changes to it. No amendment can become valid until it is ratified by three-fourths of all of the states. The British system of government was part of the basis of the final document. But significant changes were necessary to meet the needs of a partnership of states that were tied together as a single federation, yet sovereign in their own local affairs. This constitution established a system of government that was unique and advanced far beyond other systems of its day.

The constitution binds the states in a governmental unity in everything that affects the welfare of all. At the same time, it recognizes the right of the people of each state to independence of action in matters that relate only to them. Since the Federal Constitution is the law of the land, all other laws must conform to it.

The debates conducted during the Constitutional Congress represent the issues and the arguments that led to the compromises in the final document. The debates also reflect the concerns of the Founding Fathers that the rights of the people be protected from abrogation by the government itself and the determination that no branch of government should have enough power to continually dominate the others. There is a **system of checks and balances.**

Bill Of Rights - The first ten amendments to the United States Constitution dealing with civil liberties and civil rights. James Madison was credited with writing a majority of them. They are in brief:

1.   **Freedom of Religion.**
2.   **Right To Bear Arms.**
3.   **Security from the quartering of troops in homes.**
4.   **Right against unreasonable search and seizures.**
5.   **Right against self-incrimination.**
6.   **Right to trial by jury, right to legal council.**
7.   **Right to jury trial for civil actions.**
8.   **No cruel or unusual punishment allowed.**
9.   **These rights shall not deny other rights the people enjoy.**
10.   **Powers not mentioned in the Constitution shall be retained by the states or the people.**

Skill 16.2   Demonstrate an understanding of the U.S. election process and the roles of political parties, pressure groups, and special interests in the U.S. political system

The political party system in the U.S. has five main objects or lines of action:

1. To influence government policy,
2. To form or shape public opinion,
3. To win elections,
4. To choose between candidates for office,
5. To procure salaried posts for party leaders and workers.

The U.S. electoral process has many and varied elements, from simple voting to complex campaigning for office.

First of all, American citizens vote. They vote for laws and statues and referenda and elected officials. They have to register in order to vote, and at that time they can declare their intended membership in a political party. America has a large list of political parties, which have varying degrees of membership. The Democratic and Republican Parties are the two with the most money and power, but other political parties abound. In some cases, people who are registered members of a political party are allowed to vote for only members of that political party.   Elections are held at the local, state and national level at designated times throughout the year.

Candidates affiliate themselves with political parties. Candidates then go about the business of campaigning, which includes getting the word on out on their candidacy, what they believe in, and what they will do if elected. Candidates sometimes get together for debates, to showcase their views on important issues of the day and how those views differ from those of their opponents. Candidates give public speeches, attend public functions, and outline their views to reporters, for coverage in newspapers and magazines and on radio and television. On Election Day candidates hope they've done enough. The results of elections are made known very quickly, sometimes instantly, thanks to computerized vote tallying. Once results are finalized, winning candidates give victory speeches and losing candidates give concession speeches.

Voters technically have the option to **recall** elected candidates; such a measure, however, is drastic and requires a large number of signatures to get the motion on the ballot and then a large number of votes to have the measure approved. As such, recalls of elected candidates are relatively rare. One widely publicized recall in recent years was that of California Governor Gray Davis, who was replaced by Arnold Schwarzenegger.

Another method of removing public officials from office is **impeachment**. This is also rare but still a possibility. Both houses of the state or federal government get involved, and both houses have to approve the impeachment measures by a large margin. In the case of the federal government, the House of Representatives votes to impeach a federal official and the Senate votes to convict or acquit. Conviction means that the official must leave office immediately; acquittal results in no penalties or fines.

The **College of Electors**—or the Electoral College, as it is more commonly known—has a long and distinguished history of mirroring the political will of the American voters. On some occasions, the results have not been entirely reflective of the popular vote.

Article II of the Constitution lists the specifics of the Electoral College. The Founding Fathers included the Electoral College as one of the famous "checks and balances" for two reasons: 1) to give states with small populations more equal weight in the presidential election, and 2) they didn't trust the common man to be able to make an informed decision on which candidate would make the best president.

Technically, the electors do not have to vote for anyone. The Constitution does not require them to do so. And throughout the history of presidential elections, some have indeed voted for someone else. But tradition holds that the electors vote for the candidate chosen by their state, and so the vast majority of electors do just that. The Electoral College meets a few weeks after the presidential election. Mostly, their meeting is a formality. When all the electoral votes are counted, the candidate with the most votes wins. In most cases, the candidate who wins the popular vote also wins in the Electoral College. However, this has not always been the case.

In 2000 in Florida, the election was decided by the Supreme Court. The Democratic Party's nominee was Vice-President Al Gore. A presidential candidate himself back in 1988, Gore had served as vice-president for both of President Bill Clinton's terms. As such, he was both a champion of Clinton's successes and a reflection of his failures. The Republican Party's nominee was George W. Bush, governor of Texas and son of former President George Bush. He campaigned on a platform of a strong national defense and an end to questionable ethics in the White House. The election was hotly contested, and many states went down to the wire, being decided by only a handful of votes. The one state that seemed to be flip-flopping as Election Day turned into Election Night was Florida. In the end, Gore won the popular vote, by nearly 540,000 votes. But he didn't win the electoral vote. The vote was so close in Florida that a recount was necessary under federal law. Eventually, the Supreme Court weighed in and stopped all the recounts. The last count had Bush winning by less than a thousand votes. That gave him Florida and the White House.

Lobbyists are a very visible and time-honored part of the political process. They wield power to varying degrees, depending on the issues involved and how much the parties they represent want to maintain the status quo or effect change. A lobbyist is someone who works for a political cause by attempting to influence lawmakers to vote a certain way on issues of the day. For example, a lobbyist for an oil production company would urge lawmakers not to increase existing or create new taxes on oil. This urging can take many forms, among them direct communication, letter-writing or phone-in campaigns designed to stir up public sentiment for or against an issue or set of issues. Lobbyists also serve to make lawmakers aware of information that they might not have, including how other lawmakers view the important issues of the day and they make other lobbyists aware of information.

Citizens wishing to engage in the political process to a greater degree have several paths open, such as participating in local government. Counties, states, and sometimes neighborhoods are governed by locally elected boards or councils that meet publicly. Citizens are usually able to address these boards, bringing their concerns and expressing their opinions on matters being considered. Citizens may even wish to stand for local election and join a governing board, or seek support for higher office.

Supporting a political party is another means by which citizens can participate in the political process. Political parties endorse certain platforms that express general social and political goals, and support member candidates in election campaigns. Political parties make use of much volunteer labor, with supporters making telephone calls, distributing printed material and campaigning for the party's causes and candidates. Political parties solicit donations to support their efforts as well. Contributing money to a political party is another form of participation citizens can undertake.

The vehicle by which a candidate gets the most exposure these days is **media** advertising, specifically television advertising. This is the most expensive kind of advertising but it also has the potential to reach the widest audience. TV ad prices can run into the hundreds of thousands of dollars, depending on when they run; but they have the potential to reach perhaps millions of viewers. Other forms of advertising include radio and Web ads, signs and billboards, and flyers.

The sources of funds needed to run a successful political campaign are varied. A candidate might have a significant amount of money in his or her own personal coffers. In rare cases, the candidate finances the entire campaign. However, the most prevalent source of money is outside donations. A candidate's friends and family might donate funds to the campaign, as well as the campaign workers themselves. State and federal governments will also contribute to most regional or national campaigns, provided that the candidate can prove that he or she can raise a certain amount of money first. The largest source of campaign finance money, however, comes from so-called "special interests." A large company such as an oil company or a manufacturer of electronic goods will want to keep prices or tariffs down and so will want to make sure that laws lifting those prices or tariffs aren't passed.

To this end, the company will contribute money to the campaigns of candidates who are likely to vote to keep those prices or tariffs down. A candidate is not obligated to accept such a donation, of course, and further is not obligated to vote in favor of the interests of the special interest; however, doing the former might create a shortage of money and doing the latter might ensure that no further donations come from that or any other special interest. An oil company wants to protect its interests, and its leaders don't very much care which political candidate is doing that for them as long as it is being done.

Another powerful source of support for a political campaign is **special interest groups** of a political nature. These are not necessarily economic powers but rather groups whose people want to effect political change or ensure that such change doesn't take place, depending on the status of the laws at the time. A good example of a special interest group is a pro-life group or a pro-choice group. The abortion issue is still a divisive one in American politics, and many groups will want to protect or defend or ban—depending on which side they're on—certain rights and practices. This kind of social group usually has a large number of dedicated individuals who do much more than vote: They organize into political action committees attend meetings and rallies, and work to make sure that their message gets out to a wide audience. Methods of spreading the word often include media advertising on behalf of their chosen candidates. This kind of expenditure is no doubt welcomed by the candidates, who will get the benefit of the exposure but won't have to spend that money because someone else is signing the checks.

Skill 16.3 **Analyze the ways in which citizens participate in and influence the political process in the United States (e.g., the role of public opinion and citizen action in shaping public policy)**

A person who lives in a democratic society theoretically has a list of rights guaranteed to him or her by the government. In the United States, this is the Constitution and its Amendments. Among these very important rights are:

- the right to speak out in public;
- the right to pursue any religion;
- the right for a group of people to gather in public for *any* reason that doesn't fall under a national security cloud;
- the right *not* to have soldiers stationed in your home;
- the right *not* to be forced to testify against yourself in a court of law;
- the right to a speedy and public trial by a jury of your peers;
- the right *not* to the victim of cruel and unusual punishment;
- and the right to avoid unreasonable search and seizure of your person, your house, and your vehicle.

The average citizen of an authoritarian country has little if any of these rights and must watch his or her words, actions, and even magazine subscriptions and Internet visits in order to avoid *the appearance* of disobeying one of the many oppressive laws that help the government govern its people.

Both the democratic-society and the authoritarian-society citizens can serve in government. They can even run for election and can be voted in by their peers. One large difference exists, however: In an authoritarian society, the members of government will most likely be of the same political party. A country with this setup, like China, will have a government that includes representatives elected by the Chinese people, but all of those elected representatives will belong to the Communist Party, which runs the government and the country. When the voters cast their ballot, only Communist Party members are listed. In fact, in many cases, only one candidate is on the ballot for each office. China, in fact, chooses its head of government through a meeting of the Party leaders. In effect, the Party is higher in the governmental hierarchy than the leader of the country. Efforts to change this governmental structure and practice are discouraged.

On the other side of this spectrum is the citizen of the democratic society, who can vote for whomever he or she wants to and can run for any office he or she wants to. On those ballots will appear names and political parties that run the spectrum, including the Communist Party. Theoretically, *any* political party can get its candidates on ballots locally, statewide, or nationwide; varying degrees of effort have to be put in to do this, of course. Building on the First Amendment freedom to peacefully assembly, American citizens can have political party meetings, fund-raisers, and even conventions without fearing reprisals from the Government.

In a civil society, people are certainly free to pursue business interests both private and public. Private activities are less regulated than public ones, but public activities are not discouraged or dissuaded, as long as they don't violate laws or other people's rights.

In America and in other countries as well, a person has the right to pursue any kind of business strategy he or she wants. The age of Internet advertising and marketing has created opportunities for new and different businesses. Rather than discourage people from starting businesses, the American government and its various associated entities actually encourage such endeavors. Prospective business owners can find whole libraries of information encouraging them and guiding them through the sometimes rigorous practice of starting a business. Entire organizations exist just to answer questions about this process.

America is a land full of groups—religious groups, political groups, social groups, and business and economic groups. All these groups meet in public and in private and the people who belong to these groups are free to associate with any groups that they choose, again as long as the practices of those groups are not illegal or harmful to other people.

Freedom to practice the faith of your choice finds extraordinary protection under US law. The First Amendment guarantees every American the right to worship as he or she sees fit, without fear of reprisal by the government. Religious organizations, however, do not, for the most part, receive funding from governments to support their efforts. The First Amendment also denies the government the right to establish a religion, meaning that it can favor no one religion over others. Entities like parochial schools, which provide both education and religious training, routinely have to seek funding in places other than the federal or state governments.

Social groups are encouraged as well. The First Amendment gives the American people the right to peaceable assembly. Social organizations are made up of people with similar interests or experiences that come together on a regular basis to discuss those interests and experiences and to pursue a joint appreciation.

Public officials have an overwhelming need to communicate. They want other people to know what they're doing and why. They want to make sure that the voters who elected them know what they're doing pursuing the agendas that are closest to their hearts. Ultimately, they want to do as much as they can to get themselves re-elected or, if term limits won't allow re-election, to leaving a memorable public legacy.

In the court of **public opinion**, the newspaper or radio offers politicians a fairly easy way to get noticed. Television began to change all that with its visual record of events. The proliferation of cable and satellite television channels has made it very difficult for a lawmaker *not* to get noticed if her or she does something remarkable these days. The Internet offers a vast, heterogeneous world of opportunities. Internet opportunities include not just news websites but personal websites and the eponymous blogs, public opinion pieces that may or may not contain factual information contrasted with the scrutiny that major media outlets such as newspapers, radio, and television undergo.

Public officials will hire people or an agency to conduct **public relations**, which is efforts to make the lawmakers look good in the eyes of their constituents. A public relations person or firm will have as its overreaching goal the happiness of the lawmaker who hired her or them and will gladly write press releases, arrange media events (like tours of schools or soup kitchens), and basically do everything else to keep their employer's name in the public eye in a good way. This includes making the lawmaker's position on important issues known to the public. Especially controversial issues will be embraced on the other side by lawmakers, and those lawmakers will want their constituents to know how they intend to vote those issues. It's also a good idea to find out what your constituents think about these issues of the day, since the fastest way to get yourself bad publicity or thrown out at re-election time is to ignore the weight of **public opinion**.

Skill 16.4 **Analyze the factors that affect attitudes toward civic life and that have expanded or limited the role of the individual in U.S. political life during the twentieth century (e.g., female suffrage, discriminatory laws, the growth of presidential primaries, the role of the media in political elections)**

The **women's rights movement** is concerned with the freedoms of women as differentiated from broader ideas of human rights. These issues are generally different from those that affect men and boys because of biological conditions or social constructs. The rights the movement has sought to protect throughout history include:
- The right to vote
- The right to work
- The right to fair wages
- The right to bodily integrity and autonomy
- The right to own property
- The right to an education
- The right to hold public office
- Marital rights
- Parental rights
- Religious rights
- The right to serve in the military
- The right to enter into legal contracts

The movement for women's rights has resulted in many social and political changes. Many of the ideas that seemed very radical merely 100 years ago are now normative. Some of the most famous leaders in the women's movement throughout American history are:

- Abigail Adams
- Susan B. Anthony
- Gloria E. Anzaldua
- Betty Friedan
- Olympe de Gouges
- Gloria Steinem
- Harriet Tubman
- Mary Wollstonecraft
- Virginia Woolf
- Germaine Greer

Many within the women's movement are primarily committed to justice and the natural rights of all people. This has led many members of the women's movement to be involved in the Black Civil Rights Movement, the gay rights movement, and the recent social movement to protect the rights of fathers.

After the Civil War, the rise of the Redeemer governments marked the beginning of the **Jim Crow** laws and official segregation. Blacks were still allowed to vote, but ways were found to make it difficult for them to do so, such as literacy tests and poll taxes. Reconstruction, which had set as its goal the reunification of the South with the North and the granting of civil rights to freed slaves was a limited success, at best, and in the eyes of blacks was considered a failure.

Take for example the Birmingham Campaign of 1963-64. A campaign was planned to use sit-in, kneel-ins in churches, and a march to the county building to launch a voter registration campaign. The City obtained an injunction forbidding all such protests. The protesters, including Martin Luther King, Jr., believed the injunction was unconstitutional, and defied it. They were arrested. While in jail, King wrote his famous Letter from Birmingham Jail. When the campaign began to falter, the "Children's Crusade" called students to leave school and join the protests. The events became news when more than 600 students were jailed. The next day more students joined the protest. **The media** was present and broadcast to the nation vivid pictures of fire hoses being used to knock down children and dogs attacking some of them. The resulting public outrage led the Kennedy administration to intervene. About a month later, a committee was formed to end hiring discrimination, arrange for the release of jailed protesters, and establish normative communication between blacks and whites. Four months later, the KKK bombed the Sixteenth Street Baptist Church, killing four girls.

Newspapers, then as now, influence the growth of political parties. Newspaper publishers and editors took sides on issues. Thus, from the very beginning, American newspapers and each new branch of the media have played an important role in helping to shape public opinion.

First and foremost, the **media** report on the actions taken and encouraged by leaders of the government. In many cases, these actions are common knowledge. Policy debates, discussions on controversial issues, struggles against foreign powers in economic and wartime endeavors—all are fodder for media reports. The First Amendment guarantees media in America the right to report on these things, and the media reporters take full advantage of that right and privilege in striving not only to inform the American public but also to keep the governmental leaders in check.

COMPETENCY 17.0 UNDERSTAND AND APPLY SKILLS RELATED TO SOCIAL STUDIES, INCLUDING GATHERING, ORGANIZATION, MAPPING, EVALUATING, INTERPRETING, AND DISPLAYING INFORMATION

Skill 17.1 Evaluate the appropriateness of various resources for meeting specified information needs (e.g., atlas, database, surveys, polls, the Internet)

The Internet and other research resources provide a wealth of information on thousands of interesting topics for students preparing presentations or projects. Using search engines like Google, Microsoft and Infotrac, students can search multiple Internet resources or databases on one subject search. Students should have an outline of the purpose of a project or research presentation that includes:

- Purpose - identity the reason for the research information
- Objective - having a clear thesis for a project will allow the students opportunities to be specific on Internet searches
- Preparation - when using resources or collecting data, students should create folders for sorting through the information. Providing labels for the folders will create a system of organization that will make construction of the final project or presentation easier and less time consuming
- Procedure - organized folders and a procedural list of what the project or presentation needs to include will create A+ work for students and A+ grading for teachers
- Visuals or artifacts - choose data or visuals that are specific to the subject content or presentation. Make sure that poster boards or Power Point presentations can be visually seen from all areas of the classroom. Teachers can provide laptop computers for Power Point presentations.

When a teacher models and instructs students in the proper use of search techniques, the teacher can minimize wasted time in preparing projects and wasted paper from students who print every search. In some school districts, students are allowed a maximum number of printed pages per week. Since students have Internet accounts for computer usage, the monitoring of printing is easily done by the school's librarian and teachers in classrooms.

Having the school's librarian or technology expert as a guest speaker in classrooms provides another method of sharing and modeling proper presentation preparation using technology. Teachers can also appoint technology experts from the students in a classroom to work with students on projects and presentations. In high schools, technology classes provide students with upper-class teacher assistants who fill the role of technology assistants.

Internet usage agreements define a number of criteria of technology use that students must agree to in order to have access to school computers. Students must exercise responsibility and accountability in adhering to technology usage during the school day. Students who violate any parts of the computer usage agreement are subject to have all access to school computers or other educational technology denied or blocked, which, for the student needing to print a paper using the school computer and printer, could make the difference in handing assignments in on time or receiving a lower grade for late assignments.

An **atlas** is a collection of maps usually bound into a book and containing geographic features, political boundaries, and perhaps social, religious and economic statistics. Atlases can be found at most libraries but they are widely available on the Internet.

Statistical **surveys** are used in social sciences to collect information on a sample of the population. With any kind of information, care must be taken to accurately record information so the results are not skewed or distorted.

Opinion Polls are used to represent the opinions of a population by asking a number of people a series of questions about a product, place, person, event or perhaps the president and then using the results to apply the answers to a larger group or population. Polls, like surveys are subject to errors in the process. Errors can occur based on who is asked the question, where they are asked, the time of day or the biases one may hold in relevance to the poll being taken.

Skill 17.2 **Interpret information presented in one or more graphic representations (e.g., graph, table, map) and translates written or graphic information from one form to the other**

Physical **locations** of the earth's surface features include the four major hemispheres and the parts of the earth's continents in them. Political **locations** are the political divisions, if any, within each continent. Both physical and political locations are precisely determined in two *ways:* (1) Surveying is done to determine boundary lines and distance from other features. (2) Exact locations are precisely determined by imaginary lines of **latitude (parallels)** and **longitude** (meridians). The intersection of these lines at right angles forms a grid, making it impossible to pinpoint an exact location of any place using any two grid coordinates.

The process of putting the features of the Earth onto a flat surface is called **projection**. All maps are really map projections. There are many different types. Each one deals in a different way with the problem of distortion. Map projections are made in a number of ways. Some are done using complicated mathematics.

However, the basic ideas behind map projections can be understood by looking at the three most common types:

(1) **<u>Cylindrical Projections</u>** - These are done by taking a cylinder of paper and wrapping it around a globe. A light is used to project the globe's features onto the paper. Distortion is least where the paper touches the globe. For example, suppose that the paper was wrapped so that it touched the globe at the equator, the map from this projection would have just a little distortion near the equator. However, in moving north or south of the equator, the distortion would increase as you moved further away from the equator. The best known and most widely used cylindrical projection is the **Mercator Projection.** It was first developed in 1569 by Gerardus Mercator, a Flemish mapmaker.

(2) **<u>Conical Projections</u>** - The name for these maps come from the fact that the projection is made onto a cone of paper. The cone is made so that it touches a globe at the base of the cone only. It can also be made so that it cuts through part of the globe in two different places. Again, there is the least distortion where the paper touches the globe. If the cone touches at two different points, there is some distortion at both of them. Conical projections are most often used to map areas in the **middle latitudes**. Maps of the United States are most often conical projections. This is because most of the country lies within these latitudes.

(3) **<u>Flat-Plane Projections</u>** - These are made with a flat piece of paper. It touches the globe at one point only. Areas near this point show little distortion. Flat-plane projections are often used to show the areas of the north and south poles. One such flat projection is called a **Gnomonic Projection**. On this kind of map all meridians appear as straight lines, Gnomonic projections are useful because any straight line drawn between points on it forms a **Great-Circle Route**.

Great-Circle Routes can best be described by thinking of a globe and when using the globe the shortest route between two points on it can be found by simply stretching a string from one point to the other. However, if the string was extended in reality, so that it took into effect the globe's curvature, it would then make a great-circle. A great-circle is any circle that cuts a sphere, such as the globe, into two equal parts. Because of distortion, most maps do not show great-circle routes as straight lines, Gnomonic projections, however, do show the shortest distance between the two places as a straight line, because of this they are valuable for navigation. They are called Great-Circle Sailing Maps.

To properly analyze a given map one must be familiar with the various parts and symbols that most modern maps use. For the most part, this is standardized, with different maps using similar parts and symbols, these can include:

The Title - All maps should have a title, just like all books should. The title tells you what information is to be found on the map.

The Legend - Most maps have a legend. A legend tells the reader about the various symbols that are used on that particular map and what the symbols represent, (also called a *map key)*.

The Grid - A grid is a series of lines that are used to find exact places and locations on the map. There are several different kinds of grid systems in use however most maps do use the longitude and latitude system, known as the **Geographic Grid System**.

Directions - Most maps have some directional system to show which way the map is being presented. Often on a map, a small compass will be present, with arrows showing the four basic directions, north, south, east, and west.

The Scale - This is used to show the relationship between a unit of measurement on the map versus the real world measure on the Earth. Maps are drawn to many different scales. Some maps show a lot of detail for a small area. Others show a greater span of distance, whichever is being used one should always be aware of just what scale is being used. For instance the scale might be something like 1 inch = 10 miles for a small area or for a map showing the whole world it might have a scale in which 1 inch = 1,000 miles. The point is that one must look at the map key in order to see what units of measurements the map is using.

Maps have four main properties. They are (1) the size of the areas shown on the map. (2) The shapes of the areas, (3) Consistent scales, and (4) Straight line directions. A map can be drawn so that it is correct in one or more of these properties. No map can be correct in all of them.

Equal areas - One property which maps can have is that of equal areas. In an equal area map, the meridians and parallels are drawn so that the areas shown have the same proportions as they do on the Earth. For example, Greenland is about 118th the size of South America, thus it will be show as 118th the size on an equal area map. The **Mercator projection** is an example of a map that does not have equal areas. In it, Greenland appears to be about the same size of South America. This is because the distortion is very bad at the poles and Greenland lies near the North Pole.

Conformal Map - A second map property is conformal, or correct shapes. There are no maps which can show very large areas of the earth in their exact shapes. Only globes can really do that, however Conformal Maps are as close as possible to true shapes. The United States is often shown by a Lambert Conformal Conic Projection Map.

Consistent Scales - Many maps attempt to use the same scale on all parts of the map. Generally, this is easier when maps show a relatively small part of the earth's surface. For example, a map of Florida might be a Consistent Scale Map. Generally maps showing large areas are not consistent-scale maps. This is so because of distortion. Often such maps will have two scales noted in the key. One scale, for example, might be accurate to measure distances between points along the Equator. Another might be then used to measure distances between the North Pole and the South Pole.

Maps showing physical features often try to show information about the elevation or **relief** of the land. **Elevation** is the distance above or below the sea level. The elevation is usually shown with colors, for instance, all areas on a map which are at a certain level will be shown in the same color.

Relief Maps - Show the shape of the land surface, flat, rugged, or steep. Relief maps usually give more detail than simply showing the overall elevation of the land's surface. Relief is also sometimes shown with colors, but another way to show relief is by using **contour lines**. These lines connect all points of a land surface which are the same height surrounding the particular area of land.

Thematic Maps - These are used to show more specific information, often on a single **theme**, or topic. Thematic maps show the distribution or amount of something over a certain given area in topics of interest such as population density, climate, economic information, cultural, political information, etc.

We use **illustrations** of various sorts because it is often easier to demonstrate a given idea visually instead of orally. Sometimes it is even easier to do so with an illustration than a description. This is especially true in the areas of education and research because humans are visually stimulated. It is a fact that any idea presented visually in some manner is always easier to understand and to comprehend than simply getting an idea across verbally, by hearing it or reading it. Throughout this document, there are several illustrations that have been presented to explain an idea in a more precise way. Sometimes these will demonstrate some of the types of illustrations available for use in the arena of political science. Among the more common illustrations used in political science are various types of **maps, graphs and charts**.

Photographs and globes are useful as well, but as they are limited in what kind of information that they can show, they are rarely used. Unless, as in the case of a photograph, it is of a particular political figure or a time that one wishes to visualize.

Although maps have advantages over globes and photographs, they do have a major disadvantage. This problem must be considered as well. The major problem of all maps comes about because most maps are flat and the Earth is a sphere. It is impossible to reproduce exactly on a flat surface an object shaped like a sphere. In order to put the earth's features onto a map they must be stretched in some way. This stretching is called **distortion.**

Distortion does not mean that maps are wrong; it simply means that they are not perfect representations of the Earth or its parts. **Cartographers,** or mapmakers, understand the problems of distortion. They try to design them so that there is as little distortion as possible in the maps.

To apply information obtained from **graphs** one must understand the two major reasons why graphs are used:

1. To present a <u>model or theory</u> visually in order to show how two or more variables interrelate.

2. To present <u>real world</u> data visually in order to show how two or more variables interrelate.

Most often used are those known as **bar graphs** and **line graphs**. Graphs themselves are most useful when one wishes to demonstrate the sequential increase, or decrease of a variable or to show specific correlations between two or more variables in a given circumstance.

Most common is the **bar graph**. Because it has an easy to see and understand way of visually showing the difference in a given set of variables. However it is limited in that it can not really show the actual proportional increase, or decrease, of each given variable to each other. (In order to show a decrease, a bar graph must show the "bar" under the starting line, thus removing the ability to really show how the various different variables would relate to each other).

Thus in order to accomplish this one must use a **line graph**. Line graphs can be of two types a **linear** or **non-linear** graph. A linear line graph uses a series of straight lines a non-linear line graph uses a curved line. Though the lines can be either straight or curved, all of the lines are called **curves**.

A line graph uses a number line or **axis.** The numbers are generally placed in order, equal distances from one another, the number line is used to represent a number, degree or some such other variable at an appropriate point on the line. Two lines are used, intersecting at a specific point. They are referred to as the X-axis and the Y-axis. The Y-axis is a vertical line the X-axis is a horizontal line. Together they form a **coordinate system.** The difference between a point on the line of the X-axis and the Y-axis is called the **slope** of the line, or the change in the value on the vertical axis divided by the change in the value on the horizontal axis. The Y-axis number is called the rise and the X-axis number is called the **run,** thus the equation for slope is:

SLOPE = RISE - (Change in value on the vertical axis)
   RUN - (Change in value on the horizontal axis)

The slope tells the amount of increase or decrease of a given **specific** variable. When using two or more variables one can plot the amount of difference between them in any given situation. This makes presenting information on a line graph more involved. It also makes it more informative and accurate than a simple bar graph. Knowledge of the term slope and what it is and how it is measured helps us to describe verbally the pictures we are seeing visually. For example, if a curve is said to have a slope of "zero", you should picture a flat line. If a curve has a slope of "one", you should picture a rising line that makes a 45-degree angle with the horizontal and vertical axis lines.

The preceding examples are of **linear** (straight line) curves. With **non-linear** curves (the ones that really do curve) the slope of the curve is constantly changing, so as a result, we must then understand that the slope of the non-linear curved line will be at a specific point. How is this done? The slope of a non-linear curve is determined by the slope of a straight line that intersects the curve at that specific point. In all graphs, an upward sloping line represents a direct relationship between the two variables. A downward slope represents an inverse relationship between the two variables. In reading any graph, one must always be very careful to understand what is being measured, what can be deduced and what cannot be deduced from the given graph.

To use **charts** correctly, one should remember the reasons one uses graphs. The general ideas are similar. It is usually a question as to which, a graph or chart, is more capable of adequately portraying the information one-wants to illustrate. One can see the difference between them and realize that in many ways graphs and charts are interrelated. One of the most common types, because it is easiest to read and understand, even for the lay person, is the **Pie-chart.** You can see pie-charts used often, especially when one is trying to illustrate the differences in percentages among various items, or when one is demonstrating the divisions of a whole.

Skill 17.3   Summarize the purpose or point of view of a historical text

A synthesis of information from multiple sources requires an understanding of the content chosen for the historical text, first of all. The writer of the synthesis will, no doubt, wish to incorporate his/her own ideas, particularly in any conclusions that are drawn, and show relationships to those of the chosen sources. That can only happen if the writer has a firm grip on what others have said or written. The focus is not so much on documentary methods but on techniques of critically examining and evaluating the ideas of others. Even so, careful documentation is extremely important in this type of presentation, particularly with regard to which particular edition is being read in the case of written sources; and date, location, etc., of online sources. The phrase "downloaded from such-and-such a website on such-and-such a date" is useful. If the conversation, interview, or speech is live, date, circumstances, and location must be indicated.

The purpose of a synthesis is to understand the works of others and to use that work in shaping a conclusion. The writer or speaker must clearly differentiate between the ideas that come from a source and his/her own.

A historical text seeks to relate or define a certain event, topic or period of time. History is the study humans through time. Historical texts can tell us what was happening at the time, what foods were eaten, what wars were being waged, who or what group was the reigning power.

COMPETENCY 18.0   **UNDERSTAND FORMAL AND INFORMAL REASONING PROCESSES, INCLUDING LOGIC AND SIMPLE PROOFS, AND APPLY PROBLEM-SOLVING TECHNIQUES AND STRATEGIES IN A VARIETY OF CONTEXTS**

Skill 18.1   **Judge the validity or logic of mathematical arguments**

A valid argument is a statement made about a pattern or relationship between elements, thought to be true, which is subsequently justified through repeated examples and logical reasoning. Another term for a valid argument is a proof.

For example, the statement that the sum of two odd numbers is always even could be tested through actual examples.

Two Odd Numbers	Sum	Validity of Statement
1+1	2 (even)	Valid
1+3	4 (even)	Valid
61+29	90 (even)	Valid
135+47	182 (even)	Valid
253+17	270 (even)	Valid
1,945+2,007	3,952 (even)	Valid
6,321+7,851	14,172 (even)	Valid

Adding two odd numbers always results in a sum that is even. It is a valid argument based on the justifications in the table above.

Here is another example. The statement that a fraction of a fraction can be determined by multiplying the numerator by the numerator and the denominator by the denominator can be proven through logical reasoning. For example, one-half of one-quarter of a candy bar can be found by multiplying ½ * ¼. The answer would be one-eighth. The validity of this argument can be demonstrated as valid with a model.

The entire rectangle represents one whole candy bar. The top half section of the model is shaded in one direction to demonstrate how much of the candy bar remains from the whole candy bar. The left quarter, shaded in a different direction, demonstrates that one-quarter of the candy bar has been given to a friend. Since the whole candy bar is not available to give out, the area that is double-shaded is the fractional part of the ½ candy bar that has been actually given away. That fractional part is one-eighth of the whole candy bar as shown in both the sketch and the algorithm.

Skill 18.2   Evaluate the sufficiency of information provided to solve a problem

Conditional statements can be diagrammed using a **Venn diagram**. A diagram can be drawn with one figure inside another figure. The inner figure represents the hypothesis. The outer figure represents the conclusion. If the hypothesis is taken to be true, then you are located inside the inner figure. If you are located in the inner figure then you are also inside the outer figure, so that proves the conclusion is true. Sometimes that conclusion can then be used as the hypothesis for another conditional, which can result in a second conclusion.

Suppose that these statements were given to you, and you are asked to try to reach a conclusion. The statements are:

> All swimmers are athletes.
> All athletes are scholars.

In "if-then" form, these would be:
> If you are a swimmer, then you are an athlete.
> If you are an athlete, then you are a scholar.

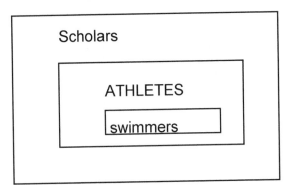

Clearly, if you are a swimmer, then you are also an athlete. This includes you in the group of scholars.

Suppose that these statements were given to you, and you are asked to try to reach a conclusion. The statements are:

> All swimmers are athletes.
> All wrestlers are athletes.

In "if-then" form, these would be:

If you are a swimmer, then you are an athlete.
If you are a wrestler, then you are an athlete.

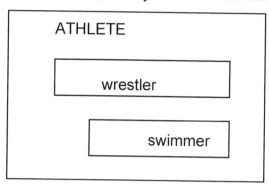

Clearly, if you are a swimmer or a wrestler, then you are also an athlete. This does NOT allow you to come to any other conclusions.

A swimmer may or may NOT also be a wrestler. Therefore, NO CONCLUSION IS POSSIBLE.

Suppose that these statements were given to you, and you are asked to try to reach a conclusion. The statements are:

All rectangles are parallelograms.
Quadrilateral ABCD is not a parallelogram.

In "if-then" form, the first statement would be:

If a figure is a rectangle, then it is also a parallelogram.

Note that the second statement is the negation of the conclusion of statement one. Remember also that the contrapositive is logically equivalent to a given conditional. That is, **"If ~ q, then ~ p"**. Since" ABCD is NOT a parallelogram " is like saying **"If ~ q,"** then you can come to the conclusion **"then ~ p"**. Therefore, the conclusion is ABCD is not a rectangle. Looking at the Venn diagram below, if all rectangles are parallelograms, then rectangles are included as part of the parallelograms. Since quadrilateral ABCD is not a parallelogram, that it is excluded from anywhere inside the parallelogram box. This allows you to conclude that ABCD can not be a rectangle either.

PARALLELOGRAMS

rectangles

quadrilateral
ABCD

Skill 19.3   Draw a valid conclusion based on stated conditions

Conditional statements are frequently written in "**if-then**" form. The "if" clause of the conditional is known as the **hypothesis**, and the "then" clause is called the **conclusion**. In a proof, the hypothesis is the information that is assumed to be true, while the conclusion is what is to be proven true. A conditional is considered to be of the form:

If p, then q
p is the hypothesis. q is the conclusion.

Conditional statements can be diagrammed using a **Venn diagram**. A diagram can be drawn with one circle inside another circle. The inner circle represents the hypothesis. The outer circle represents the conclusion. If the hypothesis is taken to be true, then you are located inside the inner circle. If you are located in the inner circle then you are also inside the outer circle, so that proves the conclusion is true.

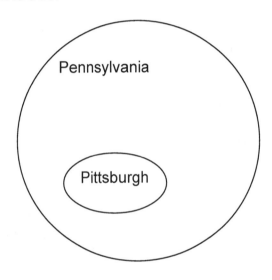

<u>Example</u>:

    If an angle has a measure of 90 degrees, then it is a right angle.

In this statement "an angle has a measure of 90 degrees" is the hypothesis.
In this statement "it is a right angle" is the conclusion.

<u>Example</u>:

    If you are in Pittsburgh, then you are in Pennsylvania.

In this statement "you are in Pittsburgh" is the hypothesis.
In this statement "you are in Pennsylvania" is the conclusion.

Skill 18.4   Apply inductive reasoning to make mathematical conjecture

Inductive thinking is the process of finding a pattern from a group of examples. That pattern is the conclusion that this set of examples seemed to indicate. It may be a correct conclusion or it may be an incorrect conclusion because other examples may not follow the predicted pattern.

Deductive thinking is the process of arriving at a conclusion based on other statements that are all known to be true, such as theorems, axiomspostulates, or postulates. Conclusions found by deductive thinking based on true statements will **always** be true.

Examples :

Suppose:
- On Monday Mr.Peterson eats breakfast at McDonalds.
- On Tuesday Mr.Peterson eats breakfast at McDonalds.
- On Wednesday Mr.Peterson eats breakfast at McDonalds.
- On Thursday Mr.Peterson eats breakfast at McDonalds again.

Conclusion: On Friday Mr. Peterson will eat breakfast at McDonalds again.

This is a conclusion based on inductive reasoning. Based on several days observations, you conclude that Mr. Peterson will eat at McDonalds. This may or may not be true, but it is a conclusion arrived at by inductive thinking.

COMPETENCY 19.0   USE A VARIETY OF APPROACHES (e.g., STIMATION, MENTAL MATH, MODELING, PATTERN RECOGNITION) TO EXPLORE MATHEMATICAL IDEAS AND SOLVE PROBLEMS

Skill 19.1   Evaluate the appropriateness of using estimation to solve a given problem

Estimation and approximation may be used to check the reasonableness of answers.

<u>Example</u>:   Estimate the answer.

$$\frac{58 \times 810}{1989}$$

58 becomes 60, 810 becomes 800 and 1989 becomes 2000.

$$\frac{60 \times 800}{2000} = 24$$

Word problems: An estimate may sometimes be all that is needed to solve a problem.

<u>Example</u>:

> Janet goes into a store to purchase a CD on sale for $13.95. While shopping, she sees two pairs of shoes, prices $19.95 and $14.50. She only has $50. Can she purchase everything?

Solve by rounding:
> $19.95→$20.00
> $14.50→$15.00
> $13.95→<u>$14.00</u>
> $49.00   Yes, she can purchase the CD and the shoes.

Skill 19.2   Use an appropriate model to illustrate a given problem

The unit rate for purchasing an item is its price divided by the number of pounds/ounces, etc. in the item. The item with the lower unit rate is the lower price.

Example: Find the item with the best unit price:

> $1.79 for 10 ounces
> $1.89 for 12 ounce
> $5.49 for 32 ounces

$$\frac{1.79}{10} = .179 \text{ per ounce} \qquad \frac{1.89}{12} = .1575 \text{ per ounce} \qquad \frac{5.49}{32} = .172 \text{ per ounce}$$

$1.89 for 12 ounces is the best price.

A second way to find the better buy is to make a proportion with the price over the number of ounces, etc. Cross multiply the proportion, writing the products above the numerator that is used. The better price will have the smaller product.

Example: Find the better buy:

> $8.19 for 40 pounds or $4.89 for 22 pounds

Find the unit price.

$$\frac{40}{8.19} = \frac{1}{x} \qquad\qquad \frac{22}{4.89} = \frac{1}{x}$$
$$40x = 8.19 \qquad\qquad 22x = 4.89$$
$$x = .20475 \qquad\qquad x = .22\overline{227}$$

Since $.20475 < .22\overline{227}$, $8.19 is less and is a better buy.

To find the amount of sales tax on an item, change the percent of sales tax into an equivalent decimal number. Then multiply the decimal number times the price of the object to find the sales tax. The total cost of an item will be the price of the item plus the sales tax.

Example: A guitar costs $120 plus 7% sales tax. How much are the sales tax and the total bill?

> 7% = .07 as a decimal   (.07)(120) = $8.40 sales tax
> $120 + $8.40 = $128.40 ← total price

<u>Example:</u> A suit costs $450 plus 6½% sales tax. How much are the sales tax and the total bill?

> 6½% = .065 as a decimal
> (.065)(450) = $29.25 sales tax
> $450 + $29.25 = $479.25 ← total price

Skill 20.3   Analyze the usefulness of a specific model or mental math procedure for exploring a given mathematical idea or problem

Examining the change in area or volume of a given figure requires first to find the existing area given the original dimensions and then finding the new area given the increased dimensions.

Sample problem:
> Given the rectangle below determine the change in area if the length is increase by 5 and the width is increased by 7.

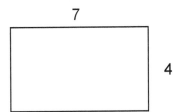

7

4

Draw and label a sketch of the new rectangle.

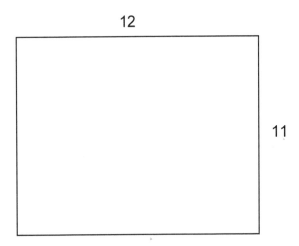

12

11

Find the areas.

Area of original = LW   Area of enlarged shape = LW
= (7)(4)   = (12)(11)
= 28 units^2 = 132 units^2

The change in area is 132 − 28 = 104 units^2.

Skill 19.4   Simplify a problem to facilitate a solution

Elapsed time problems are usually one of two types. One type of problem is the elapsed time between 2 times given in hours, minutes, and seconds. The other common type of problem is between 2 times given in months and years.

For any time of day past noon, change it into military time by adding 12 hours. For instance, 1:15 p.m. would be 13:15. Remember when you borrow a minute or an hour in a subtraction problem that you have borrowed 60 more seconds or minutes.

Example:
Find the time from 11:34:22 a.m. until 3:28:40 p.m.

```
        First change 3:28:40 p.m. to   15:28:40 p.m.
        Now subtract                 - 11:34:22 a.m.
                                             :18
```
Borrow an hour and add 60 more minutes. Subtract
```
                        14:88:40 p.m.
                      - 11:34:22 a.m.
                        3:54:18  ↔ 3 hours, 54 minutes, 18 seconds
```

Example:
John lived in Arizona from September 91 until March 95. How long is that?
```
                         year month
        March 95       =  95   03
        September 91   = - 91   09
```

Borrow a year, change it into 12 more months, and subtract.
```
                         year month
        March 95       =  94   15
        September 91   = - 91   09
                          3 yr 6 months
```

Example:
A race took the winner 1 hr. 58 min. 12 sec. on the first half of the race and 2 hr. 9 min. 57 sec. on the second half of the race. How much time did the entire race take?

```
        1 hr. 58 min. 12 sec.
      + 2 hr.  9 min. 57 sec.      Add these numbers
        3 hr. 67 min. 69 sec.
              + 1 min -60 sec.     Change 60 seconds to 1 min.
        3 hr. 68 min.  9 sec.
      + 1 hr.-60 min.      .       Change 60 minutes to 1 hr.
        4 hr.  8 min.  9 sec.  ←final answer
```

COMPETENCY 20.0 UNDERSTAND MATHEMATICAL COMMUNICATION AND THE HISTORICAL AND CULTURAL CONTEXTS OF MATHEMATICS

Skill 20.1 Use mathematical notation to represent a given relationship

Mathematical operations include addition, subtraction, multiplication and division.

Addition can be indicated by the expressions: sum, greater than, and, more than, increased by, added to.

Subtraction can be expressed by: difference, fewer than, minus, less than, decreased by.

Multiplication is shown by: product, times, multiplied by, twice.

Division is used for: quotient, divided by, ratio.

<u>Examples</u>:

7 added to a number	$n + 7$
a number decreased by 8	$n - 8$
12 times a number divided by 7	$12n \div 7$
28 less than a number	$n - 28$
the ratio of a number to 55	$\dfrac{n}{55}$
4 times the sum of a number and 21	$4(n + 21)$

Skill 20.2 Use appropriate models, diagrams, and symbols to represent mathematical concepts

Mathematical operations can be shown using manipulatives or drawings. Multiplication can be shown using arrays.

3×4 　　□□□□
　　　　　　　□□□□
　　　　　　　□□□□

Addition and subtractions can be demonstrated with symbols.

ψ ψ ψ ξ ξ ξ ξ
$3 + 4 = 7$
$7 - 3 = 4$

Fractions can be clarified using pattern blocks, fraction bars, or paper folding.

Skill 20.3   Use appropriate vocabulary to express given mathematical ideas and relationships

To read a bar graph or a pictograph, read the explanation of the scale that was used in the legend. Compare the length of each bar with the dimensions on the axes and calculate the value each bar represents. On a pictograph count the number of pictures used in the chart and calculate the value of all the pictures.

To read a circle graph, find the total of the amounts represented on the entire circle graph. To determine the actual amount that each sector of the graph represents, multiply the percent in a sector times the total amount number.

To read a chart read the row and column headings on the table. Use this information to evaluate the given information in the chart.

Skill 20.4   Apply knowledge of the role of mathematics in society and the contributions of various cultures toward the development of mathematics

Mathematics goes back before recorded history. Prehistoric cave paintings with geometrical figures and slash counting have been dated prior to 20,000 BC in Africa and France. The major early uses of mathematics were for astronomy, architecture, trading and taxation.

The early history of mathematics is found in Mesopotamia (Sumeria and Babylon), Egypt, Greece and Rome. Noted mathematicians from these times include Euclid, Pythagoras, Apollonius, Ptolemy and Archimedes.

Islamic culture from the 6th through 12th centuries drew from areas ranging from Africa and Spain to India. Through India, they also drew on China. This mix of cultures and ideas brought about developments in many areas, including the concept of algebra, our current numbering system and major developments in algebra with concepts such as zero. India was the source of many of these developments. Notable scholars of this era include Omar Khayyam and Muhammad al-Khwarizmi.

Counting boards have been found in archeological digs in Babylonia and Greece. These include the Chinese abacus whose current form dates from approximately 1200 AD. Prior to the development of the zero, a counting board or abacus was the common method used for all types of calculations.

Abelard and Fibonacci brought Islamic texts to Europe in the 12th century. By the 17th century, major new works appeared from Galileo and Copernicus (astronomy), Newton and Leibniz (calculus), and Napier and Briggs (logarithms). Other significant mathematicians of this era include René Descartes, Carl Gauss, Pierre de Fermat, Leonhard Euler and Blaise Pascal.

The growth of mathematics since 1800 has been enormous and affected nearly every area of life. Some names significant in the history of mathematics since 1800 and the work they are most know for:

- Joseph-Louis Lagrange (theory of functions and of mechanics)
- Pierre-Simon LaPlace (celestial mechanics, probability theory)
- Joseph Fourier (number theory)
- Lobachevsky and Bolyai (non-euclidean geometry)
- Charles Babbage (calculating machines, origin of the computer)
- Lady Ada Lovelace (first known program)
- Florence Nightingale (nursing, statistics of populations)
- Bernard Russel (logic)
- James Maxwell (differential calculus and analysis)
- John von Neumann (economics, quantum mechanics and game theory)
- Alan Turing (theoretical foundations of computer science)
- Albert Einstein (theory of relativity)
- Gustav Roch (topology)

COMPETENCY 21.0 UNDERSTAND SKILLS AND CONCEPTS RELATED TO NUMBER AND NUMERATION, AND APPLY THESE SKILLS AND CONCEPTS TO REAL-WORLD SITUATIONS

Skill 21.1 Use ratios, proportions, and percents to model and solve problems

Word problems involving percents can be solved by writing the problem as an equation, then solving the equation. Keep in mind that **"of" means "multiplication"** and **"is" means "equals."**

Example:
The Ski Club has 85 members. 80% of the members are able to attend the meeting. How many members attend the meeting?

Restate the problem.   What is 80% of 85?
Write an equation. $n = 0.8 \times 85$
Solve. $n = 68$
Sixty-eight members attend the meeting.

Example:
There are 64 dogs in the kennel. 48 are collies. What percent are collies?

Restate the problem.   48 is what percent of 64?
Write an equation. $48 = n \times 64$
Solve. $\frac{48}{64} = n$

$n = \frac{3}{4} = 75\%$

75% of the dogs are collies.

Example:
The auditorium was filled to 90% capacity. There were 558 seats occupied. What is the capacity of the auditorium?

Restate the problem.   90% of what number is 558?
Write an equation. $0.9n = 558$
Solve. $n = \frac{558}{.9}$

$n = 620$

The capacity of the auditorium is 620 people.

Example:
Shoes cost $42.00. Sales tax is 6%. What is the total cost of the shoes?

Restate the problem.	What is 6% of 42?
Write an equation.	$n = 0.06 \times 42$
Solve.	$n = 2.52$
Add the sales tax to the cost.	$42.00 + 2.52 = 44.52$

The total cost of the shoes, including sales tax, is $44.52.

COMMON EQUIVALENTS

- $\frac{1}{2} = 0.5 = 50\%$
- $\frac{1}{3} = 0.33\frac{1}{3} = 33\frac{1}{3}\%$
- $\frac{1}{4} = 0.25 = 25\%$
- $\frac{1}{5} = 0.2 = 20\%$
- $\frac{1}{6} = 0.16\frac{2}{3} = 16\frac{2}{3}\%$
- $\frac{1}{8} = 0.12\frac{1}{2} = 12\frac{1}{2}\%$
- $\frac{1}{10} = 0.1 = 10\%$
- $\frac{2}{3} = 0.66\frac{2}{3} = 66\frac{2}{3}\%$
- $\frac{5}{6} = 0.83\frac{1}{3} = 83\frac{1}{3}\%$
- $\frac{3}{8} = 0.37\frac{1}{2} = 37\frac{1}{2}\%$
- $\frac{5}{8} = 0.62\frac{1}{2} = 62\frac{1}{2}\%$
- $\frac{7}{8} = 0.87\frac{1}{2} = 87\frac{1}{2}\%$
- $1 = 1.0 = 100\%$

Skills 22.2   Compare and order fractions, decimals, and percents

To convert a fraction to a decimal, simply divide the numerator (top) by the denominator (bottom). Use long division if necessary.

If a decimal has a fixed number of digits, the decimal is said to be terminating. To write such a decimal as a fraction, first determine what place value the farthest right digit is in, for example: tenths, hundredths, thousandths, ten thousandths, hundred thousands, etc. Then drop the decimal and place the string of digits over the number given by the place value.

If a decimal continues forever by repeating a string of digits, the decimal is said to be repeating. To write a repeating decimal as a fraction, follow these steps.

- Let $x =$ the repeating decimal
  (ex. $x = .716716716...$)
- Multiply x by the multiple of ten that will move the decimal just to the right of the repeating block of digits.
  (ex. $1000x = 716.716716...$)
- Subtract the first equation from the second.
  (ex. $1000x - x = 716.716.716... - .716716...$)
- Simplify and solve this equation. The repeating block of digits will subtract out.
  (ex. $999x = 716$ so $x = {}^{716}\!/_{999}$)
- The solution will be the fraction for the repeating decimal.

The **exponent form** is a shortcut method to write repeated multiplication. The **base** is the factor. The **exponent** tells how many times that number is multiplied by itself.

Example:
3^4 is $3 \times 3 \times 3 \times 3 = 81$ where 3 is the base and 4 is the exponent.

x^2 *is read* "x squared"
y^3 *is read* "y cubed"
a^1 = a for all values of a; thus $17^1 = 17$
b^0 = 1 for all values of b; thus $24^0 = 1$

When 10 is raised to any power, the exponent tells the numbers of zeroes in the product.

Example:
$10^7 = 10,000,000$

Proportions can be used to solve word problems whenever relationships are compared.

Some situations include scale drawings and maps, similar polygons, speed, time and distance, cost, and comparison shopping.

<u>Example:</u>
Which is the better buy, 6 items for $1.29 or 8 items for $1.69?

Find the unit price.

$$\frac{6}{1.29} = \frac{1}{x} \qquad\qquad \frac{8}{1.69} = \frac{1}{x}$$

$6x = 1.29 \qquad\qquad\qquad 8x = 1.69$

$x = 0.215 \qquad\qquad\qquad x = 0.21125$

Thus, 6 items for $1.29 is the better buy.

<u>Example:</u>
A car travels 125 miles in 2.5 hours.. How far will it go in 6 hours?

Write a proportion comparing the distance and time.

$$\frac{miles}{hours} \qquad \frac{125}{2.5} = \frac{x}{6}$$

$2.5x = 750$

$x = 300$

Thus, the car can travel 300 miles in 6 hours.

<u>Example:</u>
The scale on a map is $\frac{3}{4}$ inch $= 6$ miles. What is the actual distance between two cities if they are $1\frac{1}{2}$ inches apart on the map?

Write a proportion comparing the scale to the actual distance.

$$\begin{array}{cc} \text{scale} & \text{actual} \\ \frac{\frac{3}{4}}{1\frac{1}{2}} & = \frac{6}{x} \end{array}$$

$\frac{3}{4}x = 1\frac{1}{2} \times 6$

$\frac{3}{4}x = 9$

$x = 12$

Thus, the actual distance between the cities is 12 miles.

Skill 21.3 **Solve problems using equivalent forms of numbers (e.g., integer, fraction, decimal, percent, exponential and scientific notation)**

The use of supplementary materials in the classroom can greatly enhance the learning experience by stimulating student interest and satisfying different learning styles. Manipulatives, models, and technology are examples of tools available to teachers.

Manipulatives are materials that students can physically handle and move. Manipulatives allow students to understand mathematic concepts by allowing them to see concrete examples of abstract processes. Manipulatives are attractive to students because they appeal to the students' visual and tactile senses. Available for all levels of math, manipulatives are useful tools for reinforcing operations and concepts. They are not, however, a substitute for the development of sound computational skills.

Models are another means of representing mathematical concepts by relating the concepts to real-world situations. Teachers must choose wisely when devising and selecting models because, to be effective, models must be applied properly. For example, a building with floors above and below ground is a good model for introducing the concept of negative numbers. It would be difficult, however, to use the building model in teaching subtraction of negative numbers.

Finally, there are many forms of **technology** available to math teachers. For example, students can test their understanding of math concepts by working on skill specific computer programs and websites. Graphing calculators can help students visualize the graphs of functions. Teachers can also enhance their lectures and classroom presentations by creating multimedia presentations.

- **See** Skills 221. and 22.2

Skill 21.4   **Analyze the number properties used in operational algorithms (e.g., multiplication, long division)**

The Order of Operations are to be followed when evaluating algebraic expressions. Follow these steps in order:

1. Simplify inside grouping characters such as parentheses, brackets, square root, fraction bar, etc.
2. Multiply out expressions with exponents.
3. Do multiplication or division, from left to right.
4. Do addition or subtraction, from left to right.

Samples of simplifying expressions with exponents:

$$(^-2)^3 = -8 \qquad\qquad ^-2^3 = ^-8$$

$$(^-2)^4 = 16 \qquad\qquad ^-2^4 = 16 \qquad \text{Note change of sign.}$$

$$(^2\!/_3)^3 = {}^8\!/_{27}$$

$$5^0 = 1$$

$$4^{-1} = {}^1\!/_4$$

COMPETENCY 22.0 UNDERSTAND AND APPLY THE PRINCIPLES AND PROPERTIES OF LINEAR ALGEBRAIC RELATIONS AND FUNCTIONS

Skill 22.1 Analyze mathematical relationships and patterns using tables, verbal rules, equations, and graphs

A relationship between two quantities can be shown using a table, graph or rule. In this example, the rule y= 9x describes the relationship between the total amount earned, y, and the total amount of $9 sunglasses sold, x.

A table using this data would appear as:

number of sunglasses sold	1	5	10	15
total dollars earned	9	45	90	135

Each *(x,y)* relationship between a pair of values is called the coordinate pair and can be plotted on a graph. The coordinate pairs *(1,9)*, *(5,45)*, *(10,90)*, and *(15,135)*, are plotted on the graph below.

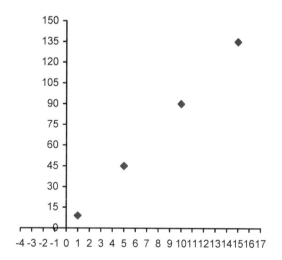

The graph above shows a linear relationship. A linear relationship is one in which two quantities are proportional to each other. Doubling *x* also doubles *y*. On a graph, a straight line depicts a linear relationship.

Another type of relationship is a nonlinear relationship. This is one in which change in one quantity does not affect the other quantity to the same extent. Nonlinear graphs have a curved line such as the graph below.

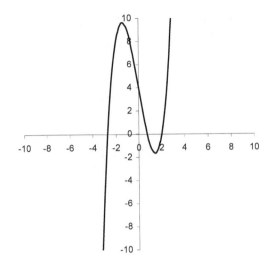

Skill 22.2   **Derive an algebraic expression to represent a real-world relationship or pattern, and recognize a real-world relationship that is represented by an algebraic expression**

The function or relationship between two quantities may be analyzed to determine how one quantity depends on the other. For example, the function below shows a relationship between y and x:

$$y=2x+1$$

The relationship between two or more variables can be analyzed using a table, graph, written description or symbolic rule. The function, y=2x+1, is written as a symbolic rule. The same relationship is also shown in the table below:

x	0	2	3	6	9
y	1	5	7	13	19

A relationship could be written in words by saying the value of y is equal to two times the value of x, plus one. This relationship could be shown on a graph by plotting given points such as the ones shown in the table above.

Another way to describe a function is as a process in which one or more numbers are input into an imaginary machine that produces another number as the output. If 5 is input, (x), into a machine with a process of x +1, the output, (y), will equal 6.

In real situations, relationships can be described mathematically. The function, y=x+1, can be used to describe the idea that people age one year on their birthday. To describe the relationship in which a person's monthly medical costs are 6 times a person's age, we could write y=6x. The monthly cost of medical care could be predicted using this function. A 20 year-old person would spend $120 per month (120=20*6). An 80 year-old person would spend $480 per month (480=80*6). Therefore, one could analyze the relationship to say: as you get older, medical costs increase $6.00 each year.

Skill 22.3   Use algebraic functions to describe given graphs, to plot points, and to determine slopes

To find the y intercept, substitute 0 for x and solve for y. This is the y intercept. The y intercept is also the value of b in $y = mx + b$.

To find the x intercept, substitute 0 for y and solve for x. This is the x intercept.

1. Find the slope and intercepts of $3x + 2y = 14$.

$$3x + 2y = 14$$
$$2y = {}^-3x + 14$$
$$y = {}^-3/2 \; x + 7$$

The slope of the line is $^-3/2$, the value of m.
The y intercept of the line is 7.

The intercepts can also be found by substituting 0 in place of the other variable in the equation.

To find the y intercept:
let $x = 0$; $3(0) + 2y = 14$
$0 + 2y = 14$
$2y = 14$
$y = 7$
$(0,7)$ is the y intercept.

To find the x intercept:
let $y = 0$; $3x + 2(0) = 14$
$3x + 0 = 14$
$3x = 14$
$x = 14/3$
$(14/3,0)$ is the x intercept.

Find the slope and the intercepts (if they exist) for these equations:

1. $5x + 7y = {}^-70$
2. $x - 2y = 14$
3. $5x + 3y = 3(5 + y)$
4. $2x + 5y = 15$

<u>Example</u>:
Sketch the graph of the line represented by $2x + 3y = 6$.

$$\text{Let } x = 0 \rightarrow 2(0) + 3y = 6$$
$$\rightarrow 3y = 6$$
$$\rightarrow y = 2$$
$$\rightarrow (0,2) \text{ is the } y \text{ intercept.}$$

$$\text{Let } y = 0 \rightarrow 2x + 3(0) = 6$$
$$\rightarrow 2x = 6$$
$$\rightarrow x = 3$$
$$\rightarrow (3,0) \text{ is the } x \text{ intercept.}$$

$$\text{Let } x = 1 \rightarrow 2(1) + 3y = 6$$
$$\rightarrow 2 + 3y = 6$$
$$\rightarrow 3y = 4$$
$$\rightarrow y = \frac{4}{3}$$
$$\rightarrow \left(1, \frac{4}{3}\right) \text{ is the third point.}$$

Plotting the three points on the coordinate system, we get the following:

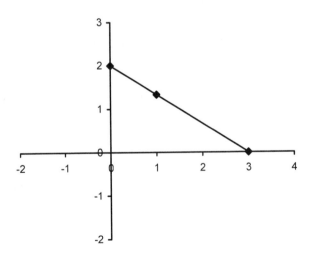

Exercise: Interpreting Slope as a Rate of Change
Connection: Social Sciences/Geography
Real-life Application: Slope is often used to describe a constant or average rate of change. These problems usually involve units of measure such as miles per hour or dollars per year.

Problem:

The town of Verdant Slopes has been experiencing a boom in population growth. By the year 2000, the population had grown to 45,000, and by 2005, the population had reached 60,000.

Communicating about Algebra:

1. Using the formula for slope as a model, find the average rate of change in population growth, expressing your answer in people per year.

Extension:

2. Using the average rate of change determined in a., predict the population of Verdant Slopes in the year 2010.

Solution:

1. Let t represent the time and p represent population growth. The two observances are represented by (t_1, p_1) and (t_2, p_2).
    1st observance = (t_1, p_1) = (2000, 45000)
    2nd observance = (t_2, p_2) = (2005, 60000)

Use the formula for slope to find the average rate of change.

$$\text{Rate of change} = \frac{p_2 - p_1}{t_2 - t_1}$$

Substitute values.

$$= \frac{60000 - 45000}{2005 - 2000}$$

Simplify

$$= \frac{15000}{5} = 3000 \, people / year$$

The average rate of change in population growth for Verdant Slopes between the years 2000 and 2005 was 3000 people/year.

$$3000\,people\,/\,year \times 5\,years = 15000\,people$$
$$60000\,people + 15000\,people = 75000\,people$$

At a continuing average rate of growth of 3000 people/year, the population of Verdant Slopes could be expected to reach 75,000 by the year 2010.

Skill 22.4 Perform algebraic operations to solve equations and inequalities

A **quadratic equation** is written in the form $ax^2 + bx + c = 0$. To solve a quadratic equation by factoring, at least one of the factors must equal zero.

Example:
Solve the equation.

$x^2 + 10x - 24 = 0$

$(x + 12)(x - 2) = 0$ Factor.

$x + 12 = 0$ or $x - 2 = 0$ Set each factor equal to 0.

$x = {}^-12 \qquad x = 2$ Solve.

Check:

$x^2 + 10x - 24 = 0$

$({}^-12)^2 + 10({}^-12) - 24 = 0 \qquad (2)^2 + 10(2) - 24 = 0$

$144 - 120 - 24 = 0 \qquad\qquad\quad 4 + 20 - 24 = 0$

$0 = 0 \qquad\qquad\qquad\qquad\qquad 0 = 0$

A quadratic equation that cannot be solved by factoring can be solved by **completing the square**.

Example:
Solve the equation.

$$x^2 - 6x + 8 = 0$$

$$x^2 - 6x = {}^-8$$ Move the constant to the right side.

$$x^2 - 6x + 9 = {}^-8 + 9$$ Add the square of half the cooeffient of x to both sides.

$$(x - 3)^2 = 1$$ Write the left side as a perfect square.

$$x - 3 = \pm\sqrt{1}$$ Take the square root of both sides.

$$x - 3 = 1 \qquad x - 3 = {}^-1$$ Solve.

$$x = 4 \qquad x = 2$$

Check:

$$x^2 - 6x + 8 = 0$$

$$4^2 - 6(4) + 8 = 0 \qquad\qquad 2^2 - 6(2) + 8 = 0$$

$$16 - 24 + 8 = 0 \qquad\qquad 4 - 12 + 8 = 0$$

$$0 = 0 \qquad\qquad\qquad 0 = 0$$

The general technique for graphing quadratics is the same as for graphing linear equations. Graphing quadratic equations, however, results in a parabola instead of a straight line.

Example:
Graph $y = 3x^2 + x - 2$.

x	$y = 3x^2 + x - 2$
$^-2$	8
$^-1$	0
0	$^-2$
1	2
2	12

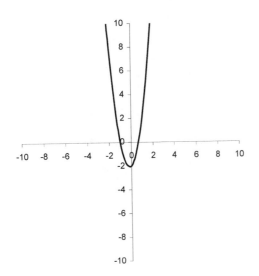

To solve a quadratic equation using the quadratic formula, be sure that your equation is in the form $ax^2 + bx + c = 0$. Substitute these values into the formula:

$$x = \frac{-b \pm \sqrt{b^2 - 4ac}}{2a}$$

<u>Example</u>:
Solve the equation.

$$3x^2 = 7 + 2x \rightarrow 3x^2 - 2x - 7 = 0$$

$$a = 3 \quad b = {}^-2 \quad c = {}^-7$$

$$x = \frac{-({}^-2) \pm \sqrt{({}^-2)^2 - 4(3)({}^-7)}}{2(3)}$$

$$x = \frac{2 \pm \sqrt{4 + 84}}{6}$$

$$x = \frac{2 \pm \sqrt{88}}{6}$$

$$x = \frac{2 \pm 2\sqrt{22}}{6}$$

$$x = \frac{1 \pm \sqrt{22}}{3}$$

COMPETENCY 23.0 UNDERSTAND THE PRINCIPLES AND PROPERTIES OF GEOMETRY, AND APPLY THEM TO MODEL AND SOLVE PROBLEMS

Skill 23.1 Apply the concepts of similarity and congruence to model and solve real-world problems

Two triangles can be proven congruent by comparing pairs of appropriate congruent corresponding parts.

SSS POSTULATE

If three sides of one triangle are congruent to three sides of another triangle, then the two triangles are congruent.

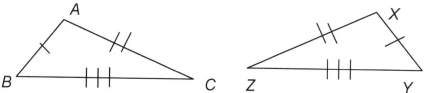

Since $AB \cong XY$, $BC \cong YZ$ and $AC \cong XZ$, then $\triangle ABC \cong \triangle XYZ$.

<u>Example</u>:
Given isosceles triangle ABC with D the midpoint of base AC, prove the two triangles formed by AD are congruent.

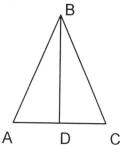

Proof:
1. Isosceles triangle ABC, D midpoint of base AC Given
2. $AB \cong BC$ An isosceles $\triangle$ has two congruent sides
3. $AD \cong DC$ Midpoint divides a line into two equal parts
4. $BD \cong BD$ Reflexive
5. $\triangle ABD \cong \triangle BCD$ SSS

SAS POSTULATE

If two sides and the included angle of one triangle are congruent to two sides and the included angle of another triangle, then the two triangles are congruent.

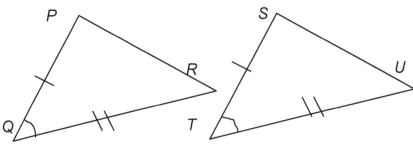

Example:

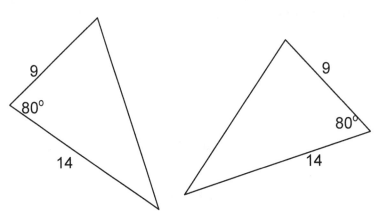

The two triangles are congruent by SAS.

ASA POSTULATE

If two angles and the included side of one triangle are congruent to two angles and the included side of another triangle, the triangles are congruent.

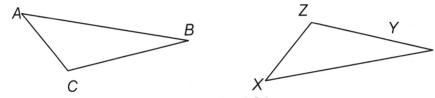

$\angle A \cong \angle X$, $\angle B \cong \angle Y$, $AB \cong XY$ then $\triangle ABC \cong \triangle XYZ$ by ASA

<u>Example:</u>
Given two right triangles with one leg of each measuring 6 cm and the adjacent angle 37°, prove the triangles are congruent.

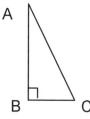 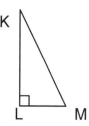

1. Right triangles *ABC* and *KLM*   Given
   $AB = KL = 6$ cm
   $\angle A = \angle K = 37°$
2. $AB \cong KL$ Figures with the same
   $\angle A \cong \angle K$ measure are congruent
3. $\angle B \cong \angle L$ All right angles are congruent.
4. $\triangle ABC \cong \triangle KLM$ ASA

<u>Example:</u>
What method would you use to prove the triangles congruent?

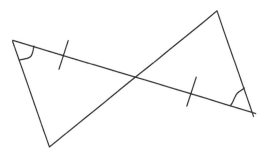

ASA because vertical angles are congruent.

Example:

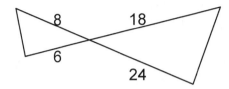

The two triangles are similar since the sides are proportional and vertical angles are congruent.

Example:
Given two similar quadrilaterals. Find the lengths of sides *x, y,* and *z.*

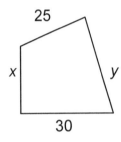
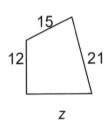

Since corresponding sides are proportional:

$$\frac{15}{25} = \frac{3}{5}$$ so the scale is $$\frac{3}{5}$$

$$\frac{12}{x} = \frac{3}{5}$$ $$\qquad \frac{21}{y} = \frac{3}{5}$$ $$\qquad \frac{z}{30} = \frac{3}{5}$$

$3x = 60$ $\qquad$ $3y = 105$ $\qquad$ $5z = 90$
$x = 20$ $\qquad$ $y = 35$ $\qquad$ $z = 18$

Polygons are similar if and only if there is a one-to-one correspondence between their vertices such that the corresponding angles are congruent and the lengths of corresponding sides are proportional.

Given the rectangles below, compare the area and perimeter.

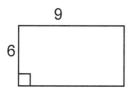

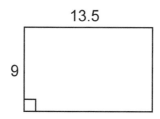

$A = LW$	$A = LW$	1. write formula
$A = (6)(9)$	$A = (9)(13.5)$	2. substitute known values
$A = 54$ sq. units	$A = 121.5$ sq. units	3. compute
$P = 2(L + W)$	$P = 2(L + W)$	1. write formula
$P = 2(6 + 9)$	$P = 2(9 + 13.5)$	2. substitute known values
$P = 30$ units	$P = 45$ units	3. compute

Notice that the areas relate to each other in the following manner:
Ratio of sides $9/13.5 = 2/3$

Multiply the first area by the square of the reciprocal $(3/2)^2$ to get the second area.

$54 \times (3/2)^2 = 121.5$

The perimeters relate to each other in the following manner
Ratio of sides $9/13.5 = 2/3$

Multiply the perimeter of the first by the reciprocal of the ratio to get the perimeter of the second

$30 \times 3/2 = 45$

A **Tessellation** is an arrangement of closed shapes that completely covers the plane without overlapping or leaving gaps. Unlike **tilings**, tessellations do not require the use of regular polygons. In art the term is used to refer to pictures or tiles mostly in the form of animals and other life forms, which cover the surface of a plane in a symmetrical way without overlapping or leaving gaps. M. C. Escher is known as the "Father" of modern tessellations. Tessellations are used for tiling, mosaics, quilts and art.

If you look at a completed tessellation, you will see the original motif repeats in a pattern. There are 17 possible ways that a pattern can be used to tile a flat surface or "wallpaper."

There are four basic transformational symmetries that can be used in tessellations: **translation, rotation, reflection,** and **glide reflection**. The transformation of an object is called its image. If the original object was labeled with letters, such as $ABCD$, the image may be labeled with the same letters followed by a prime symbol, $A'B'C'D'$.

The tessellation below is a combination of the four types of transformational symmetry we have discussed:

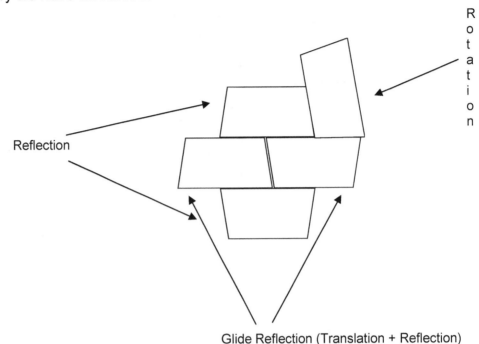

Reflection

Rotation

Glide Reflection (Translation + Reflection)

Skill 23.2   Apply knowledge of basic geometric figures to solve real-world problems involving more complex patterns

Pythagorean theorem states that the square of the length of the hypotenuse is equal to the sum of the squares of the lengths of the legs. Symbolically, this is stated as:

$$c^2 = a^2 + b^2$$

Given the right triangle below, find the missing side.

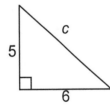

$c^2 = a^2 + b^2$	1. write formula
$c^2 = 5^2 + 6^2$	2. substitute known values
$c^2 = 61$	3. take square root
$c = \sqrt{61}$ or 7.81	4. solve

*   *   *

The Converse of the Pythagorean Theorem states that if the square of one side of a triangle is equal to the sum of the squares of the other two sides, then the triangle is a right triangle.

<u>Example</u>:
Given △XYZ, with sides measuring 12, 16 and 20 cm. Is this a right triangle?

$$c^2 = a^2 + b^2$$
$$20^2 \ \underline{?} \ 12^2 + 16^2$$
$$400 \ \underline{?} \ 144 + 256$$
$$400 = 400$$

Yes, the triangle is a right triangle.

This theorem can be expanded to determine if triangles are obtuse or acute.

If the square of the longest side of a triangle is greater than the sum of the squares of the other two sides, then the triangle is an obtuse triangle.
and
If the square of the longest side of a triangle is less than the sum of the squares of the other two sides, then the triangle is an acute triangle.

<u>Example</u>:
Given △LMN with sides measuring 7, 12, and 14 inches. Is the triangle right, acute, or obtuse?

$$14^2 \ \underline{?} \ 7^2 + 12^2$$
$$196 \ \underline{?} \ 49 + 144$$
$$196 > 193$$

Therefore, the triangle is obtuse.

<u>Real-World Example:</u> Find the area and perimeter of a rectangle if its length is 12 inches and its diagonal is 15 inches.

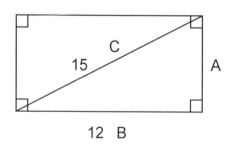

1. Draw and label sketch.

2. Since the height is still needed use Pythagorean formula to ind missing leg of the triangle.

$$A^2 + B^2 = C^2$$
$$A^2 + 12^2 = 15^2$$
$$A^2 = 15^2 - 12^2$$
$$A^2 = 81$$
$$A = 9$$

Now use this information to find the area and perimeter.

$A = LW$ $P = 2(L + W)$ 1. write formula

$A = (12)(9)$ $P = 2(12 + 9)$ 2. substitute

$A = 108 \text{ in}^2$ $P = 42$ inches   3. solve

Real-World Example: Given the figure below, find the area by dividing the polygon into smaller shapes.

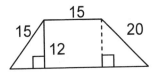

1. divide the figure into two triangles and a rectangle.

2. find the missing lengths.

3. find the area of each part.

4. find the sum of all areas.

Find base of both right triangles using Pythagorean Formula:

$a^2 + b^2 = c^2$ $a^2 + b^2 = c^2$

$a^2 + 12^2 = 15^2$ $a^2 + 12^2 = 20^2$

$a^2 = 225 - 144$ $a^2 = 400 - 144$

$a^2 = 81$ $a^2 = 256$

$a = 9$ $a = 16$

Area of triangle 1	Area of triangle 2	Area of rectangle
$A = \dfrac{1}{2}bh$	$A = \dfrac{1}{2}bh$	$A = LW$
$A = \dfrac{1}{2}(9)(12)$	$A = \dfrac{1}{2}(16)(12)$	$A = (15)(12)$
$A = 54$ sq. units	$A = 96$ sq. units	$A = 180$ sq. units

Find the sum of all three figures.

$54 + 96 + 180 = 330$ square units

Given the special right triangles below, we can find the lengths of other special right triangles.

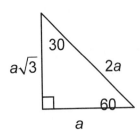 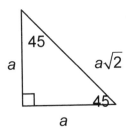

Sample problems:

1. 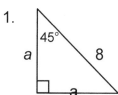 if $8 = a\sqrt{2}$ then $a = 8/\sqrt{2}$ or 5.657

2.  if $7 = a$ then $c = a\sqrt{2} = 7\sqrt{2}$ or 9.899

3. 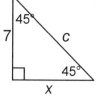 if 2a = 10 then a = 5 and $x = a\sqrt{3} = 5\sqrt{3}$ or 8.66

Given triangle right ABC, the adjacent side and opposite side can be identified for each angle A and B.

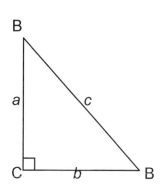

Looking at angle A, it can be determined that side b is adjacent to angle A and side a is opposite angle A.

If we now look at angle B, we see that side a is adjacent to angle b and side b is opposite angle B.

The longest side (opposite the 90 degree angle) is always called the hypotenuse.

The basic trigonometric ratios are listed below:

Sine = opposite/hypotenuse   Cosine = adjacent/hypotenuse   Tangent = opposite/adjacent

Sample problem:
1. Use triangle ABC to find the sin, cos and tan for angle A.

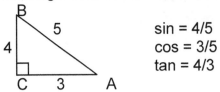

sin = 4/5
cos = 3/5
tan = 4/3

Use the basic trigonometric ratios of sine, cosine and tangent to solve for the missing sides of right triangles when given at least one of the acute angles.

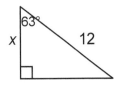

In the triangle ABC, an acute angle of 63 degrees and the length of the hypotenuse (12). The missing side is the one adjacent to the given angle.

The appropriate trigonometric ratio to use would be cosine since we are looking for the adjacent side and we have the length of the hypotenuse.

Cos$x$= $\frac{adjacent}{hypotenuse}$ 1. Write formula

Cos 63 = $\frac{x}{12}$ 2. Substitute known value

0.454 = $\frac{x}{12}$

x = 5.448   3. Solve.

Example:
Find the missing side or angle.

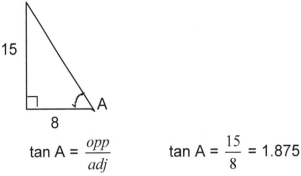

tan A = $\frac{opp}{adj}$ tan A = $\frac{15}{8}$ = 1.875

Looking on the trigonometric chart, the angle whose tangent is closest to 1.875 is 62°. Thus ∠A ≈ 62°

Example:

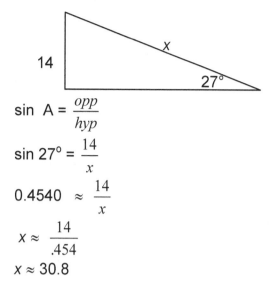

$$\sin\ A = \frac{opp}{hyp}$$

$$\sin 27° = \frac{14}{x}$$

$$0.4540 \approx \frac{14}{x}$$

$$x \approx \frac{14}{.454}$$

$$x \approx 30.8$$

Example:

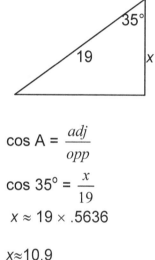

$$\cos A = \frac{adj}{opp}$$

$$\cos 35° = \frac{x}{19}$$

$$x \approx 19 \times .5636$$

$$x \approx 10.9$$

Skill 23.3   Apply inductive and deductive reasoning to solve real-world problems in geometry

Inductive thinking is the process of finding a pattern from a group of examples. That pattern is the conclusion that this set of examples seemed to indicate. It may be a correct conclusion or it may be an incorrect conclusion because other examples may not follow the predicted pattern.

Deductive thinking is the process of arriving at a conclusion based on other statements that are all known to be true, such as theorems, axioms, or postulates. Conclusions found by deductive thinking based on true statements will **always** be true.

Examples :

Suppose:
- On Monday, Mr.Peterson eats breakfast at McDonalds.
- On Tuesday, Mr.Peterson eats breakfast at McDonalds.
- On Wednesday, Mr.Peterson eats breakfast at McDonalds.
- On Thursday, Mr.Peterson eats breakfast at McDonalds again.

Conclusion: On Friday, Mr. Peterson will eat breakfast at McDonalds again.

This is a conclusion based on inductive reasoning. Based on several days' observations, you conclude that Mr. Peterson will eat at McDonalds. This may or may not be true, but it is a conclusion arrived at by inductive thinking.

Conditional statements are frequently written in "if-then" form. The "if" clause of the conditional is known as the **hypothesis**, and the "then" clause is called the **conclusion**. In a proof, the hypothesis is the information that is assumed to be true, while the conclusion is what is to be proven true. A conditional is considered to be of the form:

If p, then q

p is the hypothesis. q is the conclusion.

Conditional statements can be diagrammed using a **Venn diagram**. A diagram can be drawn with one circle inside another circle. The inner circle represents the hypothesis. The outer circle represents the conclusion. If the hypothesis is taken to be true, then you are located inside the inner circle. If you are located in the inner circle then you are also inside the outer circle, so that proves the conclusion is true.

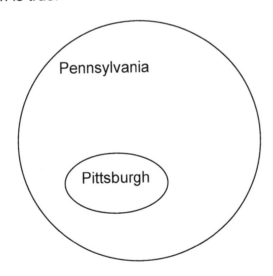

Example:
- If an angle has a measure of 90 degrees, then it is a right angle.

In this statement, "an angle has a measure of 90 degrees" is the hypothesis.
In this statement, "it is a right angle" is the conclusion.

Example:
If you are in Pittsburgh, then you are in Pennsylvania.

In this statement, "you are in Pittsburgh" is the hypothesis.
In this statement, "you are in Pennsylvania" is the conclusion.

Conditional: If p, then q

p is the hypothesis. q is the conclusion.

Inverse: If ~ p, then ~ q

Negate both the hypothesis (If not p, then not q) and the conclusion from the original conditional.

Converse : If q, then p.

Reverse the 2 clauses. The original hypothesis becomes the conclusion. The original conclusion then becomes the new hypothesis.

Contrapositive: If ~ q, then ~ p.

Reverse the 2 clauses. The If not q, then not p original hypothesis becomes the conclusion. The original conclusion then becomes the new hypothesis. THEN negate both the new hypothesis and the new conclusion.

Example:
Given the **conditional**:
- If an angle has 60°, then it is an acute angle.
- Its **inverse**, in the form "If ~ p, then ~ q", would be:
- If an angle doesn't have 60°, then it is not an acute angle.

NOTICE that the inverse is not true, even though the conditional statement was true.

Its **converse**, in the form "If q, then p", would be:

If an angle is an acute angle, then it has 60°.

NOTICE that the converse is not true, even though the conditional statement was true.

Its **contrapositive**, in the form "If q, then p", would be:

If an angle isn't an acute angle, then it doesn't have 60°.

NOTICE that the contrapositive is true, assuming the original conditional statement was true.

TIP: If you are asked to pick a statement that is logically equivalent to a given conditional, look for the contrapositive. The inverse and converse are not always logically equivalent to every conditional. The contrapositive is ALWAYS logically equivalent.

Find the inverse, converse, and contrapositive of the following conditional statement. Also, determine if each of the 4 statements is true or false.

Conditional: If $x = 5$, then $x^2 - 25 = 0$.	TRUE
Inverse: If $x \neq 5$, then $x^2 - 25 \neq 0$.	FALSE, x could be $^-5$
Converse: If $x^2 - 25 = 0$, then $x = 5$.	FALSE, x could be $^-5$
Contrapositive: If $x^2 - 25 \neq 0$, then $x \neq 5$.	TRUE
Conditional: If $x = 5$, then $6x = 30$.	TRUE
Inverse: If $x \neq 5$, then $6x \neq 30$.	TRUE
Converse: If $6x = 30$, then $x = 5$.	TRUE
Contrapositive: If $6x \neq 30$, then $x \neq 5$.	TRUE

Sometimes, as in this example, all 4 statements can be logically equivalent; however, the only statement that will always be logically equivalent to the original conditional is the contrapositive.

Conditional statements can be diagrammed using a **Venn diagram**. A diagram can be drawn with one figure inside another figure. The inner figure represents the hypothesis. The outer figure represents the conclusion. If the hypothesis is taken to be true, then you are located inside the inner figure. If you are located in the inner figure then you are also inside the outer figure, so that proves the conclusion is true. Sometimes that conclusion can then be used as the hypothesis for another conditional, which can result in a second conclusion.

Suppose that these statements were given to you, and you are asked to try to reach a conclusion. The statements are:

- All swimmers are athletes.
- All athletes are scholars.

In "if-then" form, these would be:

- If you are a swimmer, then you are an athlete.
- If you are an athlete, then you are a scholar.

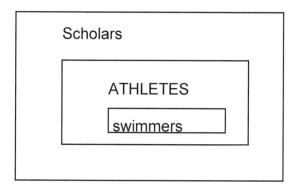

Clearly, if you are a swimmer, then you are also an athlete. This includes you in the group of scholars.

Suppose that these statements were given to you, and you are asked to try to reach a conclusion. The statements are:

- All swimmers are athletes.
- All wrestlers are athletes.

In "if-then" form, these would be:

- If you are a swimmer, then you are an athlete.
- If you are a wrestler, then you are an athlete.

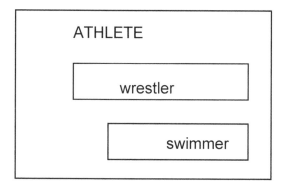

Clearly, if you are a swimmer or a wrestler, then you are also an athlete. This does NOT allow you to come to any other conclusions.

A swimmer may or may NOT also be a wrestler. Therefore, NO CONCLUSION IS POSSIBLE.

Suppose that these statements were given to you, and you are asked to try to reach a conclusion. The statements are:

- All rectangles are parallelograms.
- Quadrilateral ABCD is not a parallelogram.

In "if-then" form, the first statement would be:

- If a figure is a rectangle, then it is also a parallelogram.

Note that the second statement is the negation of the conclusion of statement one. Remember also that the contrapositive is logically equivalent to a given conditional. That is, **"If ~ q, then ~ p"**. Since "ABCD is NOT a parallelogram" is like saying **"If ~ q,"** then you can come to the conclusion **"then ~ p."** Therefore, the conclusion is ABCD is not a rectangle. Looking at the Venn diagram below, if all rectangles are parallelograms, then rectangles are included as part of the parallelograms. Since quadrilateral ABCD is not a parallelogram, that it is excluded from anywhere inside the parallelogram box. This allows you to conclude that ABCD cannot be a rectangle either.

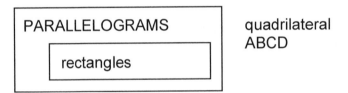

Try These:

What conclusion, if any, can be reached? Assume each statement is true, regardless of any personal beliefs.

1. If the Red Sox win the World Series, I will die. I died.
2. If an angle's measure is between 0° and 90°, then the angle is acute. Angle B is not acute.
3. Students who do well in geometry will succeed in college. Annie is doing extremely well in geometry.
4. Left-handed people are witty and charming. You are left-handed.

A counterexample is an exception to a proposed rule or conjecture that disproves the conjecture. For example, the existence of a single non-brown dog disproves the conjecture "all dogs are brown." Thus, any non-brown dog is a counterexample.

In searching for mathematic counterexamples, one should consider extreme cases near the ends of the domain of an experiment and special cases where an additional property is introduced. Examples of extreme cases are numbers near zero and obtuse triangles that are nearly flat. An example of a special case for a problem involving rectangles is a square because a square is a rectangle with the additional property of symmetry.

Example:
Identify a counterexample for the following conjectures.

1. If n is an even number, then $n + 1$ is divisible by 3.

$n = 4$
$n + 1 = 4 + 1 = 5$
5 is not divisible by 3.

2. If n is divisible by 3, then $n^2 - 1$ is divisible by 4.

$n = 6$
$n^2 - 1 = 6^2 - 1 = 35$
35 is not divisible by 4.

The only undefined terms are point, line, and plane.

Definitions are explanations of all mathematical terms except those that are undefined.

Postulates are mathematical statements that are accepted as true statements without providing a proof.

Theorems are mathematical statements that can be proven to be true based on postulates, definitions, algebraic properties, given information, and previously proved theorems.

The following algebraic postulates are frequently used as reasons for statements in 2 column geometric properties:

Addition Property:
   If $a = b$ and $c = d$, then $a + c = b + d$.

Subtraction Property:
   If a = b and c = d, then a - c = b - d.

Multiplication Property:
   If $a = b$ and $c \neq 0$, then $ac = bc$.

Division Property:
   If $a = b$ and $c \neq 0$, then $a/c = b/c$.

Reflexive Property:	$a = a$
Symmetric Property:	If $a = b$, then $b = a$.
Transitive Property:	If $a = b$ and $b = c$, then $a = c$.
Distributive Property:	$a(b + c) = ab + ac$
Substitution Property:	If $a = b$, then b may be substituted for a in any other expression (a may also be substituted for b).

In a 2 column proof, the left side of the proof should be the given information, or statements that could be proved by deductive reasoning. The right column of the proof consists of the reasons used to determine that each statement to the left was verifiably true. The right side can identify given information, or state theorems, postulates, definitions, or algebraic properties used to prove that particular line of the proof is true.

To write indirect proofs, assume the opposite of the conclusion. Keep your hypothesis and given information the same. Proceed to develop the steps of the proof, looking for a statement that contradicts your original assumption or some other known fact. This contradiction indicates that the assumption you made at the beginning of the proof was incorrect; therefore, the original conclusion has to be true.

COMPETENCY 24.0   UNDERSTAND CONCEPTS, PRINCIPLES, SKILLS AND PROCEDURES RELATED TO MEASUREMENT, STATISTICS AND PROBABILITY; AND DEMONSTRATE AN ABILITY TO US ETHIS UNDERSTANDING TO DESCRIBE AND COMPARE PHENOMENA AND EVALUATE AND INTERPRET DATA, AND TO APPLY MATHEMATICAL EXPECTATIONS TO REAL-WORLD PHENOMENA

Skill 24.1   **Estimate and convert measurements using standard and nonstandard units**

The units of **length** in the customary system are inches, feet, yards and miles.

> 12 inches (in.) = 1 foot (ft.)
> 36 in. = 1 yard (yd.)
> 3 ft. = 1 yd.
> 5280 ft. = 1 mile (mi.)
> 760 yd. = 1 mi.

To change from a **larger unit to a smaller unit, multiply**.
To change from a **smaller unit to a larger unit, divide**.

Example:
     4 mi. = _____ yd.
     Since 1760 yd. = 1 mile, multiply $4 \times 1760 = 7040$ yd.

Example:
     21 in. = _____ ft.
     $21 \div 12 = 1\frac{3}{4}$ ft.

The units of **weight** are ounces, pounds and tons.

> 16 ounces (oz.) = 1 pound (lb.)
> 2,000 lb. = 1 ton (T.)

Example:
     $2\frac{3}{4}$ T. = _____ lb.
     $2\frac{3}{4} \times 2,000 = 5,500$ lb.

The units of **capacity** are fluid ounces, cups, pints, quarts, and gallons.

> 8 fluid ounces (fl. oz.) = 1 cup (c.)
> 2 c. = 1 pint (pt.)
> 4 c. = 1 quart (qt.)
> 2 pt. = 1 qt.
> 4 qt. = 1 gallon (gal.)

Example1:
  3 gal. = _____ qt.
  $3 \times 4 = 12$ qt.

Example:
  $1 \frac{1}{4}$ cups = _____ oz.
  $1 \frac{1}{4} \times 8 = 10$ oz.

Example:
  7 c. = _____ pt.
  $7 \div 2 = 3 \frac{1}{2}$ pt.

Square units can be derived with knowledge of basic units of length by squaring the equivalent measurements.

> 1 square foot (sq. ft.) = 144 sq. in.
> 1 sq. yd. = 9 sq. ft.
> 1 sq. yd. = 1296 sq. in.

Example:
  14 sq. yd. = _____ sq. ft.
  $14 \times 9 = 126$ sq. ft.

METRIC UNITS

The metric system is based on multiples of <u>ten</u>. Conversions are made by simply moving the decimal point to the left or right.

kilo-	1000	thousands
hecto-	100	hundreds
deca-	10	tens
nit		
deci-	.1	tenths
centi-	.01	hundredths
milli-	.001	thousandths

The basic unit for **length** is the meter. One meter is approximately one yard.

The basic unit for **weight** or mass is the gram.   A paper clip weighs about one gram.

The basic unit for **volume** is the liter. One liter is approximately a quart.

These are the most commonly used units.

1 m = 100 cm	1000 mL= 1 L	1000 mg = 1 g
1 m = 1000 mm	1 kL = 1000 L	1 kg = 1000 g
1 cm = 10 mm		
1000 m = 1 km		

The prefixes are commonly listed from left to right for ease in conversion.

K H D U D C M

Example:
>63 km = _____ m
>Since there are 3 steps from Kilo to Unit, move the decimal point 3 places to the right.
>63 km = 63,000 m

Example:
>14 mL = _____ L
>Since there are 3 steps from Milli to Unit, move the decimal point 3 places to the left.
>14 mL = 0.014 L

Example:
>56.4 cm = _____ mm
>56.4 cm = 564 mm

Example:
>9.1 m = _____ km
>9.1 m = 0.0091 km

Example 5:
>75 kg = _____ m
>75 kg = 75,000,000 m

Skill 24.2 Solve measurement problems involving volume, time, or speed

There are two types of measurement: direct measurement and indirect measurement. Direct measurement is the action of measuring something directly. The length of a boat can be measured with a measuring tape. Elapsed time can be measured with a stop watch.

Indirect measurement is measurement that is not done with a tool such as a ruler or watch. Instead, other mathematics are used to derive the desired measurement. Using similar triangles is example of indirect measurement. Similar triangles have the same angles and proportionate sides; they are different sizes. They can be used to determine the distance from one point to another without measuring directly. In the diagram below x represents the distance between two points with an unknown length.

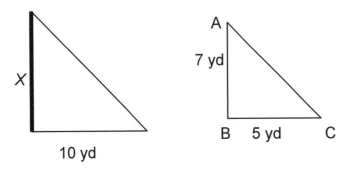

The problem can be determined by setting up the proportion below and solving for X.

$$\frac{X}{10 \text{ yd}} = \frac{7 \text{yd}}{5 \text{yd}}$$

After cross-multiplying, the equation can be written as $5X = 70$; X equals 14 yards. Without actually measuring the distance with a measuring tape or other tool, the distance between the points is determined.

Indirect measurement occurs in instances other than that of measuring length. The area of a room can be measured using a scale drawing. Measuring the weight of the moon is possible using the measurable effects the moon exerts on the earth, such as the changes in tides. Another familiar indirect measurement is the Body Mass Index (BMI), which indicates body composition. The body composition uses height and weight measurements to measure health risks.

Some problems can be solved using equations with rational expressions. First write the equation. To solve it, multiply each term by the LCD of all fractions. This will cancel out all of the denominators and give an equivalent algebraic equation that can be solved.

1. The denominator of a fraction is two less than three times the numerator. If 3 is added to both the numerator and denominator, the new fraction equals $1/2$.

   original fraction: $\dfrac{x}{3x-2}$ revised fraction: $\dfrac{x+3}{3x+1}$

$$\dfrac{x+3}{3x+1} = \dfrac{1}{2} \qquad\qquad 2x+6 = 3x+1$$

$$x = 5$$

   original fraction: $\dfrac{5}{13}$

2. Elly Mae can feed the animals in 15 minutes. Jethro can feed them in 10 minutes. How long will it take them if they work together?

   Solution: If Elly Mae can feed the animals in 15 minutes, then she could feed $1/15$ of them in 1 minute, $2/15$ of them in 2 minutes, $x/15$ of them in x minutes. In the same fashion Jethro could feed $x/10$ of them in x minutes. Together they complete 1 job. The equation is:

$$\dfrac{x}{15} + \dfrac{x}{10} = 1$$

   Multiply each term by the LCD of 30:

   $2x + 3x = 30$
   $x = 6$ minutes

3. A salesman drove 480 miles from Pittsburgh to Hartford. The next day he returned the same distance to Pittsburgh in half an hour less time than his original trip took, because he increased his average speed by 4 mph. Find his original speed.

Since distance = rate x time then time = $\dfrac{\text{distance}}{\text{rate}}$

original time − 1/2 hour = shorter return time

$$\frac{480}{x} - \frac{1}{2} = \frac{480}{x+4}$$

Multiplying by the LCD of $2x(x+4)$, the equation becomes:

$$480\left[2(x+4)\right] - 1\left[x(x+4)\right] = 480(2x)$$
$$960x + 3840 - x^2 - 4x = 960x$$
$$x^2 + 4x - 3840 = 0$$
$$(x+64)(x-60) = 0$$
$$x = 60 \qquad\qquad \text{60 mph is the original speed}$$
$$\qquad\qquad\qquad\qquad \text{64 mph is the faster return speed}$$

Try these:

1. Working together, Larry, Moe, and Curly can paint an elephant in 3 minutes. Working alone, it would take Larry 10 minutes or Moe 6 minutes to paint the elephant. How long would it take Curly to paint the elephant if he worked alone?

2. The denominator of a fraction is 5 more than twice the numerator. If the numerator is doubled, and the denominator is increased by 5, the new fraction is equal to 1/2. Find the original number.

3. A trip from Augusta, Maine to Galveston, Texas is 2108 miles. If one car drove 6 mph faster than a truck and got to Galveston 3 hours before the truck, find the speeds of the car and truck.

Skill 24.3 Interpret graphic and non-graphic representations of frequency distributions, percentiles, and measures of central tendency

Mean, median and mode are three measures of central tendency. The **mean** is the average of the data items. The **median** is found by putting the data items in order from smallest to largest and selecting the item in the middle (or the average of the two items in the middle). The **mode** is the most frequently occurring item.

Range is a measure of variability. It is found by subtracting the smallest value from the largest value.

Sample problem:

Find the mean, median, mode and range of the test score listed below:

85	77	65
92	90	54
88	85	70
75	80	69
85	88	60
72	74	95

Mean (X) = sum of all scores ÷ number of scores
$$= 78$$

Median = put numbers in order from smallest to largest. Pick middle number.

54, 60, 65, 69, 70, 72, 74, 75, 77, 80, 85, 85, 85, 88, 88, 90, 92, 95

                                        -- --
                                  both in middle

Therefore, median is average of two numbers in the middle or 78.5

Mode = most frequent number
$$= 85$$

Range = largest number minus the smallest number
$$= 95 - 54$$
$$= 41$$

Different situations require different information. If we examine the circumstances under which an ice cream store owner may use statistics collected in the store, we find different uses for different information.

Over a 7-day period, the store owner collected data on the ice cream flavors sold. He found the mean number of scoops sold was 174 per day. The most frequently sold flavor was vanilla. This information was useful in determining how much ice cream to order in all and in what amounts for each flavor.

In the case of the ice cream store, the median and range had little business value for the owner.

Consider the set of test scores from a math class: 0, 16, 19, 65, 65, 65, 68, 69, 70, 72, 73, 73, 75, 78, 80, 85, 88, and 92. The mean is 64.06 and the median is 71. Since there are only three scores less than the mean out of the eighteen score, the median (71) would be a more descriptive score.

Retail store owners may be most concerned with the most common dress size so they may order more of that size than any other.

*   *   *

An understanding of the definitions is important in determining the validity and use of statistical data. All definitions and applications in this section apply to ungrouped data.

- Data item: each piece of data is represented by the letter X.
- Mean: the average of all data represented by the symbol $\overline{X}$.
- Range: difference between the highest and lowest value of data items.
- Sum of the Squares: sum of the squares of the differences between each item and the mean. $Sx^2 = (X - \overline{X})^2$
-

Variance: the sum of the squares quantity divided by the number of items. (the lower case Greek letter sigma squared (σ^2)represents variance).

$$\frac{Sx^2}{N} = \sigma^2$$ The larger the value of the variance the larger the spread

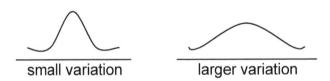

small variation   larger variation

Standard Deviation: the square root of the variance. The lower case Greek letter sigma (σ) is used to represent standard deviation. $\sigma = \sqrt{\sigma^2}$

Most statistical calculators have standard deviation keys on them and should be used when asked to calculate statistical functions. It is important to become familiar with the calculator and the location of the keys needed.

Sample Problem:
Given the ungrouped data below, calculate the mean, range, standard deviation and the variance.

| 15 | 22 | 28 | 25 | 34 | 38 |
| 18 | 25 | 30 | 33 | 19 | 23 |

Mean $(\overline{X}) = 25.8333333$

Range: $38 - 15 = 23$

Standard deviation $(\sigma) = 6.6936952$

Variance $(\sigma^2) = 44.805556$

To make a **bar graph** or a **pictograph**, determine the scale to be used for the graph. Then determine the length of each bar on the graph or determine the number of pictures needed to represent each item of information. Be sure to include an explanation of the scale in the legend.

Example:
A class had the following grades: 4 A's, 9 B's, 8 C's, 1 D, 3 F's. Graph these on a bar graph and a pictograph.

Pictograph

Grade	Number of Students
A	☺☺☺☺
B	☺☺☺☺☺☺☺☺☺
C	☺☺☺☺☺☺☺☺
D	☺
F	☺☺☺

Bar graph

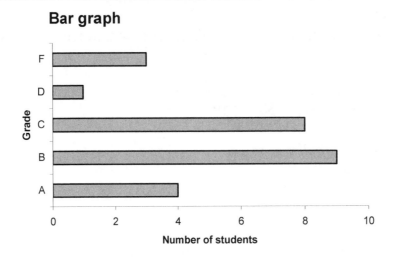

To make a **line graph**, determine appropriate scales for both the vertical and horizontal axes (based on the information to be graphed). Describe what each axis represents and mark the scale periodically on each axis. Graph the individual points of the graph and connect the points on the graph from left to right.

Example:
Graph the following information using a line graph.

The number of National Merit finalists/school year

	90-'91	91-'92	92-'93	93-'94	94-'95	95-'96
Central	3	5	1	4	6	8
Wilson	4	2	3	2	3	2

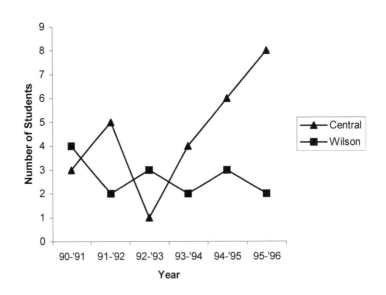

To make a **circle graph**, total all the information that is to be included on the graph. Determine the central angle to be used for each sector of the graph using the following formula:

$$\frac{\text{information}}{\text{total information}} \times 360° = \text{degrees in central } \sphericalangle$$

Lay out the central angles to these sizes, label each section and include its percent.

Example:
Graph this information on a circle graph:

Monthly expenses:
Rent, $400
Food, $150
Utilities, $75
Clothes, $75
Church, $100
Misc., $200

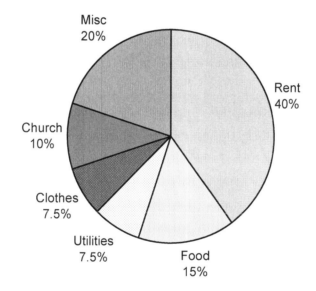

To read a bar graph or a pictograph, read the explanation of the scale that was used in the legend. Compare the length of each bar with the dimensions on the axes and calculate the value each bar represents. On a pictograph count the number of pictures used in the chart and calculate the value of all the pictures.

To read a circle graph, find the total of the amounts represented on the entire circle graph. To determine the actual amount that each sector of the graph represents, multiply the percent in a sector times the total amount number.

To read a chart read the row and column headings on the table. Use this information to evaluate the given information in the chart.

Histograms are used to summarize information from large sets of data that can be naturally grouped into intervals. The vertical axis indicates **frequency** (the number of times any particular data value occurs), and the horizontal axis indicates data values or ranges of data values. The number of data values in any interval is the **frequency of the interval**.

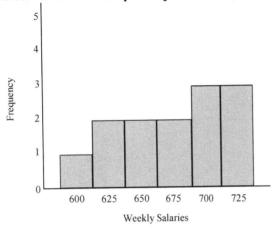

Weekly Salaries

Skill 24.4   Determine probabilities, and make predictions based on probabilities

Dependent events occur when the probability of the second event depends on the outcome of the first event. For example, consider the two events (A) it is sunny on Saturday and (B) you go to the beach. If you intend to go to the beach on Saturday, rain or shine, then A and B may be independent. If however, you plan to go to the beach only if it is sunny, then A and B may be dependent. In this situation, the probability of event B will change depending on the outcome of event A.

Suppose you have a pair of dice, one red and one green. If you roll a three on the red die and then roll a four on the green die, we can see that these events do not depend on the other. The total probability of the two independent events can be found by multiplying the separate probabilities.

$$P(A \text{ and } B) = P(A) \times P(B)$$
$$= 1/6 \times 1/6$$
$$= 1/36$$

Many times, however, events are not independent. Suppose a jar contains 12 red marbles and 8 blue marbles. If you randomly pick a red marble, replace it and then randomly pick again, the probability of picking a red marble the second time remains the same. However, if you pick a red marble, and then pick again without replacing the first red marble, the second pick becomes dependent upon the first pick.

$$P(\text{Red and Red}) \text{ with replacement} = P(\text{Red}) \times P(\text{Red})$$
$$= 12/20 \times 12/20$$
$$= 9/25$$

$$P(\text{Red and Red}) \text{ without replacement} = P(\text{Red}) \times P(\text{Red})$$
$$= 12/20 \times 11/19$$
$$= 33/95$$

Odds are defined as the ratio of the number of favorable outcomes to the number of unfavorable outcomes. The sum of the favorable outcomes and the unfavorable outcomes should always equal the total possible outcomes.

For example, given a bag of 12 red and 7 green marbles compute the odds of randomly selecting a red marble.

$$\text{Odds of red} = \frac{12}{19} : \frac{7}{19} \text{ or } 12{:}7.$$
$$\text{Odds of not getting red} = \frac{7}{19} : \frac{12}{19} \text{ or } 7{:}12.$$

In the case of flipping a coin, it is equally likely that a head or a tail will be tossed. The odds of tossing a head are 1:1. This is called even odds.

COMPETENCY 25.0   **UNDERSTAND THE INTERRELATIONSHIPS AMONG THE PHYSICAL AND LIFE SCIENCES AND THE CONNECTIONS AMONG SCIENCE, TECHNOLOGY, AND SOCIETY**

Skill 25.1   **Apply principles of mathematics, science, and technology to model a given situation (e.g., the movement of energy and nutrients between a food chain and the physical environment)**

The tools of modeling and mathematics can be used to help us understand and predict behavior of natural systems. Let's look at an example: the movement of carbon through the biological and geological world.

The first step in preparing our model is to draw a diagram representing the various components and the relationships between them. Below, carbon reserves are shown as squares and converting processes as circles. This is a simplified diagram, with only a few of the important components of the carbon cycle:

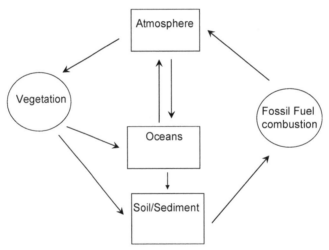

Next, we would like to attach mathematical quantities and equations to describe these relationships. In this and many other situations in the natural world, not all these quantities and exact relationships will be known. Thus the equations and their coefficients must be approximated and estimated. In the carbon cycle, we can write chemical equations for the various exchanges of carbon, such as that for aerobic respiration: $C_6H_{12}O_6 + 6O_2 \rightarrow 6CO_2 + 6H_2O$. Additionally, we can make yearly estimates for how much carbon is stored in the various reservoirs and how much is transformed by the processes. To make visualization simple, we can add these numbers to our diagram (all quantities are in GigaTons or GigaTons/yr):

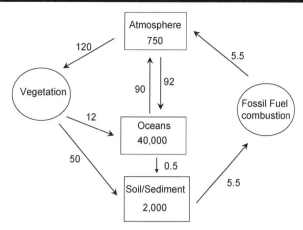

Finally, with all the relationships elucidated, we can use our model to make predictions. In the carbon cycle example, we can predict what might happen if fossil fuel combustion rates were increased or vegetation was killed. The ability to make predictions about the results of changes in a system, without actually performing an experiment, is one of the most useful aspects of modeling. Computer simulations are often employed for highly complex natural systems, in which the number of relationships is high and the equations are complicated.

Skill 25.2   Analyze the effects of changes in environmental conditions (e.g., temperature, availability of water and sunlight) on plant and animal health, growth, and development

Natural phenomena affect the make up and functioning of ecosystems both directly and indirectly. For example, floods and volcanic eruptions can destroy the fixed portions of an ecosystem, such as plants and microbes. Mobile elements, such as animals, must evacuate or risk injury or death. After a catastrophic event, species of microbes and plants begin to repopulate the ecosystem, beginning a line of secondary succession that eventually leads to the return of higher-level species. Often the area affected by the event returns to something like its original state.

Volcanic eruptions produce large amounts of molten lava and expel large amounts of ash and gas. Molten lava kills and destroys any living organisms it contacts. However, when lava cools and hardens, it provides a rich environment for growth of microbes and plants. Volcanic eruptions also affect ecosystems indirectly. Studies show that the ash and gas released by eruptions can cause a reduction in the area temperature for several years. The volcanic aerosol reflects the Sun's rays and creates clouds that have the same effect. In addition, sulfuric acid released by the volcano suppresses the production of greenhouse gases that damage the ozone layer.

Floods destroy microbes and vegetation and kill or force the evacuation of animals. Only when floodwaters recede can an ecosystem begin to return to normal. Floods, however, also have indirect effects. For example, floods can cause permanent soil erosion and nutrient depletion. Such disruptions of the soil can delay and limit an ecosystem's recovery.

Succession is an orderly process of replacing a community that has been damaged or has begun where no life previously existed. Primary succession occurs where life never existed before, as in a flooded area or a new volcanic island. Secondary succession takes place in communities that were once flourishing but disturbed by some source, either man or nature, but not totally stripped. A climax community is a community that is established and flourishing.

A limiting factor is the component of a biological process that determines how quickly or slowly the process proceeds. Photosynthesis is the main biological process determining the rate of ecosystem productivity, the rate at which an ecosystem creates biomass. Thus, in evaluating the productivity of an ecosystem, potential limiting factors are light intensity, gas concentrations, and mineral availability. The Law of the Minimum states that the required factor in a given process that is most scarce controls the rate of the process.

One potential limiting factor of ecosystem productivity is light intensity because photosynthesis requires light energy. Light intensity can limit productivity in two ways. First, too little light limits the rate of photosynthesis because the required energy is not available. Second, too much light can damage the photosynthetic system of plants and microorganisms thus slowing the rate of photosynthesis. Decreased photosynthesis equals decreased productivity.

Another potential limiting factor of ecosystem productivity is gas concentrations. Photosynthesis requires carbon dioxide. Thus, increased concentration of carbon dioxide often results in increased productivity. While carbon dioxide is often not the ultimate limiting factor of productivity, increased concentration can indirectly increase rates of photosynthesis in several ways. First, increased carbon dioxide concentration often increases the rate of nitrogen fixation (available nitrogen is another limiting factor of productivity). Second, increased carbon dioxide concentration can decrease the pH of rain, improving the water source of photosynthetic organisms.

Finally, mineral availability also limits ecosystem productivity. Plants require adequate amounts of nitrogen and phosphorus to build many cellular structures. The availability of the inorganic minerals phosphorus and nitrogen often is the main limiting factor of plant biomass production. In other words, in a natural environment phosphorus and nitrogen availability most often limits ecosystem productivity, rather than carbon dioxide concentration or light intensity.

Interrelationships among organisms within a community

There are many interactions that may occur between different species living together. Predation, parasitism, competition, commensalisms, and mutualism are the different types of relationships populations have amongst each other.

Predation and **parasitism** result in a benefit for one species and a detriment for the other. Predation is when a predator eats its prey. The common conception of predation is of a carnivore consuming other animals. This is one form of predation. Although not always resulting in the death of the plant, herbivory is a form of predation. Some animals eat enough of a plant to cause death. Parasitism involves a predator that lives on or in their hosts, causing detrimental effects to the host. Insects and viruses living off and reproducing in their hosts is an example of parasitism. Many plants and animals have defenses against predators. Some plants have poisonous chemicals that will harm the predator if ingested and some animals are camouflaged so they are harder to detect.

Competition is when two or more species in a community use the same resources. Competition is usually detrimental to both populations. Competition is often difficult to find in nature because competition between two populations is not continuous. Either the weaker population will no longer exist, or one population will evolve to utilize other available resources.

Symbiosis is when two species live close together. Parasitism is one example of symbiosis described above. Another example of symbiosis is commensalisms. **Commensalism** occurs when one species benefits from the other without harmful effects. **Mutualism** is when both species benefit from the other. Species involved in mutualistic relationships must co-evolve to survive. As one species evolves, the other must as well if it is to be successful in life. The grouper and a species of shrimp live in a mutualistic relationship. The shrimp feed off parasites living on the grouper; thus the shrimp are fed and the grouper stays healthy. Many microorganisms are in mutualistic relationships.

Skill 25.3   Analyze the effects of human activities (e.g., burning fossil fuels, clear-cutting forests) on the environment and the benefits and limitations of science and technology

Humans have a tremendous impact on the world's natural resources. The world's natural water supplies are affected by human use. Waterways are major sources for recreation and freight transportation. Oil and wastes from boats and cargo ships pollute the aquatic environment. The aquatic plant and animal life is affected by this contamination. To obtain drinking water, contaminants such as parasites, pollutants and bacteria are removed from raw water through a purification process involving various screening, conditioning and chlorination steps. Most uses of water resources, such as drinking and crop irrigation, require fresh water. Only 2.5% of water on Earth is fresh water, and more than two thirds of this fresh water is frozen in glaciers and polar ice caps. Consequently, in many parts of the world, water use greatly exceeds supply. This problem is expected to increase in the future.

Plant resources also make up a large part of the world's natural resources. Plant resources are renewable and can be re-grown and restocked. Plant resources can be used by humans to make clothing, buildings and medicines, and can also be directly consumed. Forestry is the study and management of growing forests. This industry provides the wood that is essential for use as construction timber or paper. Cotton is a common plant found on farms of the Southern United States. Cotton is used to produce fabric for clothing, sheets, furniture, etc. Another example of a plant resource that is not directly consumed is straw, which is harvested for use in plant growth and farm animal care. The list of plants grown to provide food for the people of the world is extensive. Major crops include corn, potatoes, wheat, sugar, barley, peas, beans, beets, flax, lentils, sunflowers, soybeans, canola, and rice. These crops may have alternate uses as well. For example, corn is used to manufacture cornstarch, ethanol fuel, high fructose corn syrup, ink, biodegradable plastics, chemicals used in cosmetics and pharmaceuticals, adhesives, and paper products.

Other resources used by humans are known as "non-renewable" resources. Such resources, including fossil fuels, cannot be re-made and do not naturally reform at a rate that could sustain human use. Non-renewable resources are therefore depleted and not restored. Presently, non-renewable resources provide the main source of energy for humans. Common fossil fuels used by humans are coal, petroleum and natural gas, which all form from the remains of dead plants and animals through natural processes after millions of years. Because of their high carbon content, when burnt these substances generate high amounts of energy as well as carbon dioxide, which is released back into the atmosphere increasing global warming. To create electricity, energy from the burning of fossil fuels is harnessed to power a rotary engine called a turbine. Implementation of the use of fossil fuels as an energy source provided for large-scale industrial development.

Mineral resources are concentrations of naturally occurring inorganic elements and compounds located in the Earth's crust that are extracted through mining for human use. Minerals have a definite chemical composition and are stable over a range of temperatures and pressures. Construction and manufacturing rely heavily on metals and industrial mineral resources. These metals may include iron, bronze, lead, zinc, nickel, copper, tin, etc. Other industrial minerals are divided into two categories: bulk rocks and ore minerals. Bulk rocks, including limestone, clay, shale and sandstone, are used as aggregate in construction, in ceramics or in concrete. Common ore minerals include calcite, barite and gypsum. Energy from some minerals can be utilized to produce electricity fuel and industrial materials. Mineral resources are also used as fertilizers and pesticides in the industrial context.

Deforestation for urban development has resulted in the extinction or relocation of several species of plants and animals. Animals are forced to leave their forest homes or perish amongst the destruction. The number of plant and animal species that have become extinct due to deforestation is unknown. Scientists have only identified a fraction of the species on Earth. It is known that if the destruction of natural resources continues, there may be no plants or animals successfully reproducing in the wild.

The current energy crisis is largely centered on the uncertain future of fossil fuels. The supplies of fossil fuels are limited and fast declining. Additionally, most oil is now derived from a highly politically volatile area of the world. Finally, continuing to produce energy from fossils fuels is unwise given the damage done by both the disruption to the environment necessary to harvest them and the byproducts of their combustion cause pollution. The various detrimental effects of fossil fuels are listed later in this section.

It is important to recognize that a real energy crisis has vast economic implications. Oil, currently the most important fossil fuel, is needed for heating, electricity, and as a raw material for the manufacture of many items, particularly plastics. Additionally, the gasoline made from oil is important in transporting people and goods, including food and other items necessary for life. A disruption in the oil supply often causes rising prices in all sectors and may eventually trigger recession.

Alternative, sustainable energy sources must be found for both economic and ecological reasons.

Skill 25.4   Evaluate the use of science and technology in solving problems related to the effects of human activities on the environment (e.g., recycling, energy conservation)

o   *See Skill 25.3*

COMPETENCY 26.0   UNDERSTAND THE PRINCIPLES OF LIFE SCIENCE (INCLUDING BIOLOGY AND ECOLOGY), AND USE THIS UNDERSTANDING TO INTERPRET, ANALYZE, AND EXPLAIN PHENOMENA

Skill 26.1   Infer the life science principle (e.g., adaptation, homeostasis) illustrated in a given situation

Adaptation

Darwin defined the theory of Natural Selection in the mid-1800s. Through the study of finches on the Galapagos Islands, Darwin theorized that nature selects the traits that are advantageous to the organism. Those that do not possess the desirable trait die and do not pass on their genes. Those more fit to survive reproduce, thus increasing that gene in the population. Darwin listed four principles to define natural selection:

1. The individuals in a certain species vary from generation to generation.
2. Some of the variations are determined by the genetic makeup of the species.
3. More individuals are produced than will survive.
4. Some genes allow for better survival of an animal.

Causes of evolution - Certain factors increase the chances of variability in a population, thus leading to evolution. Items that increase variability include mutations, sexual reproduction, immigration, and large population. Items that decrease variation would be natural selection, emigration, small population, and random mating.

Sexual selection - Genes that happen to come together determine the makeup of the gene pool. Animals that use mating behaviors may be successful or unsuccessful. An animal that lacks attractive plumage or has a weak mating call will not attract the female, thereby eventually limiting that gene in the gene pool. Mechanical isolation, where sex organs do not fit the female, has an obvious disadvantage.

Homeostasis

All living organisms respond and adapt to their environments. Homeostasis is the result of regulatory mechanisms that help maintain an organism's internal environment within tolerable limits.

The molecular composition of the immediate environment outside of the organism is not the same as it is inside and the temperature outside may not be optimal for metabolic activity within the organism. Homeostasis is the control of these differences between internal and external environments. There are three homeostatic systems to regulate these differences.

Osmo-regulation deals with maintenance of the appropriate level of water and salts in body fluids for optimum cellular functions.

Excretion is the elimination of metabolic waste products from the body including excess water.

Thermoregulation maintains the internal, or core, body temperature of the organism within a tolerable range for metabolic and cellular processes. For example, in humans and mammals, constriction and dilation of blood vessels near the skin help maintain body temperature.

Skill 26.2   Analyze relationships among the components of an ecological community

Essential elements are recycled through an ecosystem. At times, the element needs to be "fixed" in a useable form. Cycles are dependent on plants, algae and bacteria to fix nutrients for use by animals.

Water cycle - 2% of all the available water is fixed and held in ice or the bodies of organisms. Available water includes surface water (lakes, ocean, and rivers) and ground water (aquifers, wells). 96% of all available water is from ground water. Water is recycled through the processes of evaporation and precipitation. The water present now is the water that has been here since our atmosphere formed.

Carbon cycle - Ten percent of all available carbon in the air (from carbon dioxide gas) is fixed by photosynthesis. Plants fix carbon in the form of glucose; animals eat the plants and are able to obtain their source of carbon. When animals release carbon dioxide through respiration, the plants again have a source of carbon to fix.

Nitrogen cycle - Eighty percent of the atmosphere is in the form of nitrogen gas. Nitrogen must be fixed and taken out of the gaseous form to be incorporated into an organism. Only a few genera of bacteria have the correct enzymes to break the triple bond between nitrogen atoms. These bacteria live within the roots of legumes (peas, beans, alfalfa) and add bacteria to the soil so it may be taken up by the plant. Nitrogen is necessary to make amino acids and the nitrogenous bases of DNA.

Phosphorus cycle - Phosphorus exists as a mineral and is not found in the atmosphere. Fungi and plant roots have structures called mycorrhizae that are able to fix insoluble phosphates into useable phosphorus. Urine and decayed matter returns phosphorus to the earth where it can be fixed in the plant. Phosphorus is needed for the backbone of DNA and for the manufacture of ATP.

Major characteristics of world biomes and communities, including succession and interrelationships of organisms.

Ecology is the study of organisms, where they live and their interactions with the environment. A **population** is a group of the same species in a specific area. A **community** is a group of populations residing in the same area. Communities that are ecologically similar in regards to temperature, rainfall and the species that live there are called **biomes**. Specific biomes include:

Marine - covers 75% of the earth. This biome is organized by the depth of the water. The intertidal zone is from the tide line to the edge of the water. The littoral zone is from the water's edge to the open sea. It includes coral reef habitats and is the most densely populated area of the marine biome. The open sea zone is divided into the epipelagic zone and the pelagic zone. The epipelagic zone receives more sunlight and has a larger number of species. The ocean floor is called the benthic zone and is populated with bottom feeders.

Tropical Rain Forest - temperature is constant (25 degrees C), rainfall exceeds 200 cm. per year. Located around the area of the equator, the rain forest has abundant, diverse species of plants and animals.

Savanna - temperatures range from 0-25 degrees C depending on the location. Rainfall is from 90 to 150 cm per year. Plants include shrubs and grasses. The savanna is a transitional biome between the rain forest and the desert.

Desert - temperatures range from 10-38 degrees C. Rainfall is under 25   cm per year. Plant species include xerophytes and succulents. Lizards, snakes and small mammals are common animals.

Temperate Deciduous Forest - temperature ranges from -24 to 38 degrees C. Rainfall is between 65 to 150 cm per year. Deciduous trees are common, as well as deer, bear and squirrels.

Taiga - temperatures range from -24 to 22 degrees C. Rainfall is between 35 to 40 cm per year. Taiga is located very north and very south of the equator, getting close to the poles. Plant life includes conifers and plants that can withstand harsh winters. Animals include weasels, mink, and moose.

Tundra - temperatures range from -28 to 15 degrees C. Rainfall is limited, ranging from 10 to 15 cm per year. The tundra is located even further north and south than the taiga. Common plants include lichens and mosses. Animals include polar bears and musk ox.

Polar or Permafrost - temperature ranges from -40 to 0 degrees C. It rarely gets above freezing. Rainfall is below 10 cm per year. Most water is bound up as ice. Life is limited.

Succession - Succession is an orderly process of replacing a community that has been damaged or beginning one where no life previously existed. Primary succession occurs after a community has been totally wiped out by a natural disaster or where life never existed before, as in a flooded area. Secondary succession takes place in communities that were once flourishing but were disturbed by some source, either man or nature, but were not totally stripped. A climax community is a community that is established and flourishing.

Definitions of feeding relationships:

> **Parasitism** - two species that occupy a similar place; the parasite benefits from the relationship, the host is harmed.
> **Commensalism** - two species that occupy a similar place; neither species is harmed or benefits from the relationship.
> **Mutualism (symbiosis)**- two species that occupy a similar place; both species benefit from the relationship.
> **Competition** - two species that occupy the same habitat or eat the same food are said to be in competition with each other.
> **Predation** - animals that eat other animals are called predators. The animals they feed on are called the prey. Population growth depends upon competition for food, water, shelter, and space. The amount of predators determines the amount of prey, which in turn affects the number of predators.
> **Carrying Capacity** - this is the total amount of life a habitat can support. Once the habitat runs out of food, water, shelter, or space, the carrying capacity decreases, and then stabilizes.

Ecological Problems - nonrenewable resources are fragile and must be conserved for use in the future. Man's impact and knowledge of conservation will control our future.

Biological magnification - chemicals and pesticides accumulate along the food chain. Tertiary consumers have more accumulated toxins than animals at the bottom of the food chain.

Simplification of the food web - Three major crops feed the world (rice, corn, wheat). The planting of these foods wipe out habitats and push animals residing there into other habitats causing overpopulation or extinction.

Fuel sources - strip mining and the overuse of oil reserves have depleted these resources. At the current rate of consumption, conservation or alternate fuel sources will guarantee our future fuel sources.

Pollution - although technology gives us many advances, pollution is a side effect of production. Waste disposal and the burning of fossil fuels have polluted our land, water and air. Global warming and acid rain are two results of the burning of hydrocarbons and sulfur.

Global warming - rainforest depletion and the use of fossil fuels and aerosols have caused an increase in carbon dioxide production. This leads to a decrease in the amount of oxygen which is directly proportional to the amount of ozone. As the ozone layer depletes, more heat enters our atmosphere and is trapped. This causes an overall warming effect which may eventually melt polar ice caps, causing a rise in water levels and changes in climate which will affect weather systems world-wide.

Endangered species - construction of homes to house people in our overpopulated world has caused the destruction of habitat for other animals leading to their extinction.

Overpopulation - the human race is still growing at an exponential rate. Carrying capacity has not been met due to our ability to use technology to produce more food and housing. Space and water can not be manufactured and eventually our non-renewable resources will reach a crisis state. Our overuse affects every living thing on this planet.

Biotic factors - living things in an ecosystem; plants, animals, bacteria, fungi, etc. If one population in a community increases, it affects the ability of another population to succeed by limiting the available amount of food, water, shelter and space.

Abiotic factors - non-living aspects of an ecosystem; soil quality, rainfall, and temperature. Changes in climate and soil can cause effects at the beginning of the food chain, thus limiting or accelerating the growth of populations.

Abiotic factors vary in the environment. It is also difficult to determine the types and numbers of organisms that exist in that environment. Factors which determine the types and numbers of organisms of a species in an ecosystem are called limiting factors. Many limiting factors restrict the growth of populations in nature.

Carrying capacity is the maximum number of organisms the resources of an ecosystem can support. The carrying capacity of the environment is limited by the available abiotic and biotic resources (limiting factors), as well as the ability of ecosystems to recycle the residue of dead organisms through the activities of bacteria and fungi.

The arrival of human species has greatly altered the biotic and abiotic factors for much of life on earth. An example of this would include how annual average temperature common to the Arctic restricts the growth of trees, as the subsoil is permanently frozen. Another example is the effect that climate change has on migratory birds. The anticipated increase in cloudiness over the arctic could itself become a factor in ozone depletion. The clouds, formed from condensed nitric acid and water, tend to increase snowfall, which accelerates depletion of stratospheric nitrogen. There is a circular relationship between how biotic and abiotic factors influence environment conditions and then how environmental conditions in turn affect biotic and abiotic factors.

Although bacteria and fungi may cause disease, they are also beneficial for use as medicines and food. Penicillin is derived from a fungus that is capable of destroying the cell wall of bacteria. Most antibiotics work in this way. Viral diseases have been fought through the use of vaccination, where a small amount of the virus is introduced so the immune system is able to recognize it upon later infection. Antibodies are more quickly manufactured when the host has had prior exposure. Viruses are difficult to treat because antibiotics are ineffective against them. That is why doctors do not usually prescribe antibiotics for those who have a cold or the flu—common viral infections. While some yeast can cause illness, Brewer's yeast is a fungus that humans use to make bread and to ferment wine. In addition, many microbes are decomposers, helping to clear away dead organisms and clean the forest floor of debris.

Skill 26.3 Analyze the factors that contribute to change in organisms and species over time

Gregor Mendel is recognized as the father of genetics. His work in the late 1800's is the basis of our knowledge of genetics. Although unaware of the presence of DNA or genes, Mendel realized there were factors (now known as genes) that were transferred from parents to their offspring. Mendel worked with pea plants and fertilized the plants himself, keeping track of subsequent generations which led to the Mendelian laws of genetics. Mendel found that two "factors" governed each trait, one from each parent. Traits or characteristics came in several forms, known as alleles. For example, the trait of flower color had white alleles and purple alleles. Mendel formed three laws:

- **Law of dominance** - in a pair of alleles, one trait may cover up the allele of the other trait. Example: brown eyes are dominant to blue eyes.
- **Law of segregation** - only one of the two possible alleles from each parent is passed on to the offspring from each parent. (During meiosis, the haploid number insures that half the sex cells get one allele, half get the other).

- **Law of independent assortment** - alleles sort independently of each other. (Many combinations are possible depending on which sperm ends up with which egg. Compare this to the many combinations of hands possible when dealing a deck of cards).
  1. **monohybrid cross** - a cross using only one trait.
  2. **dihybrid cross** - a cross using two traits. More combinations are possible.

Punnet squares - these are used to show the possible ways that genes combine and indicate probability of the occurrence of a certain genotype or phenotype. One parent's genes are put at the top of the box and the other parent at the side of the box. Genes combine on the square just like numbers that are added in addition tables we learned in elementary school.

Example: Monohybrid Cross - four possible gene combinations
Example: Dihybrid Cross - sixteen possible gene combinations

Human genetics, including relationships between genotypes and phenotypes and causes and effects of disorders.

SOME DEFINITIONS TO KNOW -

Dominant - the stronger of the two traits. If a dominant gene is present, it will be expressed. Shown by a capital letter.

Recessive - the weaker of the two traits. In order for the recessive gene to be expressed, there must be two recessive genes present. Shown by a lower case letter.

Homozygous - (purebred) having two of the same genes present; an organism may be homozygous dominant with two dominant genes or homozygous recessive with two recessive genes.

Heterozygous - (hybrid) having one dominant gene and one recessive gene. The dominant gene will be expressed due to the Law of Dominance.

Genotype - the genes the organism has. Genes are represented with letters. AA, Bb, and tt are examples of genotypes.

Phenotype - how the trait is expressed in an organism. Blue eyes, brown hair, and red flowers are examples of phenotypes.

Incomplete dominance - neither gene masks the other; a new phenotype is formed. For example, red flowers and white flowers may have equal strength. A heterozygote (Rr) would have pink flowers. If a problem occurs with a third phenotype, incomplete dominance is occurring.

Co-dominance - genes may form new phenotypes. The ABO blood grouping is an example of co-dominance. A and B are of equal strength and O is recessive. Therefore, type A blood may have the genotypes of AA or AO, type B blood may have the genotypes of BB or BO, type AB blood has the genotype A and B, and type O blood has two recessive O genes.

Linkage - genes that are found on the same chromosome usually appear together unless crossing over has occurred in meiosis. (Example - blue eyes and blonde hair)

Lethal alleles - these are usually recessive due to the early death of the offspring. If a 2:1 ratio of alleles is found in offspring, a lethal gene combination is usually the reason. Some examples of lethal alleles include sickle cell anemia, tay-sachs and cystic fibrosis. Usually the coding for an important protein is affected.

Inborn errors of metabolism - these occur when the protein affected is an enzyme. Examples include PKU (phenylketonuria) and albanism.

Polygenic characters - many alleles code for a phenotype. There may be as many as twenty genes that code for skin color. This is why there is such a variety of skin tones. Another example is height. A couple of medium height may have very tall offspring.

Sex linked traits - the Y chromosome found only in males (XY) carries very little genetic information, whereas the X chromosome found in females (XX) carries very important information. Since men have no second X chromosome to cover up a recessive gene, the recessive trait is expressed more often in men. Women need the recessive gene on both X chromosomes to show the trait. Examples of sex linked traits include hemophilia and color-blindness.

Sex influenced traits - traits are influenced by the sex hormones. Male pattern baldness is an example of a sex influenced trait. Testosterone influences the expression of the gene. Mostly men loose their hair due to this trait.

DNA and DNA REPLICATION

The modern definition of a gene is a unit of genetic information. DNA makes up genes which in turn make up the chromosomes. DNA is wound tightly around proteins in order to conserve space. The DNA/protein combination makes up the chromosome. DNA controls the synthesis of proteins, thereby controlling the total cell activity. DNA is capable of making copies of itself.

Review of DNA structure:

1. Made of nucleotides; a five carbon sugar, phosphate group and nitrogen base (either adenine, guanine, cytosine or thymine).
2. Consists of a sugar/phosphate backbone which is covalently bonded. The bases are joined down the center of the molecule and are attached by hydrogen bonds which are easily broken during replication.
3. The amount of adenine equals the amount of thymine and the amount of cytosine equals the amount of guanine.
4. The shape is that of a twisted ladder called a double helix. The sugar/phosphates make up the sides of the ladder and the base pairs make up the rungs of the ladder.

DNA Replication

Enzymes control each step of the replication of DNA. The molecule untwists. The hydrogen bonds between the bases break and serve as a pattern for replication. Free nucleotides found inside the nucleus join on to form a new strand. Two new pieces of DNA are formed which are identical. This is a very accurate process. There is only one mistake for every billion nucleotides added. This is because there are enzymes (polymerases) present that proofread the molecule. In eukaryotes, replication occurs in many places along the DNA at once. The molecule may open up at many places like a broken zipper. In prokaryotic circular plasmids, replication begins at a point on the plasmid and goes in both directions until it meets itself.

Base pairing rules are important in determining a new strand of DNA sequence. For example say our original strand of DNA had the sequence as follows:

1. A T C G G C A A T A G C   This may be called our sense strand as it contains a sequence that makes sense or codes for something.
   The complementary strand (or other side of the ladder) would follow base pairing rules (A bonds with T and C bonds with G) and would read:
2. T A G C C G T T A T C G   When the molecule opens up and nucleotides join on, the base pairing rules create two new identical strands of DNA
   A T C G G C A A T A G C   and   A T C G G C A A T A G C
   T A G C C G T T A T C G   T A G C C G T T A T C G

Protein Synthesis

It is necessary for cells to manufacture new proteins for growth and repair of the organism. Protein Synthesis is the process that allows the DNA code to be read and carried out of the nucleus into the cytoplasm in the form of RNA. This is where the ribosomes are found, which are the sites of protein synthesis. The protein is then assembled according to the instructions on the DNA. There are several types of RNA. Familiarize yourself with where they are found and their function.

Messenger RNA - (mRNA) copies the code from DNA in the nucleus and takes it to the ribosomes in the cytoplasm.
Transfer RNA - (tRNA) free floating in the cytoplasm. Its job is to carry and position amino acids for assembly on the ribosome.
Ribosomal RNA - (rRNA) found in the ribosomes. They make a place for the proteins to be made. rRNA is believed to have many important functions, so much research is currently being done currently in this area.

Along with enzymes and amino acids, the RNA's function is to assist in the building of proteins. There are two stages of protein synthesis:

Transcription - this phase allows for the assembly of mRNA and occurs in the nucleus where the DNA is found. The DNA splits open and the mRNA reads the code and "transcribes" the sequence onto a single strand of mRNA. For example, if the code on the DNA is T A C C T C G T A C G A , the mRNA will make a complementary strand reading: A U G G A G C A U G C U (Remember that uracil replaces   thymine in RNA.) Each group of three bases is called a **codon**. The codon   will eventually code for a specific amino acid to be carried to the ribosome. "Start" codons begin the building of the protein and "stop" codons end transcription. When the stop codon is reached, the mRNA separates from the DNA and leaves the nucleus for the cytoplasm.

Translation - this is the assembly of the amino acids to build the protein and occurs in the cytoplasm. The nucleotide sequence is translated to choose the correct amino acid sequence. As the rRNA translates the code at the ribosome, tRNA's that contain an **anticodon** seek out the correct amino acid and bring it back to the ribosome. For example, using the codon sequence from the example above:

the mRNA reads A U G / G A G / C A U / G C U
the anticodons are U A C / C U C / G U A / C G A
the amino acid sequence would be: Methionine (start) - Glu - His - Ala.

 *Be sure to note if the table you are given is written according to the codon sequence or the anticodon sequence. It will be specified.

This whole process is accomplished through the assistance of **activating enzymes**. Each of the twenty amino acids has their own enzyme. The enzyme binds the amino acid to the tRNA. When the amino acids get close to each other on the ribosome, they bond together using peptide bonds. The start and stop codons are called nonsense codons. There is one start codon (AUG) and three stop codons. (UAA, UGA and UAG). Addition mutations will cause the whole code to shift, thereby producing the wrong protein or, at times, no protein at all.

Skill 26.4   Analyze processes that contribute to the continuity of life (e.g., life cycles; the role of growth, repair, and maintenance)

Life has defining properties. Some of the more important processes and properties associated with life are as follows:

- Order – an organism's complex organization.
- Reproduction – life only comes from life (biogenesis).
- Energy utilization – organisms use and make energy to do many kinds of work.
- Growth and development – DNA directed growth and development.
- Adaptation to the environment – occurs by homeostasis (ability to maintain a certain status), response to stimuli, and evolution.

Recognize the levels of organization
Life is highly organized. The organization of living systems builds on levels from small to increasingly more large and complex. All aspects, whether it is a cell or an ecosystem, have the same requirements to sustain life. Life is organized from simple to complex in the following way:

Atoms→molecules→organelles→cells→tissues→organs→organ systems→organism

Viruses are neither living nor non-living; they greatly affect other living things by disrupting cell activity. They are considered to be obligate parasites because they reproduce only inside living things.
There are two types of viral reproductive cycles:

1. **Lytic cycles** - the virus enters the host cell and makes copies of its nucleic acids and protein coats and reassembles. It then lyses or breaks out of the host cell and infects other nearby cells, repeating the process.
2. **Lysogenic cycle** - the virus may remain dormant within the cells until something initiates it to break out of the cell. Herpes is an example of a lysogenic virus.

Monera consists of single celled organisms that do not have a nucleus, but have nuclear material inside the cells. This group consists of bacteria and blue green bacteria, which exist as uni- or multi-cellular organisms. Blue green bacteria are small one-celled organisms that are photosynthetic, since they have the green pigment, chlorophyll. Bacteria reproduce asexually (from a single parent) by fission, in which on organism divides into two. The chromosome of the bacterial cell, which is circular, makes a copy of itself and then the cell divides resulting in two identical cells. If the conditions for asexual reproduction are ideal, a bacterium can reproduce in about 20 minutes.

Bacteria reproduce by binary fission. This asexual process is simply dividing the bacterium in half. All new organisms are exact clones of the parent.

Protists are larger than bacteria and are of three types – animal like, plant like and fungus like. Animal like protests reproduce asexually by fission (by dividing into two) and spores. These are special cells that develop into new organisms. Plant like protests reproduce by fission, spores and by gametes and conjugation, which is somewhat similar to sexual reproduction. Fungus, like protests, form spores and reproduce.

Mushrooms, molds, mildews, yeasts, rusts and smuts come under fungi. Fungi are of three kinds – sporangium fungi, club fungi and sac fungi. Sporangium fungi (molds) reproduce by forming spores in sporangia, which are specialized structures producing spores. Club fungi (mushrooms etc.) reproduce by spores, which are produced in club shaped structures within the gills. These gills are located in the cap of the fungi. Sac fungi (yeasts) reproduce by budding (parent cell forming a bud, which ultimately breaks) and spores produced in the sacs.

Reproduction in plants is accomplished through alternation of generations. Simply stated, a haploid stage in the plant's life history alternates with a diploid stage. The diploid sporophyte divides by meiosis to reduce the chromosome number to the haploid gametophyte generation. The haploid gametophytes undergo mitosis to produce gametes (sperm and eggs). Then, the haploid gametes fertilize to return to the diploid sporophyte stage.

The non-vascular plants need water to reproduce. The vascular non-seeded plants reproduce with spores and also need water to reproduce. Gymnosperms use seeds for reproduction and do not require water.

Angiosperms are the most numerous and are therefore the main focus of reproduction in this section. The sporophyte is the dominant phase in reproduction. Angiosperm reproductive structures are the flowers.

The male gametophytes are pollen grains and the female gametophytes are embryo sacs that are inside of the ovules. The male pollen grains are formed in the anthers at the tips of the stamens. The ovaries enclose the female ovules. Therefore, the stamen is the reproductive organ of the male and the carpel is the reproductive organ of
the female.

In a process called **pollination**, the pollen grains are released from the anthers and carried by animals and the wind and land on the carpels. The sperm is released to fertilize the eggs. Angiosperms reproduce through a method of double fertilization. Two sperms fertilize an ovum. One sperm produces the new plant and the other forms the food supply for the developing plant (endosperm).

The ovule develops into a seed and the ovary develops into a fruit. The fruit is then carried by wind or animals and the seeds are dispersed to form new plants.

The development of the egg to form a plant occurs in three stages: growth, morphogenesis, the development of form, and cellular differentiation (the acquisition of a cell's specific structure and function).

Asexual reproduction is quicker and is very beneficial to the organisms and the offspring are identical. In sexual reproduction, there is the chance factor and the offspring are different from each other except for identical twins.

The higher animals use various methods to attract the opposite sex to improve their chances of mating – attractive plumage in birds, various sounds, smells etc.

Reproduction in animals occurs both asexually and sexually. Reproduction in simple animals like sponges happens by breaking off a piece of the organism, which in turn develops into an individual. Sexual reproduction occurs by union of egg and sperm.

Fish need water for reproduction. The female fish lays a huge number of eggs and male fish releases sperms into the water and fertilization takes place in water. Most of the mammals give birth to offspring and care for them. There are two groups of mammals that are different. The marsupials have a pouch to care for their young ones and the other group lays eggs and embryos develop from those eggs.

COMPETENCY 27.0 UNDERSTAND THE PRINCIPLES OF PHYSICAL SCIENCE (INCLUDING EARTH SCIENCE, CHEMISTRY, AND PHYSICS), AND USE THIS UNDERSTANDING TO INTERPRET, ANALYZE, AND EXPLAIN PHENOMENA

Skill 27.1 Analyze factors and processes related to celestial and atmospheric phenomena (e.g., seasonal changes, the phases of the moon)

Earth is the third planet away from the sun in our solar system. Earth's numerous types of motion and states of orientation greatly effect global conditions, such as seasons, tides and lunar phases. The Earth orbits the Sun with a period of 365 days. During this orbit, the average distance between the Earth and Sun is 93 million miles. The shape of the Earth's orbit around the Sun deviates from the shape of a circle only slightly. This deviation, known as the Earth's eccentricity, has a very small affect on the Earth's climate. The Earth is closest to the Sun at perihelion, occurring around January 2nd of each year, and farthest from the Sun at aphelion, occurring around July 2nd. Because the Earth is closest to the sun in January, the northern winter is slightly warmer than the southern winter.

Seasons
The rotation axis of the Earth is not perpendicular to the orbital (ecliptic) plane. The axis of the Earth is tilted 23.45° from the perpendicular. The tilt of the Earth's axis is known as the obliquity of the ecliptic, and is mainly responsible for the four seasons of the year by influencing the intensity of solar rays received by the Northern and Southern Hemispheres. The four seasons, spring, summer, fall and winter, are extended periods of characteristic average temperature, rainfall, storm frequency and vegetation growth or dormancy. The effect of the Earth's tilt on climate is best demonstrated at the solstices, the two days of the year when the Sun is farthest from the Earth's equatorial plane. At the Summer Solstice (June Solstice), the Earth's tilt on its axis causes the Northern Hemisphere to lean toward the Sun, while the southern hemisphere leans away. Consequently, the Northern Hemisphere receives more intense rays from the Sun and experiences summer during this time, while the Southern Hemisphere experiences winter. At the Winter Solstice (December Solstice), it is the Southern Hemisphere that leans toward the sun and thus experiences summer. Spring and fall are produced by varying degrees of the same leaning toward or away from the Sun.

Tides

The orientation of and gravitational interaction between the Earth and the Moon are responsible for the ocean tides that occur on Earth. The term "tide" refers to the cyclic rise and fall of large bodies of water. Gravitational attraction is defined as the force of attraction between all bodies in the universe. At the location on Earth closest to the Moon, the gravitational attraction of the Moon draws seawater toward the Moon in the form of a tidal bulge. On the opposite side of the Earth, another tidal bulge forms in the direction away from the Moon because at this point, the Moon's gravitational pull is the weakest. "Spring tides" are especially strong tides that occur when the Earth, Sun and Moon are in line, allowing both the Sun and the Moon to exert gravitational force on the Earth and increase tidal bulge height. These tides occur during the full moon and the new moon. "Neap tides" are especially weak tides occurring when the gravitational forces of the Moon and the Sun are perpendicular to one another. These tides occur during quarter moons.

Lunar Phases

The Earth's orientation in respect to the solar system is also responsible for our perception of the phases of the moon. As the Earth orbits the Sun with a period of 365 days, the Moon orbits the Earth every 27 days. As the moon circles the Earth, its shape in the night sky appears to change. The changes in the appearance of the moon from Earth are known as "lunar phases." These phases vary cyclically according to the relative positions of the Moon, the Earth and the Sun. At all times, half of the Moon is facing the Sun and is thus illuminated by reflecting the Sun's light. As the Moon orbits the Earth and the Earth orbits the Sun, the half of the moon that faces the Sun changes. However, the Moon is in synchronous rotation around the Earth, meaning that nearly the same side of the moon faces the Earth at all times. This side is referred to as the near side of the moon. Lunar phases occur as the Earth and Moon orbit the Sun and the fractional illumination of the Moon's near side changes.

When the Sun and Moon are on opposite sides of the Earth, observers on Earth perceive a "full moon," meaning the moon appears circular because the entire illuminated half of the moon is visible. As the Moon orbits the Earth, the Moon "wanes" as the amount of the illuminated half of the Moon that is visible from Earth decreases. A gibbous moon is between a full moon and a half moon, or between a half moon and a full moon. When the Sun and the Moon are on the same side of Earth, the illuminated half of the moon is facing away from Earth, and the moon appears invisible. This lunar phase is known as the "new moon." The time between each full moon is approximately 29.53 days.

A list of all lunar phases includes:

- New Moon: the moon is invisible or the first signs of a crescent appear
- Waxing Crescent: the right crescent of the moon is visible
- First Quarter: the right quarter of the moon is visible Waxing Gibbous: only the left crescent is not illuminated
- Full Moon: the entire illuminated half of the moon is visible
- Waning Gibbous: only the right crescent of the moon is not illuminated
- Last Quarter: the left quarter of the moon is illuminated
- Waning Crescent: only the left crescent of the moon is illuminated

Viewing the moon from the Southern Hemisphere would cause these phases to occur in the opposite order.

Dry air is composed of three basic components; dry gas, water vapor, and solid particles (dust from soil, etc.).

The most abundant dry gases in the atmosphere are:

(N_2)	Nitrogen	78.09 %
(O_2)	Oxygen	20.95 %
(AR)	Argon	0.93 %
(CO_2)	Carbon Dioxide	0.03 %

The atmosphere is divided into four main layers based on temperature. These layers are labeled Troposphere, Stratosphere, Mesosphere, Thermosphere.

Troposphere - this layer is the closest to the earth's surface and all weather phenomena occurs here as it is the layer with the most water vapor and dust. Air temperature decreases with increasing altitude. The average thickness of the Troposphere is 7 miles (11 km).

Stratosphere - this layer contains very little water, clouds within this layer are extremely rare. The Ozone layer is located in the upper portions of the stratosphere. Air temperature is fairly constant but does increase somewhat with height due to the absorption of solar energy and ultra violet rays from the ozone layer.

Mesosphere - air temperature again decreases with height in this layer. It is the coldest layer with temperatures in the range of -100^0 C at the top..

Thermosphere - extends upward into space. Oxygen molecules in this layer absorb energy from the sun, causing temperatures to increase with height. The lower part of the thermosphere is called the Ionosphere. Here charged particles or ions and free electrons can be found. When gases in the Ionosphere are excited by solar radiation, the gases give off light and glow in the sky. These glowing lights are called the Aurora Borealis in the Northern Hemisphere and Aurora Australis in Southern Hemisphere. The upper portion of the Thermosphere is called the Exosphere. Gas molecules are very far apart in this layer. Layers of Exosphere are also known as the Van Allen Belts and are held together by earth's magnetic field.

Cloud types
- **Cirrus clouds** - White and feathery; high in the sky
- **Cumulus** – thick, white, fluffy
- **Stratus** – layers of clouds cover most of the sky
- **Nimbus** – heavy, dark clouds that represent thunderstorm clouds

Variations on the clouds mentioned above include Cumulo-nimbus and Strato-nimbus.

El Niño refers to a sequence of changes in the ocean and atmospheric circulation across the Pacific Ocean. The water around the equator is unusually hot every two to seven years. Trade winds normally blow east to west across the equatorial latitudes, piling warm water into the western Pacific. A huge mass of heavy thunderstorms usually forms in the area and produces vast currents of rising air that displace heat poleward. This helps create the strong mid-latitude jet streams. The world's climate patterns are disrupted by this change in location of thunderstorm activity.

Air masses moving toward or away from the Earth's surface are called air currents. Air moving parallel to Earth's surface is called **wind**. Weather conditions are generated by winds and air currents carrying large amounts of heat and moisture from one part of the atmosphere to another. Wind speeds are measured by instruments called anemometers.

The wind belts in each hemisphere consist of convection cells that encircle Earth like belts. There are three major wind belts on Earth: (1) trade winds (2) prevailing westerlies, and (3) polar easterlies. Wind belt formation depends on the differences in air pressures that develop in the doldrums, the horse latitudes, and the Polar Regions. The Doldrums surround the equator. Within this belt heated air usually rises straight up into Earth's atmosphere. The Horse latitudes are regions of high barometric pressure with calm and light winds and the Polar Regions contain cold dense air that sinks to the Earth's surface.

Winds caused by local temperature changes include sea breezes, and land breezes.

Sea breezes are caused by the unequal heating of the land and an adjacent, large body of water. Land heats up faster than water. The movement of cool ocean air toward the land is called a sea breeze. Sea breezes usually begin blowing about mid-morning; ending about sunset.

A breeze that blows from the land to the ocean or a large lake is called a **land breeze.**

Monsoons are huge wind systems that cover large geographic areas and that reverse direction seasonally. The monsoons of India and Asia are examples of these seasonal winds. They alternate wet and dry seasons. As denser cooler air over the ocean moves inland, a steady seasonal wind called a summer or wet monsoon is produced.

The air temperature at which water vapor begins to condense is called the **dew point.**

Relative humidity is the actual amount of water vapor in a certain volume of air compared to the maximum amount of water vapor this air could hold at a given temperature.

Knowledge of types of storms

A **thunderstorm** is a brief, local storm produced by the rapid upward movement of warm, moist air within a cumulo-nimbus cloud. Thunderstorms always produce lightning and thunder, and are accompanied by strong wind gusts and heavy rain or hail.

A severe storm with swirling winds that may reach speeds of hundreds of km per hour is called a **tornado**. Such a storm is also referred to as a "twister". The sky is covered by large cumulo-nimbus clouds and violent thunderstorms; a funnel-shaped swirling cloud may extend downward from a cumulo-nimbus cloud and reach the ground. Tornadoes are storms that leave a narrow path of destruction on the ground.

A swirling, funnel-shaped cloud that **extends** downward and touches a body of water is called a **waterspout.**

Hurricanes are storms that develop when warm, moist air, carried by trade winds, rotates around a low-pressure "eye". A large, rotating, low-pressure system accompanied by heavy precipitation and strong winds is called a tropical cyclone (better known as a hurricane). In the Pacific region, a hurricane is called a typhoon.

Storms that occur only in the winter are known as blizzards or ice storms. A **blizzard** is a storm with strong winds, blowing snow and frigid temperatures. An **ice storm** consists of falling rain that freezes when it strikes the ground, covering everything with a layer of ice.

Skill 27.2   Analyze the forces that shape the earth's surface (e.g., volcanism, erosion)

Movement of tectonic plates.

Data obtained from many sources led scientists to develop the theory of plate tectonics. This theory is the most current model that explains not only the movement of the continents, but also the changes in the earth's crust caused by internal forces.

Plates are rigid blocks of earth's crust and upper mantle. These rigid solid blocks make up the lithosphere. The earth's lithosphere is broken into nine large sections and several small ones. These moving slabs are called plates. The major plates are named after the continents they are "transporting."

The plates float on and move with a layer of hot, plastic-like rock in the upper mantle. Geologists believe that the heat currents circulating within the mantle cause this plastic zone of rock to slowly flow, carrying along the overlying crustal plates.

Movement of these crustal plates creates areas where the plates diverge as well as areas where the plates converge. A major area of divergence is located in the Mid-Atlantic. Currents of hot mantle rock rise and separate at this point of divergence creating new oceanic crust at the rate of 2 to 10 centimeters per year. Convergence is when the oceanic crust collides with either another oceanic plate or a continental plate. The oceanic crust sinks forming an enormous trench and generating volcanic activity. Convergence also includes continent to continent plate collisions. When two plates slide past one another a transform fault is created.

These movements produce many major features of the earth's surface, such as mountain ranges, volcanoes, and earthquake zones. Most of these features are located at plate boundaries, where the plates interact by spreading apart, pressing together, or sliding past each other. These movements are very slow, averaging only a few centimeters a year.

Boundaries form between spreading plates where the crust is forced apart in a process called rifting. Rifting generally occurs at mid-ocean ridges. Rifting can also take place within a continent, splitting the continent into smaller landmasses that drift away from each other, thereby forming an ocean basin between them. The Red Sea is a product of rifting. As the seafloor spreading takes place, new material is added to the inner edges of the separating plates. In this way the plates grow larger, and the ocean basin widens. This is the process that broke up the super continent Pangaea and created the Atlantic Ocean.

Boundaries between plates that are colliding are zones of intense crustal activity. When a plate of ocean crust collides with a plate of continental crust, the more dense oceanic plate slides under the lighter continental plate and plunges into the mantle. This process is called **subduction**, and the site where it takes place is called a subduction zone. A subduction zone is usually seen on the sea-floor as a deep depression called a trench.

The crustal movement which is identified by plates sliding sideways past each other produces a plate boundary characterized by major faults that are capable of unleashing powerful earth-quakes. The San Andreas Fault forms such a boundary between the Pacific Plate and the North American Plate.

Orogeny is the term given to natural mountain building.

A mountain is terrain that has been raised high above the surrounding landscape by volcanic action, or some form of tectonic plate collisions. The plate collisions could be intercontinental or ocean floor collisions with a continental crust (subduction). The physical composition of mountains would include igneous, metamorphic, or sedimentary rocks; some may have rock layers that are tilted or distorted by plate collision forces.

There are many different types of mountains. The physical attributes of a mountain range depends upon the angle at which plate movement thrust layers of rock to the surface. Many mountains (Adirondacks, Southern Rockies) were formed along high angle faults.

Folded mountains (Alps, Himalayas) are produced by the folding of rock layers during their formation. The Himalayas are the highest mountains in the world and contain Mount Everest which rises almost 9 km above sea level. The Himalayas were formed when India collided with Asia. The movement which created this collision is still in process at the rate of a few centimeters per year.

Fault-block mountains (Utah, Arizona, and New Mexico) are created when plate movement produces tension forces instead of compression forces. The area under tension produces normal faults and rock along these faults is displaced upward.

Dome mountains are formed as magma tries to push up through the crust but fails to break the surface. Dome mountains resemble a huge blister on the earth's surface.

Upwarped mountains (Black Hills of S.D.) are created in association with a broad arching of the crust. They can also be formed by rock thrust upward along high angle faults.

Volcanism is the term given to the movement of magma through the crust and its emergence as lava onto the earth's surface. Volcanic mountains are built up by successive deposits of volcanic materials.

An active volcano is one that is presently erupting or building to an eruption. A dormant volcano is one that is between eruptions but still shows signs of internal activity that might lead to an eruption in the future. An extinct volcano is said to be no longer capable of erupting. Most of the world's active volcanoes are found along the rim of the Pacific Ocean, which is also a major earthquake zone. This curving belt of active faults and volcanoes is often called the Ring of Fire. The world's best known volcanic mountains include: Mount Etna in Italy and Mount Kilimanjaro in Africa. The Hawaiian Islands are actually the tops of a chain of volcanic mountains that rise from the ocean floor.

There are three types of volcanic mountains: shield volcanoes, cinder cones and composite volcanoes.

Shield Volcanoes are associated with quiet eruptions. Lava emerges from the vent or opening in the crater and flows freely out over the earth's surface until it cools and hardens into a layer of igneous rock. A repeated lava flow builds this type of volcano into the largest volcanic mountain. Mauna Loa found in Hawaii, is the largest volcano on earth.

Cinder Cone Volcanoes are associated with explosive eruptions as lava is hurled high into the air in a spray of droplets of various sizes. These droplets cool and harden into cinders and particles of ash before falling to the ground. The ash and cinder pile up around the vent to form a steep, cone-shaped hill called the cinder cone. Cinder cone volcanoes are relatively small but may form quite rapidly.

Composite Volcanoes are described as being built by both lava flows and layers of ash and cinders. Mount Fuji in Japan, Mount St. Helens in Washington, USA and Mount Vesuvius in Italy are all famous composite volcanoes.

Mechanisms of producing mountains

Mountains are produced by different types of mountain-building processes. Most major mountain ranges are formed by the processes of folding and faulting.

Folded Mountains are produced by the folding of rock layers. Crustal movements may press horizontal layers of sedimentary rock together from the sides, squeezing them into wavelike folds. Up-folded sections of rock are called anticlines; down-folded sections of rock are called synclines. The Appalachian Mountains are an example of folded mountains with long ridges and valleys in a series of anticlines and synclines formed by folded rock layers.

Faults are fractures in the earth's crust which have been created by either tension or compression forces transmitted through the crust. These forces are produced by the movement of separate blocks of crust.

Faultings are categorized on the basis of the relative movement between the blocks on both sides of the fault plane. The movement can be horizontal, vertical or oblique.

A dip-slip fault occurs when the movement of the plates is vertical and opposite. The displacement is in the direction of the inclination, or dip, of the fault. Dip-slip faults are classified as normal faults when the rock above the fault plane moves down relative to the rock below.

Reverse faults are created when the rock above the fault plane moves up relative to the rock below. Reverse faults having a very low angle to the horizontal are also referred to as thrust faults.

Faults in which the dominant displacement is horizontal movement along the trend or strike (length) of the fault are called **strike-slip faults**. When a large strike-slip fault is associated with plate boundaries it is called a **transform fault**. The San Andreas Fault in California is a well-known transform fault.

Faults that have both vertical and horizontal movement are called **oblique-slip faults**.

When lava cools, igneous rock is formed. This formation can occur either above ground or below ground.

Intrusive rock includes any igneous rock that was formed below the earth's surface. Batholiths are the largest structures of intrusive type rock and are composed of near granite materials; they are the core of the Sierra Nevada Mountains.

Extrusive rock includes any igneous rock that was formed at the earth's surface.

Dikes are old lava tubes formed when magma entered a vertical fracture and hardened. Sometimes magma squeezes between two rock layers and hardens into a thin horizontal sheet called a **sill**. A **laccolith** is formed in much the same way as a sill, but the magma that creates a laccolith is very thick and does not flow easily. It pools and forces the overlying strata creating an obvious surface dome.

A **caldera** is normally formed by the collapse of the top of a volcano. This collapse can be caused by a massive explosion that destroys the cone and empties most if not all of the magma chamber below the volcano. The cone collapses into the empty magma chamber forming a caldera.

An inactive volcano may have magma solidified in its pipe. This structure, called a volcanic neck, is resistant to erosion and today may be the only visible evidence of the past presence of an active volcano.

Glaciation

A continental glacier covered a large part of North America during the most recent ice age. Evidence of this glacial coverage remains as abrasive grooves, large boulders from northern environments dropped in southerly locations, glacial troughs created by the rounding out of steep valleys by glacial scouring, and the remains of glacial sources called cirques that were created by frost wedging the rock at the bottom of the glacier. Remains of plants and animals found in warm climate have been discovered in the moraines and out wash plains help to support the theory of periods of warmth during the past ice ages.

The Ice Age began about 2 -3 million years ago. This age saw the advance and retreat of glacial ice over millions of years. Theories relating to the origin of glacial activity include Plate Tectonics, where it can be demonstrated that some continental masses, now in temperate climates, were at one time blanketed by ice and snow. Another theory involves changes in the earth's orbit around the sun, changes in the angle of the earth's axis, and the wobbling of the earth's axis. Support for the validity of this theory has come from deep ocean research that indicates a correlation between climatic sensitive micro-organisms and the changes in the earth's orbital status.

About 12,000 years ago, a vast sheet of ice covered a large part of the northern United States. This huge, frozen mass had moved southward from the northern regions of Canada as several large bodies of slow-moving ice, or glaciers. A time period in which glaciers advance over a large portion of a continent is called an ice age. A glacier is a large mass of ice that moves or flows over the land in response to gravity. Glaciers form among high mountains and in other cold regions.

There are two main types of glaciers: valley glaciers and continental glaciers. Erosion by valley glaciers is characteristic of U-shaped erosion. They produce sharp peaked mountains such as the Matterhorn in Switzerland. Erosion by continental glaciers often rides over mountains in their paths leaving smoothed, rounded mountains and ridges.

Erosion is the inclusion and transportation of surface materials by another moveable material, usually water, wind, or ice. The most important cause of erosion is running water. Streams, rivers, and tides are constantly at work removing weathered fragments of bedrock and carrying them away from their original location.

A stream erodes bedrock by the grinding action of the sand, pebbles and other rock fragments. This grinding against each other is called abrasion. Streams also erode rocks by dissolving or absorbing their minerals. Limestone and marble are readily dissolved by streams.

The breaking down of rocks at or near to the earth's surface is known as **weathering**. Weathering breaks down these rocks into smaller and smaller pieces. There are two types of weathering: physical weathering and chemical weathering.

Physical weathering is the process by which rocks are broken down into smaller fragments without undergoing any change in chemical composition. Physical weathering is mainly caused by the freezing of water, the expansion of rock, and the activities of plants and animals.

Frost wedging is the cycle of daytime thawing and refreezing at night. This cycle causes large rock masses, especially the rocks exposed on mountain tops, to be broken into smaller pieces.

The peeling away of the outer layers from a rock is called exfoliation. Rounded mountain tops are called exfoliation domes and have been formed in this way. Chemical weathering is the breaking down of rocks through changes in their chemical composition. An example would be the change of feldspar in granite to clay. Water, oxygen, and carbon dioxide are the main agents of chemical weathering. When water and carbon dioxide combine chemically, they produce a weak acid that breaks down rocks.

Deposition, also known as sedimentation, is the term for the process by which material from one area is slowly deposited into another area. This is usually due to the movement of wind, water, or ice containing particles of matter. When the rate of movement slows down, particles filter out and remain behind, causing a build up of matter. Note that this is a result of matter being eroded and removed from another site.

Skill 27.3   Distinguish between physical and chemical properties of matter and between physical and chemical changes in matter

Physical and chemical properties of matter (e.g., mass, volume, density, chemical reactivity).

Everything in our world is made up of **matter**, whether it is a rock, a building, an animal, or a person. Matter is defined by its characteristics: It takes up space and it has mass.

Mass is a measure of the amount of matter in an object. Two objects of equal mass will balance each other on a simple balance scale no matter where the scale is located. For instance, two rocks with the same amount of mass that are in balance on earth will also be in balance on the moon. They will feel heavier on earth than on the moon because of the gravitational pull of the earth. So, although the two rocks have the same mass, they will have different **weight.**

Weight is the measure of the earth's pull of gravity on an object. It can also be defined as the pull of gravity between other bodies. The units of weight measurement commonly used are the pound (English measure) and the kilogram (metric measure).

In addition to mass, matter also has the property of volume. **Volume** is the amount of cubic space that an object occupies. Volume and mass together give a more exact description of the object. Two objects may have the same volume, but different mass, or the same mass but different volumes, etc. For instance, consider two cubes that are each one cubic centimeter, one made from plastic, one from lead. They have the same volume, but the lead cube has more mass. The measure that we use to describe the cubes takes into consideration both the mass and the volume.

Density is the mass of a substance contained per unit of volume. If the density of an object is less than the density of a liquid, the object will float in the liquid. If the object is denser than the liquid, then the object will sink.

Density is stated in grams per cubic centimeter (g/cm^3) where the gram is the standard unit of mass. To find an object's density, you must measure its mass and its volume. Then divide the mass by the volume ($D = m/V$).
To discover an object's density, first use a balance to find its mass. Then calculate its volume. If the object is a regular shape, you can find the volume by multiplying the length, width, and height together. However, if it is an irregular shape, you can find the volume by seeing how much water it displaces. Measure the water in the container before and after the object is submerged. The difference will be the volume of the object.

Specific gravity is the ratio of the density of a substance to the density of water. For instance, the specific density of one liter of turpentine is calculated by comparing its mass (0.81 kg) to the mass of one liter of water (1 kg):

$$\frac{\text{mass of 1 L alcohol}}{\text{mass of 1 L water}} = \frac{0.81 \text{ kg}}{1.00 \text{ kg}} = 0.81$$

Physical properties and chemical properties of matter describe the appearance or behavior of a substance. A **physical property** can be observed without changing the identity of a substance. For instance, you can describe the color, mass, shape, and volume of a book. **Chemical properties** describe the ability of a substance to be changed into new substances. Baking powder goes through a chemical change as it changes into carbon dioxide gas during the baking process.

Matter constantly changes. A **physical change** is a change that does not produce a new substance. The freezing and melting of water is an example of physical change. A **chemical change** (or chemical reaction) is any change of a substance into one or more other substances. Burning materials turn into smoke; a seltzer tablet fizzes into gas bubbles.

The **phase of matter** (solid, liquid, or gas) is identified by its shape and volume.

A **solid** has a definite shape and volume. A **liquid** has a definite volume, but no shape. A **gas** has no shape or volume because it will spread out to occupy the entire space of whatever container it is in.

While plasma is really a type of gas, its properties are so unique that it is considered a unique phase of matter. **Plasma is a gas that has been ionized**, meaning that at least one electron has been removed from some of its atoms. Plasma shares some characteristics with gas, specifically, the **high kinetic energy** of its molecules. Thus, plasma exists as a diffuse "cloud," though it sometimes includes tiny grains (this is termed dusty plasma). What most distinguishes plasma from gas is that it is **electrically conductive** and exhibits a strong response to electromagnetic fields. This property is a consequence of the **charged particles that result from the removal of electrons** from the molecules in the plasma.

Energy is the ability to cause change in matter. Applying heat to a frozen liquid changes it from solid back to liquid. Continue heating it and it will boil and give off steam, a gas.

Evaporation is the change in phase from liquid to gas. **Condensation** is the change in phase from gas to liquid.

Characteristics of elements, compounds, and mixtures.

An **element** is a substance that can not be broken down into other substances. To date, scientists have identified 109 elements: 89 are found in nature and 20 are synthetic.

An **atom** is the smallest particle of the element that retains the properties of that element. All of the atoms of a particular element are the same. The atoms of each element are different from the atoms of other elements.

Elements are assigned an identifying symbol of one or two letters. The symbol for oxygen is O and stands for one atom of oxygen. However, because oxygen atoms in nature are joined together is pairs, the symbol O_2 represents oxygen. This pair of oxygen atoms is a molecule. A **molecule** is the smallest particle of substance that can exist independently and has all of the properties of that substance. A molecule of most elements is made up of one atom. However, oxygen, hydrogen, nitrogen, and chlorine molecules are made of two atoms each.

A **compound** is made of two or more elements that have been chemically combined. Atoms join together when elements are chemically combined. The result is that the elements lose their individual identities when they are joined. The compound that they become has different properties.

We use a formula to show the elements of a chemical compound. A **chemical formula** is a shorthand way of showing what is in a compound by using symbols and subscripts. The letter symbols let us know what elements are involved and the number subscript tells how many atoms of each element are involved. No subscript is used if there is only one atom involved. For example, carbon dioxide is made up of one atom of carbon (C) and two atoms of oxygen (O_2), so the formula would be represented as CO_2.

Substances can combine without a chemical change. A **mixture** is any combination of two or more substances in which the substances keep their own properties. A fruit salad is a mixture. So is an ice cream sundae, although you might not recognize each part if it is stirred together. Colognes and perfumes are the other examples. You may not readily recognize the individual elements. However, they can be separated.

Compounds and **mixtures** are similar in that they are made up of two or more substances. However, they have the following opposite characteristics:

Compounds:
- Made up of one kind of particle
- Formed during a chemical change
- Broken down only by chemical changes
- Properties are different from its parts
- Has a specific amount of each ingredient.

Mixtures:
- Made up of two or more particles
- Not formed by a chemical change
- Can be separated by physical changes
- Properties are the same as its parts.
- Does not have a definite amount of each ingredient.

Common compounds are **acids, bases, salts**, and **oxides** and are classified according to their characteristics.

An **acid** contains one element of hydrogen (H). Although it is never wise to taste a substance to identify it, acids have a sour taste. Vinegar and lemon juice are both acids, and acids occur in many foods in a weak state. Strong acids can burn skin and destroy materials. Common acids include:

Sulfuric acid (H_2SO_4)	-	Used in medicines, alcohol, dyes, and car batteries.
Nitric acid (HNO_3)	-	Used in fertilizers, explosives, cleaning materials.
Carbonic acid (H_2CO_3)	-	Used in soft drinks.
Acetic acid ($HC_2H_3O_2$)	-	Used in making plastics, rubber, photographic film, and as a solvent.

Bases have a bitter taste and the stronger ones feel slippery. Like acids, strong bases can be dangerous and should be handled carefully. All bases contain the elements oxygen and hydrogen (OH). Many household cleaning products contain bases. Common bases include:

Sodium hydroxide	NaOH	-	Used in making soap, paper, vegetable oils, and refining petroleum.
Ammonium hydroxide	NH_4OH	-	Making deodorants, bleaching compounds, cleaning compounds.
Potassium hydroxide	KOH	-	Making soaps, drugs, dyes, alkaline batteries, and purifying industrial gases.
Calcium hydroxide	$Ca(OH)_2$	-	Making cement and plaster

An **indicator** is a substance that changes color when it comes in contact with an acid or a base. Litmus paper is an indicator. Blue litmus paper turns red in an acid. Red litmus paper turns blue in a base.

A substance that is neither acid nor base is **neutral**. Neutral substances do not change the color of litmus paper.

Salt is formed when an acid and a base combine chemically. Water is also formed. The process is called **neutralization**. Table salt (NaCl) is an example of this process. Salts are also used in toothpaste, Epsom salts, and cream of tartar. Calcium chloride ($CaCl_2$) is used on frozen streets and walkways to melt the ice. **Oxides** are compounds that are formed when oxygen combines with another element. Rust is an oxide formed when oxygen combines with iron.

Symbols, formulas, and equations for common elements and compounds, and their reactions

One or more substances are formed during a **chemical reaction**. Also, energy is released during some chemical reactions. Sometimes the energy release is slow and sometimes it is rapid. In a fireworks display, energy is released very rapidly. However, the chemical reaction that produces tarnish on a silver spoon happens very slowly.

Chemical equilibrium is defined as occurring when the quantities of reactants and products are at a 'steady state' and no longer shifting, but the reaction may still proceed forward and backward. The rate of forward reaction must equal the rate of backward reaction.

In one kind of chemical reaction, two elements combine to form a new substance. We can represent the reaction and the results in a chemical equation. Carbon and oxygen form carbon dioxide. The equation can be written:

$$C \quad + \quad O_2 \quad \rightarrow \quad CO_2$$

C	+	O_2	$\rightarrow$	CO_2
1 atom of carbon	+	2 atoms of oxygen	$\rightarrow$ $\rightarrow$	1 molecule of carbon dioxide

No matter is ever gained or lost during a chemical reaction; therefore the chemical equation must be *balanced.* This means that there must be the same number of atoms on both sides of the equation. Remember that the subscript numbers indicate the number of atoms in the elements. If there is no subscript, assume there is only one atom.

In a second kind of chemical reaction, the molecules of a substance split forming two or more new substances. An electric current can split water molecules into hydrogen and oxygen gas.

$2H_2O$	$\rightarrow$	$2H_2$	+	O_2
2 molecules of water	$\rightarrow$	2 molecules of hydrogen	+	1 molecule of oxygen

The number of molecules is shown by the number in front of an element or compound. If no number appears, assume that it is 1 molecule.
A third kind of chemical reaction is when elements change places with each other. An example of one element taking the place of another is when iron changes places with copper in the compound copper sulfate:

$CuSo_4$	+	Fe	$\rightarrow$	$FeSO_4$	+	Cu
copper sulfate	+	iron (steel wool)		iron sulfate	+	copper

Sometimes two sets of elements change places. In this example, an acid and a base are combined:

HCl	+	NaOH	$\rightarrow$	NaCl	+	H_2O
hydrochloric acid		sodium hydroxide		sodium chloride (table salt)		water

Matter can change, but it cannot be created or destroyed. The sample equations show two things:

1. In a chemical reaction, matter is changed into one or more different kinds of matter.
2. The amount of matter present before and after the chemical reaction is the same.

Many chemical reactions give off energy. Like matter, energy can change form but it can be neither created nor destroyed during a chemical reaction. This is the **law of conservation of energy.**

Characteristics of types of chemical bonding (e.g., covalent, ionic, metallic, hydrogen)

The outermost electrons in the atoms are called **valence electrons.** Because they are the ones involved in the bonding process, they determine the properties of the element.

A **chemical bond** is a force of attraction that holds atoms together. When atoms are bonded chemically, they cease to have their individual properties. For instance, hydrogen and oxygen combine into water and no longer look like hydrogen and oxygen. They look like water.

A **covalent bond** is formed when two atoms share electrons. Recall that atoms whose outer shells are not filled with electrons are unstable. When they are unstable, they readily combine with other unstable atoms. By combining and sharing electrons, they act as a single unit. Covalent bonding happens among nonmetals. Covalent bonds are always polar between two non-identical atoms.

Covalent compounds are compounds whose atoms are joined by covalent bonds. Table sugar, methane, and ammonia are examples of covalent compounds.

An **ionic bond** is a bond formed by the transfer of electrons. It happens when metals and nonmetals bond. Before chlorine and sodium combine, the sodium has one valence electron and chlorine has seven. Neither valence shell is filled, but the chlorine's valence shell is almost full. During the reaction, the sodium gives one valence electron to the chlorine atom. Both atoms then have filled shells and are stable. Something else has happened during the bonding. Before the bonding, both atoms were neutral. When one electron was transferred, it upset the balance of protons and electrons in each atom. The chlorine atom took on one extra electron and the sodium atom released one atom. The atoms have now become ions. **Ions** are atoms with an unequal number of protons and electrons. To determine whether the ion is positive or negative, compare the number of protons (+charge) to the electrons (-charge). If there are more electrons the ion will be negative. If there are more protons, the ion will be positive.

Compounds that result from the transfer of metal atoms to nonmetal atoms are called **ionic compounds.** Sodium chloride (table salt), sodium hydroxide (drain cleaner), and potassium chloride (salt substitute) are examples of ionic compounds.

Spontaneous diffusion occurs when random motion leads particles to increase entropy by equalizing concentrations. Particles tend to move into places of lower concentration. For example, sodium will move into a cell if the concentration is greater outside than inside the cell. Spontaneous diffusion keeps cells balanced.

Metallic bonding exist only in metals, such as aluminum, gold, copper, and iron. In metals, each atom is bonded to several other metal atoms, and their electrons are free to move throughout the metal structure. This special situation is responsible for the unique properties of metals, such as their high conductivity. For example, a piece of copper metal has a certain arrangement of copper atoms. The valence electrons of these atoms are free to move about the piece of metal and are attracted to the positive cores of copper, thus holding the atoms together. The model that tends to be applied is Band Theory but for now we can imagine the metal ions held together by this "sea" of electrons. This allows the metal to be bent and distorted without the structure breaking.

Hydrogen bonding is an example of dipole-dipole interaction. An everyday example of this is in water. The oxygen-hydrogen bond is polar, oxygen being the more electronegative element. The molecule is therefore polar (the molecule is not linear but has a bent, V shape). This is extenuated by the two lone pairs of electrons on the oxygen atom. One end of the molecule is partially negative while the two hydrogen atoms become partially positive. The molecules of water are attracted to one another, with the slightly positive hydrogens attracted to the negative "ends" (the oxygens) of other water molecules. This intermolecular attraction is termed "hydrogen bonding", and acts almost like a glue holding the molecules of water together.

In the case of water the effect on the physical properties of water are quite astounding. The boiling point of water, for example, is much greater than would be the case if such bonding did not exist. This fact alone should make the human race (and the rest of life) grateful for hydrogen bonding since water would otherwise be a gas at room temperature. Further, hydrogen bonds can occur within and between other molecules. For instance, the two strands of a DNA molecule are held together by hydrogen bonds. Hydrogen bonding between water molecules and the amino acids of proteins are involved in maintaining the protein's proper shape.

Types of chemical reactions and their characteristics

There are four kinds of chemical reactions:
In a **composition reaction**, two or more substances combine to form a compound.

$$A + B \rightarrow AB$$
i.e. silver and sulfur yield silver dioxide

In a **decomposition reaction**, a compound breaks down into two or more simpler substances.

$$AB \rightarrow A + B$$
i.e. water breaks down into hydrogen and oxygen

In a **single replacement reaction**, a free element replaces an element that is part of a compound.

$$A + BX \rightarrow AX + B$$
i.e. iron plus copper sulfate yields iron sulfate plus copper

In a **double replacement reaction**, parts of two compounds replace each other. In this case, the compounds seem to switch partners.

$$AX + BY \rightarrow AY + BX$$
i.e. sodium chloride plus mercury nitrate yields sodium nitrate plus mercury chloride

Skill 27.4 Infer the physical science principle (e.g., effects of common forces, conservation of energy) illustrated in a given situation

Types and characteristics of forces (e.g., electrical, magnetic, nuclear, gravitational, frictional)

Dynamics is the study of the relationship between motion and the forces affecting motion. **Force** causes motion.

Mass and weight are not the same quantities. An object's **mass** gives it a reluctance to change its current state of motion. It is also the measure of an object's resistance to acceleration. The force that the earth's gravity exerts on an object with a specific mass is called the object's weight on earth. Weight is a force that is measured in Newtons. Weight (W) = mass times acceleration due to gravity (**W = mg**). To illustrate the difference between mass and weight, picture two rocks of equal mass on a balance scale. If the scale is balanced in one place, it will be balanced everywhere, regardless of the gravitational field. However, the weight of the stones would vary on a spring scale, depending upon the gravitational field. In other words, the stones would be balanced both on earth and on the moon. However, the weight of the stones would be greater on earth than on the moon.

Surfaces that touch each other have a certain resistance to motion. This resistance is **friction.**

1. The materials that make up the surfaces will determine the magnitude of the frictional force.
2. The frictional force is independent of the area of contact between the two surfaces.
3. The direction of the frictional force is opposite to the direction of motion.
4. The frictional force is proportional to the normal force between the two surfaces in contact.

Static friction describes the force of friction of two surfaces that are in contact but do not have any motion relative to each other, such as a block sitting on an inclined plane. **Kinetic friction** describes the force of friction of two surfaces in contact with each other when there is relative motion between the surfaces. When an object moves in a circular path, a force must be directed toward the center of the circle in order to keep the motion going. This constraining force is called **centripetal force**. Gravity is the centripetal force that keeps a satellite circling the earth.

Electrical force is the influential power resulting from electricity as an attractive or repulsive interaction between two charged objects. The electric force is determined using Coulomb's law. As shown below, the appropriate unit on charge is the Coulomb (C) and the appropriate unit on distance is meters (m). Use of these units will result in a force expressed in units of Newtons. The demand for these units emerges from the units on Coulomb's constant.

$F_{elect} = k \cdot Q_1 \cdot Q_2 / d^2$

There is something of a mystery as to how objects affect each other when they are not in mechanical contact. Newton wrestled with the concept of "action-at-a-distance" (as Electrical Force is now classified) and eventually concluded that it was necessary for there to be some form of ether, or intermediate medium, which made it possible for one object to transfer force to another. We now know that no ether exists. It is possible for objects to exert forces on one another without any medium to transfer the force. From our fluid notion of electrical forces, however, we still associate forces as being due to the exchange of something between the two objects. The electrical field force acts between two charges, in the same way that the gravitational field force acts between two masses.

Magnetic Force- Magnetized items interact with other items in very specific ways. If a magnet is brought close enough to a ferromagnetic material (that is not magnetized itself) the magnet will strongly attract the ferromagnetic material regardless of orientation. Both the north and south pole of the magnet will attract the other item with equal strength. IN opposition, diamagnetic materials weakly repel a magnetic field. This occurs regardless of the north/south orientation of the field. Paramagnetic materials are weakly attracted to a magnetic field. This occurs regardless of the north/south orientation of the field. **Calculating** the attractive or repulsive magnetic force between two magnets is, in the general case, an extremely complex operation, as it depends on the shape, magnetization, orientation and separation of the magnets.

In the **Nuclear Force** the protons in the nucleus of an atom are positively charged. If protons interact, they are usually pushed apart by the electromagnetic force. However, when two or more nuclei come VERY close together, the nuclear force comes into play. The nuclear force is a hundred times stronger than the electromagnetic force so the nuclear force may be able to "glue" the nuclei together so fusion can happen. The nuclear force is also known as the strong force. The nuclear force keeps together the most basic of elementary particles, the quarks. Quarks combine together to form the protons and neutrons in the atomic nucleus.

The **force of gravity** is the force at which the earth, moon, or other massively large object attracts another object towards itself. By definition, this is the weight of the object. All objects upon earth experience a force of gravity that is directed "downward" towards the center of the earth. The force of gravity on earth is always equal to the weight of the object as found by the equation:

Fgrav = m * g
where g = 9.8 m/s^2 (on Earth)
and m = mass (in kg)

Push and pull –Pushing a volleyball or pulling a bowstring applies muscular force when the muscles expand and contract. Elastic force is when any object returns to its original shape (for example, when a bow is released).

Rubbing – Friction opposes the motion of one surface past another. Friction is common when slowing down a car or sledding down a hill.

Pull of gravity – is a force of attraction between two objects. Gravity questions can be raised not only on earth but also between planets and even black hole discussions.

Forces on objects at rest – The formula **F= m/a** is shorthand for force equals mass over acceleration. An object will not move unless the force is strong enough to move the mass. Also, there can be opposing forces holding the object in place. For instance, a boat may want to be forced by the currents to drift away but an equal and opposite force is a rope holding it to a dock.

Forces on a moving object - Overcoming inertia is the tendency of any object to oppose a change in motion. An object at rest tends to stay at rest. An object that is moving tends to keep moving.

Inertia and circular motion – The centripetal force is provided by the high banking of the curved road and by friction between the wheels and the road. This inward force that keeps an object moving in a circle is called centripetal force.

The relationship between heat, forms of energy, and work (mechanical, electrical, etc.) are the **Laws of Thermodynamics.** These laws deal strictly with systems in thermal equilibrium and not those within the process of rapid change or in a state of transition. Systems that are nearly always in a state of equilibrium are called **reversible systems.**

The first law of thermodynamics is a restatement of conservation of energy. The change in heat energy supplied to a system (Q) is equal to the sum of the change in the internal energy (U) and the change in the work done by the system against internal forces. $\Delta Q = \Delta U + \Delta W$

The second law of thermodynamics is stated in two parts:

1. No machine is 100% efficient. It is impossible to construct a machine that only absorbs heat from a heat source and performs an equal amount of work because some heat will always be lost to the environment.
2. Heat can not spontaneously pass from a colder to a hotter object. An ice cube sitting on a hot sidewalk will melt into a little puddle, but it will never spontaneously cool and form the same ice cube. Certain events have a preferred direction called the **arrow of time.**

Entropy is the measure of how much energy or heat is available for work. Work occurs only when heat is transferred from hot to cooler objects. Once this is done, no more work can be extracted. The energy is still being conserved, but is not available for work as long as the objects are the same temperature. Theory has it that, eventually, all things in the universe will reach the same temperature. If this happens, energy will no longer be usable.

COMPETENCY 28.0   APPLY INQUIRY SKILLS AND PROCESSES TO COMMUNICATE SCIENTIFIC INFORMATION AND INTERPRET NATURAL PHENOMENA

Skill 28.1   Draw conclusions and make generalizations based on examination of given experimental results

Science may be defined as a body of knowledge that is systematically derived from study, observations and experimentation. Its goal is to identify and establish principles and theories that may be applied to solve problems. Pseudoscience, on the other hand, is a belief that is not warranted. There is no scientific methodology or application. Some of the more classic examples of pseudoscience include witchcraft, alien encounters, or any topics that are explained by hearsay.

Scientific inquiry starts with observation. Observation is a very important skill by itself, since it leads to experimentation and finally communicating the experimental findings to the society / public. After observing, a question is formed, which starts with "why" or "how." To answer these questions, experimentation is necessary. Between observation and experimentation, there are three more important steps. These are: gathering information (or researching about the problem), hypothesis, and designing the experiment.

Designing an experiment is very important since it involves identifying control, constants, independent variables and dependent variables. A control / standard is something we compare our results with at the end of the experiment. It is like a reference. Constants are the factors we have to keep constant in an experiment to get reliable results. Independent variables are factors we change in an experiment. It is very important to bear in mind that there should be more constants than variables to obtain reproducible results in an experiment.

Classifying is grouping items according to their similarities. It is important for students to realize relationships and similarity as well as differences to reach a reasonable conclusion in a lab experience.

After the experiment is done, it is repeated and results are graphically presented. The results are then analyzed and conclusions drawn.

It is the responsibility of the scientists to share the knowledge they obtain through their research.

After the conclusion is drawn, the final step is communication. In this age, lot of emphasis is put on the way and the method of communication. The conclusions must be communicated by clearly describing the information using accurate data, visual presentation like graphs (bar/line/pie), tables/charts, diagrams, artwork, and other appropriate media like power point presentation. Modern technology must be used whenever it is necessary. The method of communication must be suitable to the audience.

Written communication is as important as oral communication. This is essential for submitting research papers to scientific journals, newspapers, other magazines etc.

Skill 28.2   Interpret data presented in one or more graphs, charts, or tables to determine patterns or relationships

Graphing is an important skill to visually display collected data for analysis. The two types of graphs most commonly used are the **line graph** and the **bar graph** (histogram). Line graphs are set up to show two variables represented by one point on the graph. The X axis is the horizontal axis and represents the dependent variable. Dependent variables are those that would be present independently of the experiment. A common example of a dependent variable is time. Time proceeds regardless of anything else occurring. The Y axis is the vertical axis and represents the independent variable. Independent variables are manipulated by the experiment, such as the amount of light, or the height of a plant. Graphs should be calibrated at equal intervals. If one space represents one day, the next space may not represent ten days. A "best fit" line is drawn to join the points and may not include all the points in the data. Axes must always be labeled, for the graph to be meaningful. A good title will describe both the dependent and the independent variable. Bar graphs are set up similarly in regards to axes, but points are not plotted. Instead, the dependent variable is set up as a bar where the X axis intersects with the Y axis. Each bar is a separate item of data and is not joined by a continuous line.

Whenever scientists begin an experiment or project they must decide what pieces of data they are going to collect. This data could be qualitative or quantitative. Scientists use a variety of methods to gather and analyze this data. Some possibilities including storing the data in a table and analyzing the data using a graph. Scientists will also make notes of their observations, what they see, hear, smell, etc., throughout the experiment. Scientists are then able to use the data and observations to make inferences and draw conclusions about a question or problem.

Several steps should be followed in the interpretation and evaluation of data.

First the scientist should **apply critical analysis and thinking strategies** asking questions about the accuracy of the data and the procedures of the experiment and procurement of the data.

Second is to **determine the important of information and its relevance to the essential question**. Any experiment may produce a plethora of data, not all of which is necessary to consider when analyzing the hypothesis. The useful information must them be **separated into component parts**.

At this point the scientist may then **make inferences, identify trends, and interpret data**. The final step is to determine the most appropriate method of communicating this these inferences and conclusions to the intended audience.

Skill 28.3   Apply mathematical rules or formulas (including basic statistics) to analyze given experimental or observational data

Science uses the metric system as it is accepted worldwide and allows easier comparison among experiments done by scientists around the world. Learn the following basic units and prefixes:

> **meter** - measure of length
> **liter** - measure of volume
> **gram** - measure of mass

deca-(meter, liter, gram)= 10X the base unit   **deci** = 1/10 the base unit
hecto-(meter, liter, gram)= 100X the base unit   **centi** = 1/100 the base unit
kilo-(meter, liter, gram) = 1000X the base unit   **milli** = 1/1000 the base unit

Moles = mass X 1 mole/molecular weight
For example, to determine the moles of 20 grams of water, you would take the mass of the water (20 g) and multiply it by 1 mole of water divided by the molecular weight of a molecule of water (18 g).

Percent solution and **proportions** are basically the same thing. To find percent volume, divide the grams of the substance by the amount of the solvent. For example, 20 grams of salt divided by 100 ml of water would result in a 20% solution of saltwater. To determine percent mass, divide the ml of substance being mixed by the amount of solvent. Percent mass is not used as often as percent volume.

Rate is determined by dividing the change in distance (or the independent variable) by the change in time. If a plant grew four inches in two days, the rate of growth would be two inches per day.

Skill 28.4   Evaluate the appropriateness of different types of graphic representations to communicate given scientific data

There are a multitude of graphs available to communicate scientific data. The choice of which graph to use is based on the available data, the conclusion to be drawn, and the audience for which the data is meant. At the early elementary level students should be able to organize and display data using pictures, tallies, tables, charts or bar graphs. Late elementary students should be able to use line graphs, line plots and stem-and-leaf graphs as well.

Some common types of graphs and charts include:

Pie Charts emphasize the relationship between the whole and each part of that whole. Pie charts should only be used if you want to show proportions. An example of this would be to show what proportion of a population is affected by a certain type of pollution.

Column/Bar Charts are the most common types of all charts. It is a simple chart that allows the user to compare values. Bar charts are often used to analyze longitudinal data over a period of time.

Scatter Charts are used when you need to display two related sets of data on one chart, often when you need to make predictions based on the data. Such a chart may be used when you are trying to graph the height and weight of the average Blue Back Whale, of the number of animal attacks in an area versus the reduction in forest acreage.

Line Charts should only be used when there is a period of time in the data. These charts are ideal for representing trends. For example, if you wanted to chart the increase in the world population over a 10 year period, the line chart would be an excellent choice.

Area Charts emphasize the differences between two or more sets of data. When using this chart it is important to get the layering correct. Failure to do so results in smaller sets of data being completely obscured by larger ones.

These are very general types of graphs. Once these basic graphs are mastered, they may be manipulated to create a graph for the specific data you wish to communicate. It is important to remember that graphs can send a very powerful message to people and that the use of images makes a much more vivid impact than only numbers. Graphs also have the capability to strengthen implications about data based on the type of graph, colors used, and other tools. Examine carefully where your data came from, what it is telling you, and what you want it to say to others. It is possible to make exactly the same data appear to have completely different meanings.

COMPETENCY 29.0   UNDERSTAND PRINCIPLES AND PROCEDURES RELATED TO THE DESIGN AND IMPLEMENTATION OF OBSERVATIONAL AND EXPERIMENTAL SCIENTIFIC INVESTIGATIONS

Skill 29.1   Distinguish among the features of a given experimental design (e.g., dependent and independent variables, control and experimental groups)

The scientific method is the basic process behind science. It involves several steps beginning with hypothesis formulation and working through to the conclusion.

Posing a question

Although many discoveries happen by chance, the standard thought process of a scientist begins with forming a question to research. The more limited the question, the easier it is to set up an experiment to answer it.

Form a hypothesis

Once the question is formulated take an educated guess about the answer to the problem or question. This 'best guess' is your hypothesis.

Doing the test

To make a test fair, data from an experiment must have a **variable** or any condition that can be changed such as temperature or mass. A good test will try to manipulate as few variables as possible so as to see which variable is responsible for the result. This requires a second example of a **control**. A control is an extra setup in which all the conditions are the same except for the variable being tested.

Observe and record the data

Reporting of the data should state specifics of how the measurements were calculated. A graduated cylinder needs to be read with proper procedures. As beginning students, technique must be part of the instructional process so as to give validity to the data.

Drawing a conclusion

After recording data, you compare your data with that of other groups. A conclusion is the judgment derived from the data results.

Graphing data

Graphing utilizes numbers to demonstrate patterns. The patterns offer a visual representation, making it easier to draw conclusions.

Apply knowledge of designing and performing investigations.

Normally, knowledge is integrated in the form of a lab report. A report has many sections. It should include a specific **title** and tell exactly what is being studied.

The **abstract** is a summary of the report written at the beginning of the paper. The **purpose** should always be defined and will state the problem. The purpose should include the **hypothesis** (educated guess) of what is expected from the outcome of the experiment. The entire experiment should relate to this problem.

It is important to describe exactly what was done to prove or disprove a hypothesis. A **control** is necessary to prove that the results occurred from the changed conditions and would not have happened normally. Only one variable should be manipulated at a time. **Observations** and **results** of the experiment should be recorded including all results from data. Drawings, graphs and illustrations should be included to support information. Observations are objective, whereas analysis and interpretation is subjective. A **conclusion** should explain why the results of the experiment either proved or disproved the hypothesis.

A scientific theory is an explanation of a set of related observations based on a proven hypothesis. A scientific law usually lasts longer than a scientific theory and has more experimental data to support it.

Variables

The procedure used to obtain data is important to the outcome. Experiments consist of **controls** and **variables**. A control is the experiment run under normal conditions. The variable includes a factor that is changed. In biology, the variable may be light, temperature, pH, time, etc. The differences in tested variables may be used to make a prediction or form a hypothesis. Only one variable should be tested at a time. One would not alter both the temperature and pH of the experimental subject.

An **independent variable** is one that is changed or manipulated by the researcher. This could be the amount of light given to a plant or the temperature at which bacteria is grown. The **dependent variable** is that which is influenced by the independent variable.

Skill 29.2 Formulate hypotheses based on reasoning and preliminary results or information

In any scientific investigation / experimentation, hypothesis is an important component.

Hypothesis is otherwise called an educated guess, which means that a guess is made on the basis of information that is obtained through various resources and also at times after a set of initial experimentation.

Keeping these two points in mind, let us look at hypothesis from different angles. To discuss this meaningfully, we need to look at the process of scientific investigation. As we are aware of, scientific investigation uses scientific method because it is objective and is made up of a series of steps. When these steps are followed truthfully, in the order they are presented, we get reliable results. The first step of any investigation is the identification of a problem. The next step is the research or gathering information. Internet is a great source of information / knowledge. The fact is that nothing can replace a person's experience and practical knowledge. The information that can be obtained from internet on any given topic is vast and extensive. It is a great advantage to have that much information, which gives more options, ideas etc. Some times it is not humanly possible to sift through all the information obtained, but the important thing is to be precise, specific and narrowing it down to our problem. After going through the relevant information, some ideas are crystallized. These are the potential hypotheses. After careful examination and elimination, a hypothesis is selected.

This *hypothesis is strictly based on information* which is backed by others' experimental results.

There are more ways than one to formulate a hypothesis. There are no rules governing this process.

Another way of formulating a hypothesis is by *reasoning.* Reasoning is a very important skill that needs to be incorporated in our regular teaching. This is something that has to be taught to our students to reason in Math, to reason in Science and also in other areas of learning. Reasoning involves observing, identifying processes and arriving at conclusions.

For example, when we use a fertilizer for the purpose of increasing the growth of our plants, we need to reason that the nutrients that are provided in the fertilizers are essential for plant growth. Also we need to reason that not all soils are rich in nitrogen and not all plants have nitrogen fixing bacteria on their roots. It also involves connecting ideas. The ideas here are - plants need nitrogen, all plants do not have nitrogen fixers on their roots, all soils are not rich in nitrogen, continuously using soils for crops depletes natural nutrients from soils. When related thoughts like these are connected, the result is the formulation of some hypotheses like plants need external sources of nutrition.

The third method of formulating hypothesis is based on results obtained from *preliminary experiments.* These simple, not well organized experiments could be referred to as activities that are used in the Elementary grades. These are simple because the problem is not identified, not much information is gathered, and variables are not specified. These activities sometimes yield good results. An example for this is - an activity for volcanic eruption. In this activity, we use sodium bicarbonate, vinegar and red food color to make it a spectacular eruption. Suppose it didn't erupt like Mt. Edna, what are the reasons for the failure of volcanic eruption? The reason is distilled vinegar, which has almost lost its strength. This could be developed into hypothesis itself - the strength of vinegar. In this way, we will be able to formulate sound hypotheses, even from failed activities.

Skill 29.3   Evaluate the validity of a scientific conclusion in a given situation

Scientific conclusion is an important step and also the last in the scientific method. A conclusion is a summary, summing up at the end of an investigation. Validity of a conclusion is a very important component in experimentation. The validity of conclusions is the degree to which conclusions we make about our data are reasonable, whether the investigation is qualitative or quantitative. Conclusions are very important because these are the end products of investigation. The general public is mainly concerned about the outcome of the investigation rather than the details or the methodology of the investigation. The society is interested in the usefulness of the investigation rather than the correctness of it.

Let us take an example and further discuss the issue of the validity of conclusions.

A problem is identified for a research investigation. It is "the effect of different fertilizers on the growth of black bean plant, which grows very fast. Black bean is a very common plant.

The control is black bean given only water. The constants are - pot size, plant size, age of plant, quantity of soil, soil brand, frequency of watering, volume of water given, time of watering (AM / PM), location of pots, frequency of measuring plant height, quantity of fertilizer given. The independent variables are the three types of fertilizers - A,B, and C. The dependent variable is the height of the plant measured once in 48 hours in the PM around 8.

Ideally, any experiment for Elementary students should last for no more than a week, otherwise they get tired and lose motivation to carry on. The experiment is all set to go. After a week, the experiment has ended. The students got data, the growth of black bean plants in different fertilizers. They found that (to illustrate the point), fertilizer B is the best followed by A and C. We need to keep in mind that the students got only one set of results. The first step they have to do to validate their conclusion is to repeat the same experiment at least twice. After repeating the experiment twice, the students have three sets of data on hand. The next step in this process is to study their data and trying to find trends / patterns. After that they can conclude confidently that fertilizer B is the best followed by A and C. Sometimes it may not happen like that fertilizer C may be the best followed by B and A. This change in the observations could happen only because the experiment was repeated twice. The pattern here changed and a new pattern emerged. When the students conclude that fertilizer C is best, their conclusions are valid because they are backed by data since the experiment was repeated twice.

Validity of conclusions is dependent on reliability of data. The data are reliable only when the experiment is repeated and the results are reproducible.

Data have to be repeatable, even when done in any part of the world under the same set of conditions and then only the data are called reliable and the experiment will have credibility and the conclusions that are made are valid.

Skill 29.4 Apply procedures for the care and humane treatment of animals and the safe and appropriate use of equipment in the laboratory

Dissections - Animals which are not obtained from recognized sources should not be used. Decaying animals or those of unknown origin may harbor pathogens and/or parasites. Specimens should be rinsed before handling. Latex gloves are desirable. If gloves are not available, students with sores or scratches should be excused from the activity. Formaldehyde is a carcinogen and should be avoided or disposed of according to district regulations. Students objecting to dissections for moral reasons should be given an alternative assignment.

Live specimens - No dissections may be performed on living mammalian vertebrates or birds. Lower order life and invertebrates may be used. Biological experiments may be done with all animals except mammalian vertebrates or birds. No physiological harm may result to the animal. All animals housed and cared for in the school must be handled in a safe and humane manner. Animals are not to remain on school premises during extended vacations unless adequate care is provided. Many state laws stipulate that any instructor who intentionally refuses to comply with the laws may be suspended or dismissed.

Microbiology - Pathogenic organisms must never be used for experimentation. Students should adhere to the following rules at all times when working with microorganisms to avoid accidental contamination:

- Treat all microorganisms as if they were pathogenic.
- Maintain sterile conditions at all times

If you are taking a national level exam you should check the Department of Education for your state for safety procedures. You will want to know what your state expects of you not only for the test but also for performance in the classroom and for the welfare of your students.

Bunsen burners - Hot plates should be used whenever possible to avoid the risk of burns or fire. If Bunsen burners are used, the following precautions should be followed:

1. Know the location of fire extinguishers and safety blankets and train students in their use. Long hair and long sleeves should be secured and out of the way.
2. Turn the gas all the way on and make a spark with the striker. The preferred method to light burners is to use strikers rather than matches.
3. Adjust the air valve at the bottom of the Bunsen burner until the flame shows an inner cone.
4. Adjust the flow of gas to the desired flame height by using the adjustment valve.
5. Do not touch the barrel of the burner (it is hot).

Graduated Cylinder - These are used for precise measurements. They should always be placed on a flat surface. The surface of the liquid will form a meniscus (lens-shaped curve). The measurement is read at the bottom of this curve.

Balance - Electronic balances are easier to use, but more expensive. An electronic balance should always be tarred (returned to zero) before measuring and used on a flat surface. Substances should always be placed on a piece of paper to avoid spills and/or damage to the instrument. Triple beam balances must be used on a level surface. There are screws located at the bottom of the balance to make any adjustments. Start with the largest counterweight first and proceed toward the last notch that does not tip the balance. Do the same with the next largest, etc until the pointer remains at zero. The total mass is the total of all the readings on the beams. Again, use paper under the substance to protect the equipment.

Buret – A buret is used to dispense precisely measured volumes of liquid. A stopcock is used to control the volume of liquid being dispensed at a time.

Light microscopes are commonly used in laboratory experiments. Several procedures should be followed to properly care for this equipment:

- Clean all lenses with lens paper only.
- Carry microscopes with two hands; one on the arm and one on the base.
- Always begin focusing on low power, then switch to high power.
- Store microscopes with the low power objective down.
- Always use a coverslip when viewing wet mount slides.
- Bring the objective down to its lowest position, then focus by moving up to avoid breaking the slide or scratching the lens.

Wet mount slides should be made by placing a drop of water on the specimen and then putting a glass coverslip on top of the drop of water. Dropping the coverslip at a forty-five degree angle will help in avoiding air bubbles. Total magnification is determined by multiplying the ocular (usually 10X) and the objective (usually 10X on low, 40X on high).

DOMAIN VI.   **HEALTH AND FITNESS**

COMPETENCY 30.0   **UNDERSTAND BASIC PRINCIPLES AND PRACTICES OF PERSONAL, INTERPERSONAL, AND COMMUNITY HEALTH AND SAFETY; AND APPLY RELATED ATTITUDES, KNOWLEDGE, AND SKILLS (E.G., DECISION MAKING, PROBLEM SOLVING) TO PROMOTE PERSONAL WELL-BEING.**

SKILL 30.1   **Apply decision-making and problem-solving skills and procedures in individual and group situations, including situations related to personal well-being, self-esteem, and interpersonal relationships**

There is an important relationship to consider between physical activity and the development of personal identity and emotional and mental well-being, most notably the impact of positive body image and self-concept. Instructors can help children develop positive body image and self-concept by creating opportunities for the children to experience successes in physical activities and to develop a comfort level with their bodies. This is an important contributor to their personal and physical confidence.

SOCIAL HEALTH

For most people, the development of social roles and appropriate social behaviors occurs during childhood. Physical play between parents and children, as well as between siblings and peers, serves as a strong regulator in the developmental process. Chasing games, roughhousing, wrestling, or practicing sport skills such as jumping, throwing, catching, and striking, are some examples of childhood play. These activities may be competitive or non-competitive and are important for promoting social and moral development of both boys and girls. Unfortunately, fathers will often engage in this sort of activity more with their sons than their daughters. Regardless of the sex of the child, both boys and girls enjoy these types of activities.

Physical play during infancy and early childhood is central to the development of social and emotional competence. Research shows that children who engage in play that is more physical with their parents, particularly with parents who are sensitive and responsive to the child, exhibited greater enjoyment during the play sessions and were more popular with their peers. Likewise, these early interactions with parents, siblings, and peers are important in helping children become more aware of their emotions and to learn to monitor and regulate their own emotional responses. Children learn quickly through watching the responses of their parents which behaviors make their parents smile and laugh and which behaviors cause their parents to frown and disengage from the activity.

If children want the fun to continue, they engage in the behaviors that please others. As children near adolescence, they learn through rough-and-tumble play that there are limits to how far they can go before hurting someone (physically or emotionally), which results in termination of the activity or later rejection of the child by peers. These early interactions with parents and siblings are important in helping children learn appropriate behavior in the social situations of sport and physical activity.

Children learn to assess their social competence (i.e., ability to get along with and acceptance by peers, family members, teachers and coaches) in sport through the feedback received from parents and coaches. Initially, authority figures teach children, "You can't do that because I said so." As children approach school age, parents begin the process of explaining why a behavior is right or wrong because children continuously ask, "why?"

Similarly, when children engage in sports, they learn about taking turns with their teammates, sharing playing time, and valuing rules. They understand that rules are important for everyone and without these regulations, the game would become unfair. The learning of social competence is continuous as we expand our social arena and learn about different cultures. A constant in the learning process is the role of feedback as we assess the responses of others to our behaviors and comments.

In addition to the development of social competence, sport participation can help youth develop other forms of self-competence. Most important among these self-competencies is self-esteem. Self-esteem is how we judge our worth and indicates the extent to which an individual believes he is capable, significant, successful and worthy. Educators have suggested that one of the biggest barriers to success in the classroom today is low self-esteem.

Children develop self-esteem by evaluating abilities and by evaluating the responses of others. Children actively observe parents' and coaches' responses to their performances, looking for signs of approval or disapproval of their behavior. Children often interpret feedback and criticism as either a negative or a positive response to the behavior. In sports, research shows that the coach is a critical source of information that influences the self-esteem of children.

Little League baseball players whose coaches use a "positive approach" to coaching (e.g. more frequent encouragement, positive reinforcement for effort and corrective, instructional feedback), had significantly higher self-esteem ratings over the course of a season than children whose coaches used these techniques less frequently. The most compelling evidence supporting the importance of coaches' feedback was found for those children who started the season with the lowest self-esteem ratings and increased considerably their self-assessment and self-worth. In addition to evaluating themselves more positively, low self-esteem children evaluated their coaches more positively than did children with higher self-esteem who played for coaches who used the "positive approach." Moreover, studies show that 95 percent of children who played for coaches trained to use the positive approach signed up to play baseball the next year, compared with 75 percent of the youth who played for untrained adult coaches.

We cannot overlook the importance of enhanced self-esteem on future participation. A major part of the development of high self-esteem is the pride and joy that children experience as their physical skills improve. Children will feel good about themselves as long as their skills are improving. If children feel that their performance during a game or practice is not as good as that of others, or as good as they think mom and dad would want, they often experience shame and disappointment.

Some children will view mistakes made during a game as a failure and will look for ways to avoid participating in the task if they receive no encouragement to continue. At this point, it is critical that adults (e.g., parents and coaches) intervene to help children to interpret the mistake or "failure." We must teach children that a mistake is not synonymous with failure. Rather, a mistake shows us that we need a new strategy, more practice, and/or greater effort to succeed at the task.

Physical education activities can promote positive social behaviors and traits in a number of different ways. Instructors can foster improved relations with adults and peers by making students active partners in the learning process and delegating responsibilities within the class environment to students. Giving students leadership positions (e.g. team captain) can give them a heightened understanding of the responsibilities and challenges facing educators.

Team-based physical activities like team sports promote collaboration and cooperation. In such activities, students learn to work together, both pooling their talents and minimizing the weaknesses of different team members, in order to achieve a common goal. The experience of functioning as a team can be very productive for development of loyalty between children, and seeing their peers in stressful situations that they can relate to can promote a more compassionate and considerate attitude among students. Similarly, the need to maximize the strengths of each student on a team (who can complement each other and compensate for weaknesses) is a powerful lesson about valuing and respecting diversity and individual differences. Varying students between leading and following positions in a team hierarchy are good ways to help students gain a comfort level being both followers and leaders.

Fairness is another trait that physical activities, especially rules-based sports, can foster and strengthen. Children are by nature very rules-oriented, and have a keen sense of what they believe is and isn't fair. Fair play, teamwork, and sportsmanship are all values that stem from proper practice of the spirit of physical education classes. Of course, a pleasurable physical education experience goes a long way towards promoting an understanding of the innate value of physical activity throughout the life cycle.

Finally, communication is another skill that improves enormously through participation in sports and games. Students will come to understand that skillful communication can contribute to a better all-around outcome, whether it be winning the game or successfully completing a team project. They will see that effective communication helps to develop and maintain healthy personal relationships, organize and convey information, and reduce or avoid conflict.

GROUP PROCESSES AND PROBLEM SOLVING

Physical fitness activities incorporate group processes, group dynamics, and a wide range of cooperation and competition. Ranging from team sports (which are both competitive and cooperative in nature) to individual competitive sports (like racing), to cooperative team activities without a winner and loser (like a gymnastics team working together to create a human pyramid), there is a great deal of room for the development of mutual respect and support among the students, safe cooperative participation, and analytical, problem solving, teamwork, and leadership skills.

Teamwork situations are beneficial to students because they create opportunities for them to see classmates with whom they might not generally socialize, and with whom they may not even get along, in a new light. It also creates opportunities for students to develop reliance on each other and practice interdependence. Cooperation and competition can also offer opportunities for children to practice group work. These situations provide good opportunities to practice analytical thinking and problem solving in a practical setting.

The social skills and values gained from participation in physical activities are as follows:

- The ability to make adjustments to both self and others by an integration of the individual to society and the environment.
- The ability to make judgments in a group situation.
- Learning to communicate with others and be cooperative.
- The development of the social phases of personality, attitudes, and values in order to become a functioning member of society such as being considerate.
- The development of a sense of belonging and acceptance by society.
- The development of positive personality traits.
- Learning for constructive use of leisure time.
- A development of attitude that reflects good moral character.
- Respect of school rules and property.

SKILL 30.2 Analyze contemporary health-related problems (e.g., HIV, teenage pregnancy, suicide, substance abuse) in terms of their causes and effects on individuals, families, and society; and evaluate strategies for their prevention

Important contemporary health-related issues that significantly effect modern society include HIV, teenage pregnancy, suicide, and substance abuse.

HIV

The human immunodefiency virus (HIV) can devastate both individuals and society. Advances in treatment options, namely pharmaceuticals, have greatly improved the prospects of those who contract the disease. However, due to the expense of treatment, many people, especially those in underdeveloped countries, do not have access to treatment. Thus, prevention is still of utmost importance.

HIV is a retrovirus that attacks the human immune system and causes AIDS (acquired immunodefiency syndrome). AIDS is a failure of the immune system that allows normally benign viruses and bacteria to infect the body causing life-threatening conditions.

Humans acquire HIV through contact with bodily fluids of infected individuals. For example, transfer of blood, semen, vaginal fluid, and breast milk can cause HIV infection. The best means of prevention of HIV is sexual abstinence outside of marriage, practicing safe sex, and avoiding the use of injected drugs.

Because HIV is a sexually transmitted disease, it disproportionably affects people in the prime of their lives. Infected persons are often heads of households and families and key economic producers. Thus, the impact of HIV on society is particularly damaging. Not only are the costs of treatment great, but families often lose their mothers and fathers and communities lose their best producers and leaders. Society must find ways to fill these gaping voids.

SUICIDE

Suicide is particularly troubling problem. Adolescent suicide is always devastating to families and communities. The main cause of adolescent suicide is mental disease, such as depression or anxiety. When untreated, such disorders can cause intense feelings of hopelessness and despair that can lead to suicide attempts. Suicides can tear families apart, often leaving behind feelings of guilt among friends and family members. The best means of suicide prevention is close monitoring of changing behaviors in adolescents. Parents, friends, and family members should watch for and never ignore signs of depression, withdrawal from friends and activities, talk of suicide, and signs of despair and hopelessness. Proper counseling, medication, and care from mental health professionals can often prevent suicide.

TEEN PREGENANCY

Teen pregnancy hurts the mothers, children, and society by extension. Pregnancy disrupts the life of adolescent girls, often preventing them from finishing school, completing higher education, and finding quality employment. In addition, teenage girls are not emotionally or financially ready to care for children. Thus, the children of teen pregnancies may have a difficult start in life. Teen pregnancy also affects society because teenage parents often require government assistance and children of teen pregnancies often do not receive appropriate care and parenting. The best means of preventing teenage pregnancy is education about the importance of abstinence and contraception.

SUBSTANCE ABUSE

Substance abuse can lead to adverse behaviors and increased risk of injury and disease. Any substance affecting the normal functions of the body, illegal or not, is potentially dangerous and students and athletes should avoid them completely. Factors contributing to substance abuse include peer pressure, parental substance abuse, physical or psychological abuse, mental illness, and physical disability. Education, vigilance, and parental oversight are the best strategies for the prevention of substance abuse.

- Alcohol – This is a legal substance for adults but is very commonly abused. Moderate to excessive consumption can lead to an increased risk of cardiovascular disease, nutritional deficiencies, and dehydration. Alcohol also causes ill effects on various aspects of performance such as reaction time, coordination, accuracy, balance, and strength.

- Nicotine – Another legal but often abused substance that can increase the risk of cardiovascular disease, pulmonary disease, and cancers of the mouth. Nicotine consumption through smoking severely hinders athletic performance by compromising lung function. Smoking especially affects performance in endurance activities.

- Marijuana – This is the most commonly abused illegal substance. Adverse effects include a loss of focus and motivation, decreased coordination, and lack of concentration.

- Cocaine – Another illegal and somewhat commonly abused substance. Effects include increased alertness and excitability. This drug can give the user a sense of over confidence and invincibility, leading to a false sense of one's ability to perform certain activities. A high heart rate is associated with the use of cocaine, leading to an increased risk of heart attack, stroke, potentially deadly arrhythmias, and seizures.

SUBSTANCE ABUSE – TREATMENT AND ALTERNATIVES

Alternatives to substance use and abuse include regular participation in stress-relieving activities like meditation, exercise, and therapy, all of which can have a relaxing effect (a healthy habit is, for example, to train oneself to substitute exercise for a substance abuse problem). More importantly, the acquisition of longer-term coping strategies (for example, self-empowerment via practice of problem-solving techniques) is key to maintaining a commitment to alternatives to substance use and abuse.

Aspects of substance abuse treatment that we must consider include the processes of physical and psychological withdrawal from the addictive substance, acquisition of coping strategies and replacement techniques to fill the void left by the addictive substance, limiting access to the addictive substance, and acquiring self-control strategies.

Withdrawal from an addictive substance has both psychological and physical symptoms. The psychological symptoms include depression, anxiety, and strong cravings for the substance. Physical withdrawal symptoms stem from the body, adapted to a steady intake of the addictive substance, adapting to accommodate the no-longer available substance. Depending on the substance, medical intervention may be necessary.

Coping strategies and replacement techniques, as discussed earlier, center around providing the individual with an effective alternative to the addictive substance as a solution to the situations that they would feel necessitate the substance.

Limiting access to the addictive substance (opportunities for use) is important, because the symptoms of withdrawal and the experiences associated with the substance can provide a strong impetus to return to using it. Finally, recovering addicts should learn strategies of self-control and self-discipline to help them stay off of the addictive substance.

SKILL 30.3 Analyze the effects of specific practices (e.g., related to nutrition, exercise) and attitudes on lifelong personal health

NUTRITION AND WEIGHT CONTROL
Identify the components of nutrition

The components of nutrition are **carbohydrates, proteins, fats, vitamins, minerals, and water.**

Carbohydrates – the main source of energy (glucose) in the human diet. The two types of carbohydrates are simple and complex. Complex carbohydrates have greater nutritional value because they take longer to digest, contain dietary fiber, and do not excessively elevate blood sugar levels. Common sources of carbohydrates are fruits, vegetables, grains, dairy products, and legumes.

Proteins – are necessary for growth, development, and cellular function. The body breaks down consumed protein into component amino acids for future use. Major sources of protein are meat, poultry, fish, legumes, eggs, dairy products, grains, and legumes.

Fats – a concentrated energy source and important component of the human body. The different types of fats are saturated, monounsaturated, and polyunsaturated. Polyunsaturated fats are the healthiest because they may lower cholesterol levels, while saturated fats increase cholesterol levels. Common sources of saturated fats include dairy products, meat, coconut oil, and palm oil. Common sources of unsaturated fats include nuts, most vegetable oils, and fish.

Vitamins and minerals – organic substances that the body requires in small quantities for proper functioning. People acquire vitamins and minerals in their diets and in supplements. Important vitamins include A, B, C, D, E, and K. Important minerals include calcium, phosphorus, magnesium, potassium, sodium, chlorine, and sulfur.

Water – makes up 55 – 75% of the human body. Essential for most bodily functions. Attained through foods and liquids.

Determine the adequacy of diets in meeting the nutritional needs of students
Nutritional requirements vary from person-to-person. General guidelines for meeting adequate nutritional needs are: no more than 30% total caloric intake from fats (preferably 10% from saturated fats, 10% from monounsaturated fats, 10% from polyunsaturated fats), no more than 15% total caloric intake from protein (complete), and at least 55% of caloric intake from carbohydrates (mainly complex carbohydrates).

Exercise and diet help maintain proper body weight by equalizing caloric intake and caloric output.

Choosing a healthy diet

A healthy diet is essential for achieving and maintaining optimum mental and physical health. Making the decision to eat well is a powerful investment. Selecting foods that encompass a variety of healthy nutrients will help reduce your risk of developing common medical conditions and will boost your immune system while increasing your energy level.

Experts agree that the key to healthy eating is balance, variety, and moderation. Other tips include:

- Enjoy plenty of whole grains, fruits, and vegetables.
- Maintain a healthy weight.
- Eat moderate portions.
- Eat regular meals.
- Reduce but don't eliminate certain foods.
- Balance your food choices over time.
- Know your diet pitfalls.
- Make changes gradually... Remember, foods are not good or bad.

Select foods based on your total eating patterns, not whether any individual food is "good" or "bad."

EXERCISE AND DIET

Exercise and diet maintain proper body weight by equalizing caloric intake to caloric output.

Nutrition and exercise are closely related concepts important to student health. An important responsibility of physical education instructors is to teach students about proper nutrition and exercise and how they relate to each other. The two key components of a healthy lifestyle are consumption of a balanced diet and regular physical activity. Nutrition can affect physical performance. Proper nutrition produces high energy levels and allows for peak performance. Inadequate or improper nutrition can impair physical performance and lead to short-term and long-term health problems (e.g. depressed immune system and heart disease, respectively). Regular exercise improves overall health. Benefits of regular exercise include a stronger immune system, stronger muscles, bones, and joints, reduced risk of premature death, reduced risk of heart disease, improved psychological well-being, and weight management.

Skill 30.4 Analyze relationships between environmental conditions and personal and community health and safety

The sources and potential health effects of various environmental factors and methods for minimizing or coping with health risks in the environment

Environmental health demonstrates concern about environmental issues. Examples of environmental issues include outdoor air pollution, indoor air pollution, noise pollution, water contamination, radiation exposure, disposal of hazardous wastes, and recycling.

Air pollution is a primary environmental health hazard. Various air pollutants are highly dangerous. Examples of air pollutants include motor vehicle emissions such as carbon monoxide, sulfur oxide, nitrogen oxide, hydrocarbons, and airborne lead. The Clean Air Act of 1979 reduced some motor vehicle emissions; however, the levels remain dangerously high due to large numbers of vehicles on the road, long commutes, and oversized vehicles. Carpooling and the use of smaller vehicles could significantly decrease the amount of motor vehicle emissions.

Another type of pollution is indoor air pollution. The most dangerous types of indoor pollution are tobacco smoke, carbon monoxide, asbestos, radon, and lead. To prevent indoor air pollution, avoid tobacco smoking indoors and ensure that indoor areas have adequate ventilation with fresh outdoor air. Remove the sources of any pollutants. Keep appliances and heating systems in good condition and follow the regular maintenance schedule. Homes should have at least one carbon monoxide detector located near the sleeping area. Check homes for asbestos, lead, and radon. When detected, safely remove them.

Noise is an additional environmental concern. To protect the ears, keep headphones at a low level, sit at a safe distance from the speakers at concerts, and wear earplugs when exposed to loud sounds.

Another major environmental hazard is water pollution. Water pollution can cause dysentery (a severe intestinal infection), increases in hypertension (due to increased sodium content), and chemical poisoning (such as mercury poisoning). The Safe Water Drinking Act passed in 1974 requires water treatment facilities to notify consumers when they violate safe drinking water requirements; however, this regulation is not strictly enforced. To ensure safe drinking water, consumers should not assume that their facility is following the regulations. They should contact their individual facility to determine the contaminant levels in their drinking water. Additionally, consumers should avoid dumping garbage or chemicals in lakes, rivers, on the ground, or down the drain. Instead, take chemicals to a hazardous waste disposal center. Finally, everyone should practice water conservation. Methods of water conservation include installing a low-flow showerhead, running the dishwasher and washing machine only when completely full, turning off the water while brushing teeth and washing hands, taking quick showers, and watering the lawn at the coolest time of the day.

Radiation exposure is also an environmental concern. Application of a 30 SPF sunscreen every hour and the use of ultraviolet-ray-blocking sunglasses can minimize the effects of ultraviolet radiation exposure.

One final environmental concern is the proper disposal of hazardous wastes. Consumers should always read and follow label information regarding the proper disposal of household products. Recycling is the process of breaking down products to their fundamental elements for use in another product. Recycling can help reduce air, water, and soil contaminants. Consumers should buy recycled products and recycle their own household materials. Additionally, consumers should avoid one-use products, especially disposable products made of plastic, paper, and foam.

Recognizing safety principles and practices for use in the home, at school, on the playground, in and around motorized and non-motorized vehicles, on the street, in or near water, and around animals

The environment surrounding children can be hazardous without appropriate safety principles and practices. Proper safety principles and practices clearly delineated by parents and educators can ensure that children enjoy and learn from their environments without taking unnecessary risks.

Safety principles and practices for use in the home include not touching potentially hazardous appliances (like the stove and oven), kitchen items (like knives), and electrical wiring and sockets. Parents and teachers should also teach children should guidelines for safe behavior, which include not opening the door to strangers, running up and down stairs, and so forth.

Safety principles and practices for use at school include prohibitions against running outside of designated areas and time periods (for example, recess and gym class), prohibitions against violence of any kind, and rules against other unsafe behavior such as standing on chairs and tables. Rules should also be in place limiting the noise levels, so that in the event that an educator has to give safety-related instruction, all children will be able to hear.

Safety principles and practices for use on the playground include prohibitions against playing on jungle-gym apparatus in ways that are potentially unsafe (these guidelines will vary relative to the age of the children in question). There should also be rules in place limiting appropriate behavior that will tend to grow rambunctious (for example, no pushing allowed). There should also be procedures in place by which students are required to line up so the instructor can count the students before returning to class to ensure that no children are left behind.

Safety principles and practices for use in and around motorized and non-motorized vehicles include crossing the street behind cars, and not in front, so that if the child is not seen they will not accidentally be run over. If children need to cross the street in front of a car, they should do it a safe distance, not directly beside it, where their short stature might prevent them from being seen. In regard to non-motorized vehicles (for example, bicycles), children should be taught to keep out of their way, as they are still dangerous, and not to play with the parts and gears, where their hands can get stuck.

Safety principles and practices for use on the street include rules against playing in the street, or in the event of very quiet streets where parents allow their children to play, clear procedures for vacating the street in the event of a passing car (playing in the street in general should be discouraged, as it is dangerous). Children should learn to look both ways before crossing the street, to ensure that it is safe. If they find themselves in the street when a car is approaching, they should either move forward or move back, but not freeze (which is a natural reaction that can prove hazardous).

Safety principles and practices for use in or near water include not running on areas that might be wet and slippery, keeping a certain prescribed distance from the water without appropriate life-preserving equipment (depending on the swimming abilities of the children), and prohibitions against getting within a certain distance of the swimming area when no supervising adult is present.

Safety principles and practices for use around animals include keeping a safe distance until it has been indicated to the child by the owner of the animal that it is safe, not petting or touching the animal without the owner's permission, and not approaching unfamiliar animals at all, and certainly not without the permission of their parents or supervising adult. Children should also learn not to feed animals.

COMPETENCY 31.0   UNDERSTAND PHYSICAL EDUCATION CONCEPTS AND PRACTICES RELATED TO THE DEVELOPMENT OF PERSONAL WELL-BEING

SKILL 31.1   Recognize activities that promote the development of motor skills (e.g., locomotor, manipulative, body mechanics), perceptual awareness skills (e.g., body awareness, spatial and directional awareness), and fitness (e.g., endurance, flexibility)

Physical education helps individuals attain a healthy level of fitness and renders significant experiences in movement. It provides an opportunity to refine and develop motor skills, stamina, strategies and the pure pleasure of physical activity and participation. Children, infants, and the disabled are all entitled to benefit from physical education. Physical activities can be adapted by recognizing the individual's abilities, learning skills, needs, etc. This requires knowledge about the science of movement, the process of skill development, social and psychological components, physical fitness, assessment of the practices of physical activities, and development and implementation of proper and appropriate activities.

Children are at a developmental stage where their physical, emotional, motor, and social skills are not fully constructed. Children in different age groups have distinct and urgent developmental needs. A developmental need varies from child to child. Instructors should respect a child's developmental needs and pace of learning. The child should be put in an environment that stimulates him and offers challenges that are appropriate to his age, developmental needs, and ability. A child should not be forced to take up an activity. Coercion discourages the child and he/she resists learning. However, motivation and stimulants can be put within the activity to encourage the child without direct intervention of an adult. Self-motivation is the best tool for learning. Children need to challenge themselves through constant exploration and experimentation. The activity should suit the developmental age of the child so that he/she can perform it with minimal outside assistance. An adult should act as an assistant who provides help only when it is required.

The physical education program for children should be geared to suit their developmental needs (i.e., constructing their motor skills, concept of movement). Physical activity should be fun, pleasurable and aimed at developing and maintaining health. Motor skills are comprised of locomotor skills, non-locomotor skills and manipulative and coordination skills. Games like Bean Bag, parachute, hula hoop, gymnastics and ball activities that instructors can modify and adapt to suit the particular needs of children, are particularly helpful. Physical activity should have the scope to adapt itself to suit an individual child's needs and goals. For an individual incapable of using his/her legs, an instructor can incorporate wheelchair races or activities that require the use of hands.

For children in the grades 1 – 3, instructors should incorporate the concepts of movement and motor skills, allowing the child to perfect them. Concepts of movements like spatial consciousness regarding location, level or height and direction, body awareness and recognition of how the body can be manipulated to perform an activity, effort required regarding time, flow and force, relationship to the various objects and to others, are developed through various activities.

Instructors should also emphasize the significance of personal hygiene. With greater development of motor skills and concepts about movement, instructors can integrate more energetic and vigorous physical activities like volleyball, gymnastics, football, and hockey, into the physical education program. Along with these skills, instructors should select activities that develop group participation skills. It is essential to instill the values of physical education and its connection to general well-being and health. Apart from this, physical education for middle grade children should help develop a good body image and enhance their social skills. Activities like advanced volleyball, dance, and gymnastics can help to develop these areas.

A normal three-year-old should be able to walk up and down the stairs, jump from the lowest step, and land on both the feet without falling. They should also be capable of standing on one foot and balancing and kicking a large ball (though not with a lot of force). A three-year-old can jump on the same spot, ride on a small tricycle, and throw a ball (although not very straight and with limited distance). The large motor skills are more or less developed, but fine motor skills and hand-eye coordination need refining. For example, a three-year-old may not be able to dodge a ball or play games like badminton, which require greater hand-eye coordination, speed, and balance, but a three-year-old can catch a big ball thrown to him/her from a short distance.

A four-year-old is capable of walking on a straight line, hopping using one foot, and pedaling a tricycle with confidence. A four-year-old can climb ladders and trees with relative ease. A four-year-old child can run around obstacles, maneuver, and stop when necessary. A four-year-old can throw a ball a greater distance and is capable of running around in circles.

A five-year-old is capable of walking backwards, using the heel and then the toe, and is able to easily climb up and down steps by alternating feet without any outside help. Five-year-olds can touch their toes without bending at the knee and balance on a beam. They may be able to do somersaults provided it is taught in a proper and safe manner. A five-year-old can ride a tricycle with speed and dexterity, make almost ten jumps or hops without losing balance and falling, and stand on one foot for about ten seconds.

Early elementary school children have already acquired many large motor and fine motor skills. Their movement is more accurate and with purpose, though some clumsiness may persist. An elementary student is always on the run and restless. A child older than five finds pleasure in more energetic and vigorous activities. He/she can jump, hop, and throw with relative accuracy and concentrate on an activity which sustains his/her interest. However, concentration on a single activity usually does not last long. Early elementary students enjoy challenges and can benefit greatly from them.

When proper and appropriate physical education is available, by the time a child finishes the fourth grade he is able to demonstrate well-developed locomotor movements. He is also capable of manipulative and nonlocomotor movement skills like kicking and catching. He is capable of living up to challenges like balancing a number of objects or controlling a variety of things simultaneously. Children at this developmental age begin to acquire specialized movement skills like dribbling. When a child has finished eighth grade, he is able to exhibit expertise in a variety of fine and modified movements (e.g. dance steps).

Children begin to develop the necessary skills for competitive and strategic games. Despite a lack of competency in a game, they learn to enjoy the pleasure of physical activity. By the time the children finish the twelfth grade they can demonstrate competency of a number of complex and modified movements with relative ease (e.g. gymnastics, dual sports, dance). Students at this age display their interest in gaining a greater degree of competency at their favorite game or activity.

PERCEPTUAL AWARENESS SKILLS

Perceptual-motor development refers to one's ability to receive, interpret, and respond successfully to sensory signals coming from the environment. Because many of the skills acquired in school rely on the child's knowledge of his body and its relationship to the surroundings, good motor development leads directly to perceptual skill development. Development of gross motor skills lead to successful development of fine motor skills, which in turn help with learning, reading, and writing. Adolescents with perceptual-motor coordination problems are at risk for poor school performance, low self-esteem, and inadequate physical activity participation. Without a successful intervention, these adolescents are likely to continue avoiding physical activity and experience frustration and teasing from their peers. Children with weak perceptual-motor skills may be easily distracted or have difficulty with tasks requiring coordination. They spend much of their energy trying to control their bodies, exhausting them so much that they physically cannot concentrate on a teacher-led lesson.

Unfortunately, perceptual-motor coordination problems do not just go away and they don't self-repair. Practice and maturity are necessary for children to develop greater coordination and spatial awareness. Physical education lessons should emphasize activities that children enjoy doing, are sequential, and require seeing, hearing, and/or touching. Discussing with students the actual steps involved in performing a fundamental skill is a great benefit. Activities and skills that can be broken down and taught in incremental steps include running, dribbling, catching or hitting a ball, making a basket in basketball, and setting volleyball. Recommended strategies include introducing the skill, practicing in a variety of settings with an assortment of equipment, implementing lead-up games modified to ensure practice of the necessary skills, and incorporating students into an actual game situation.

CONCEPT OF BODY AWARENESS APPLIED TO PHYSICAL EDUCATION ACTIVITIES

Body awareness is a person's understanding of his or her own body parts and their capability of movement.

Instructors can assess body awareness by playing and watching a game of "Simon Says" and asking the students to touch different body parts. You can also instruct students to make their bodies into various shapes, from straight to round to twisted and varying sizes, to fit into different sized spaces.

In addition, you can instruct children to touch one part of their body to another and to use various body parts to stamp their feet, twist their neck, clap their hands, nod their heads, wiggle their noses, snap their fingers, open their mouths, shrug their shoulders, bend their knees, close their eyes, bend their elbows, or wiggle their toes.

CONCEPT OF SPATIAL AWARENESS APPLIED TO PHYSICAL EDUCATION ACTIVITIES

Spatial awareness is the ability to make decisions about an object's positional changes in space (i.e. awareness of three-dimensional space position changes). Developing spatial awareness requires two sequential phases: 1) identifying the location of objects in relation to one's own body in space, and 2) locating more than one object in relation to each object and independent of one's own body. Plan activities using different size balls, boxes, or hoops and have children move towards and away; under and over; in front of and behind; and inside, outside, and beside the objects.

CONCEPT OF EFFORT QUALITIES APPLIED TO PHYSICAL EDUCATION

Effort qualities are the qualities of movement that apply the mechanical principles of balance, time, and force).

Balance - activities for balance include having children move on their hands and feet, lean, move on lines, and balance and hold shapes while moving.

Time - activities using the concept of time can include having children move as fast as they can and as slow as they can in specified, timed movement patterns.

Force - activities using the concept of force can include having students use their bodies to produce enough force to move them through space. They can also paddle balls against walls and jump over objects of various heights.

> **SKILL 31.2   Apply safety concepts and practices associated with physical activities (e.g., doing warm-up exercises, wearing protective equipment)**

TECHNIQUES AND BENEFITS OF WARMING UP AND COOLING DOWN

Warming up is a gradual 5 to 10 minute aerobic warm-up in which the participant uses the muscles needed in the activity to follow (similar movements at a lower activity). Warm-ups also include stretching of major muscle groups after the gradual warm-up.

The benefits of warming up are:
- preparing the body for physical activity
- reducing the risk of musculoskeletal injuries
- releasing oxygen from myoglobin
- warming the body's inner core
- increasing the reaction of muscles
- bringing the heart rate to an aerobic conditioning level

Cooling down is similar to warming up - a moderate to light tapering-off vigorous activity at the end of an exercise session.
The benefits of cooling down are:
- redistributing circulation of the blood throughout the body to prevent pooling of blood
- preventing dizziness
- facilitating the removal of lactic acid

HEALTH-RELATED COMPONENTS OF PHYSICAL FITNESS

There are five health related components of physical fitness: **cardio-respiratory or cardiovascular endurance, muscle strength, muscle endurance, flexibility, and body composition.**

> **Cardiovascular endurance** – the ability of the body to sustain aerobic activities (activities requiring oxygen utilization) for extended periods.

> **Muscle strength** – the ability of muscle groups to contract and support a given amount of weight.

> **Muscle endurance** – the ability of muscle groups to contract continually over a period of time and support a given amount of weight.

> **Flexibility** – the ability of muscle groups to stretch and bend.

> **Body composition** – an essential measure of health and fitness. The most important aspects of body composition are body fat percentage and ratio of body fat to muscle.

BASIC TRAINING PRINCIPLES

The **Overload Principle** is exercising at an above normal level to improve physical or physiological capacity (a higher than normal workload).

The **Specificity Principle** is overloading a particular fitness component. In order to improve a component of fitness, you must isolate and specifically work on a single component. Metabolic and physiological adaptations depend on the type of overload; hence, specific exercise produces specific adaptations, creating specific training effects.

The **Progression Principle** states that once the body adapts to the original load/stress, no further improvement of a component of fitness will occur without the addition of an additional load.

There is also a **Reversibility-of-Training Principle** in which all gains in fitness are lost with the discontinuance of a training program.

MODIFICATIONS OF OVERLOAD

We can modify overload by varying **frequency, intensity, and time**. Frequency is the number of times we implement a training program in a given period (e.g. three days per week). Intensity is the amount of effort put forth or the amount of stress placed on the body. Time is the duration of each training session.

PRINCIPLES OF OVERLOAD, PROGRESSION, AND SPECIFICITY APPLIED TO IMPROVEMENT OF HEALTH-RELATED COMPONENTS OF FITNESS

Cardio-respiratory Fitness:

Overloading for cardio-respiratory fitness:
- **Frequency** = minimum of 3 days/week
- **Intensity** = exercising in target heart-rate zone
- **Time** = minimum of 15 minutes rate

Progression for cardiovascular fitness:
- begin at a frequency of 3 days/week and work up to no more than 6 days/week
- begin at an intensity near THR threshold and work up to 80% of THR
- begin at 15 minutes and work up to 60 minutes

Specificity for cardiovascular fitness:
- To develop cardiovascular fitness, you must perform aerobic (with oxygen) activities for at least fifteen minutes without developing an oxygen debt. Aerobic activities include, but are not limited to brisk walking, jogging, bicycling, and swimming.

Muscle Strength:

Overloading for muscle strength:
- **Frequency** = every other day
- **Intensity** = 60% to 90% of assessed muscle strength
- **Time** = 3 sets of 3 - 8 reps (high resistance with a low number of repetitions)

Progression for muscle strength:
- begin 3 days/week and work up to every other day
- begin near 60% of determined muscle strength and work up to no more than 90% of muscle strength
- begin with 1 set with 3 reps and work up to 3 sets with 8 reps

Specificity for muscle strength:
- to increase muscle strength for a specific part(s) of the body, you must target that/those part(s) of the body

Muscle endurance:

Overloading for muscle endurance:
- **Frequency** = every other day
- **Intensity** = 30% to 60% of assessed muscle strength
- **Time** = 3 sets of 12 - 20 reps (low resistance with a high number of repetitions)

Progression for muscle endurance:

- begin 3 days/week and work up to every other day
- begin at 20% to 30% of muscle strength and work up to no more than 60% of muscle strength
- begin with 1 set with 12 reps and work up to 3 sets with 20 reps

Specificity for muscle endurance:

- same as muscle strength

Flexibility:

Overloading for flexibility:

- **Frequency**: 3 to 7 days/week
- **Intensity**: stretch muscle beyond its normal length
- **Time**: 3 sets of 3 reps holding stretch 15 to 60 seconds

Progression for flexibility:

- begin 3 days/week and work up to every day
- begin stretching with slow movement as far as possible without pain, holding at the end of the range of motion (ROM) and work up to stretching no more than 10% beyond the normal ROM
- begin with 1 set with 1 rep, holding stretches 15 seconds, and work up to 3 sets with 3 reps, holding stretches for 60 seconds

Specificity for flexibility:

- ROM is joint specific

Body composition:

Overloading to improve body composition:

- **Frequency**: daily aerobic exercise
- **Intensity**: low
- **Time**: approximately one hour

Progression to improve body composition:

- begin daily
- begin a low aerobic intensity and work up to a longer duration (see cardio-respiratory progression)
- begin low-intensity aerobic exercise for 30 minutes and work up to 60 minutes

Specificity to improve body composition:

- increase aerobic exercise and decrease caloric intake

ACTIVITIES THAT PROMOTE FITNESS

The following is a list of physical activities that may reduce specific health risks, improve overall health, and develop skill-related components of physical activity.

Aerobic Dance:
Health-related components of fitness = *cardio-respiratory, body composition.*
Skill-related components of fitness = *agility, coordination.*

Bicycling:
Health-related components of fitness = *cardio-respiratory, muscle strength, muscle endurance, body composition.*
Skill-related components of fitness = *balance.*

Calisthenics:
Health-related components of fitness = *cardio-respiratory, muscle strength, muscle endurance, flexibility, body composition.*
Skill-related components of fitness = *agility.*

Circuit Training:
Health-related components of fitness = *cardio-respiratory, muscle strength, muscle endurance, body composition.*
Skill-related components of fitness = *power.*

Cross Country Skiing:
Health-related component of fitness = *cardio-respiratory, muscle strength, muscle endurance, body composition.*
Skill-related components of fitness = *agility, coordination, power.*

Jogging/Running:
Health-related components of fitness = *cardio-respiratory, body composition.*

Rope Jumping:
Health-related components of fitness = *cardio-respiratory, body composition.*
Skill-related components of fitness = *agility, coordination, reaction time, speed.*

Rowing:
Health-related components of fitness = *cardio-respiratory, muscle strength, muscle endurance, body composition.*
Skill-related components of fitness = *agility, coordination, power.*

Skating:
Health-related components of fitness = *cardio-respiratory, body composition.*
Skill-related components of fitness = *agility, balance, coordination, speed.*

<u>Swimming/Water Exercises</u>:
Health-related components of fitness = *cardio-respiratory, muscle strength, muscle endurance, flexibility, body composition.*
Skill related components of fitness = *agility, coordination.*

<u>Walking (brisk):</u>
Health-related components of fitness = *cardio-respiratory, body composition.*

SKILL 31.3   Understand skills necessary for successful participation in given sports and activities (e.g., dodging, spatial orientation, eye-body coordination)

Skills necessary for successful participation in sports and fitness activities include proprioception, spatial orientation, hand-eye coordination, and movement skills.

Proprioception – Proprioception is the sense of the relative position of neighboring parts of the body. Unlike the six external senses (sight, taste, smell, touch, hearing, and balance) by which we perceive the outside world, proprioception is an internal sense that provides feedback solely on the status of the body internally. It is the sense that indicates whether the body is moving with required effort, as well as where the various parts of the body are located in relation to each other. We can improve proprioception by training.

Spatial orientation – Spatial orientation refers to the process of aligning or positioning oneself with respect to a specific direction or reference system. Specifically, it is the relationship established between the bodys self-oriented coordinate system and an external reference frame. This happens via the integration of sensory signals from the visual, vestibular, tactile, and proprioceptive systems.

Hand-eye coordination – Hand-eye coordination is the ability of the visual perception system to coordinate the information received through the eyes to control, guide, and direct the hands in the accomplishment of a given task (examples include handwriting or catching a ball). Hand-eye coordination uses the eyes to direct attention and the hands to execute a task.

Movement skills – Movement skills center on the integration of balance and proprioceptive skills to produce movement that effectively manages the weight distribution of the body. For example, dodging is a movement skill that involves moving the body in such a way to avoid oncoming objects.

SKILL 33.4   Analyze ways in which participation in individual or group sports or physical activities can promote personal well-being (e.g., self-discipline, respect for self and others) and interpersonal skills (e.g., cooperation, leadership)

o   *See Skill 30.1*

DOMAIN VII.   **FINE ARTS**

COMPETENCY 32.0   **UNDERSTAND CONCEPTS, TECHNIQUES, AND MATERIALS ASSOCIATED WITH THE VISUAL ARTS; ANALYZE WORKS Of VISUAL ART; AND UNDERSTAND THE CULTURAL DIMENSIONS OF THE VISUAL ARTS**

Skill 32.1   **Apply knowledge of basic tools, techniques, and technologies in creating different types of artwork**

abstract
An image that reduces a subject to its essential visual elements, such as lines, shapes, and colors.

background
Those portions or areas of composition that are back of the primary or dominant subject matter or design areas.

balance
A principle of art and design concerned with the arrangement of one or more elements in a work of art so that they appear symmetrical or asymmetrical in design and proportion.

contrast
A principle of art and design concerned with juxtaposing one or more elements in opposition, so as to show their differences.

emphasis
A principle of art and design concerned with making one or more elements in a work of art stand out in such a way as to appear more important or significant.

sketch
An image-development strategy; a preliminary drawing.

texture
An element of art and design that pertains to the way something feels by representation of the tactile character of surfaces.

unity
A principle of art and design concerned with the arrangement of one or more of the elements used to create a coherence of parts and a feeling of completeness or wholeness.

Following the learning the generic ideas for the above terms and how they relate to the use of line, color, value, space, texture and shape. An excellent opportunity is to create with the students an "art sample book."

Such books could include the different variety of material that would serve as examples for students to make connections to such as sandpaper to and cotton balls to represent texture elements. Samples of square pieces of construction paper designed into various shapes to represent shape. String samples to represent the element of lines, and other examples to cover all areas. The sampling of art should also focus clearly on colors necessary for the early childhood student. Color can be introduced more in-depth when discussing intensity or the strength of the color and value which relates to the lightness or darkness of the colors. Another valuable tool regarding color is the use of a color wheel and allowing students to experiment with the mixing of colors to create their own art experience.

Skill 32.2   Analyze how the illusion of space is created in a given two-dimensional work of art (e.g., linear perspective, overlapping elements)

Students should create and experience works of art that will explore different types of subject matter, themes, and topics. Students need to understand the sensory elements and organizational principles of art and expression of images.

Students should be able to select and using mediums and processes that actively communicate and express the intended meaning or their art works, exhibits and prove competence in at least two mediums. For example, students are able to select a process or medium for their intended work of art and describe their reasons for that selection.

Students must also use the computer and electronic media to express their visual ideas and demonstrate a variety of different approaches to their selected medium. An excellent example for students to produce works using mixed media, or a work of art that uses the computer, the camera, the copy machine or other types of electronic equipment.

At any age, students should be asked to compile a variety of their best works of art using different types of media. This is typically referred to as a portfolio. Early Childhood students all the way through High School students benefit from uses of a portfolio. Teachers are then able to explain choices of media and how it was chosen and used in a variety of ways using many different topics. The portfolio should begin with an early sample of the student's work, what is called a rough draft or a sketch. It can then be tracked to see the progress of each individual throughout the course of building the portfolio. By the end of the portfolio experience the growth in uses of medium and techniques should be clear and progress can be tracked through a use of a rubric or by observation.

Some of the areas that should be mastered by students and can be modeled by the teacher include the following:

- experimentation through works of art using a variety of mediums, drawing, painting, sculpture, ceramics, printmaking, and video
- producing a collection of art works (portfolio) and using a variety of mediums, topics, themes, and subject matter
- convey meaning through which art works were chosen
- create and evaluate different art works and which types of mediums chosen
- reflection on work and others works

Some examples should include:

- mixing paint in ranges of shades and tints
- use the computer to design an idea for sculpting
- include in the portfolio works that display at least two mediums
- try to include at least ten works of art in each portfolio
- include early sketches, research and development of each project with each entry
- research a design such as a building or a landmark and design it based on the research
- paint a picture using tempra or watercolor recalling a specific experience or memory

Skill 32.3   Analyze a given two-dimensional or three-dimensional work of art in terms of its unifying elements

Teachers should be able to utilize and teach various techniques when analyzing works of art. Students will learn and then begin to apply what they have learned in the arts to all subjects across the curriculum. Using problem solving techniques and creative skills students will begin to master the techniques necessary to derive meaning from both visual and sensory aspects of art.

Students will be asked to review, respond, and analyze various types of art. Students should be critical and it is necessary that students relate art in terms of life and human aspects of life. Students should be introduced to the wide range of opportunities to explore such art. Examples may include exhibits, galleries, museums, libraries, and personal art collections.

It is imperative that students learn to research and locate such artistic opportunities that are common in today's society. Some opportunities for research include the following: reproductions, art slides, films, print materials, and electronic media. Once students are taught how to effectively research and use sources students should be expected to graduate to higher level thinking skills.

Students should be able to begin to reflect on, interpret, evaluate, and explain how works of art and various styles of art work explain social, psychological, cultural, and environmental aspects of life.

Several areas that must be mastered for students to explore and identify styles in the arts are but not limited to the following:

- understanding of various types of mediums (two-dimensional, three-dimensional & electronic images) that are appropriate for learning
- developing skills using electronic media to express visual ideas
- awareness of cultural, environmental, community opportunities that will provide options for exploring art images and consulting artists
- awareness of potential careers and professional/professions in the field of the arts
- develop a variety of ways to use art material/medium

Some examples of mastery include:

- drawing or painting a computer graphics program
- visiting a museum or art festival and writing a report telling about the experience
- engage in a interview or conversation with an artist regarding what he/she does and why they have chosen art as a profession
- mixing and painting with a range of colors

Skill 32.4   Analyze how given works of art reflect the cultures that produced them

It is important for teachers to understand and relate to students the significance of early art forms and how the have developed over time. Many early folk art tales were scarce in their art and media. However now media and illustration is a tremendous part of any literature experience for young children. Another useful example is to have students describe the early days such as cave man art and compare it to art today.

Examples such as early car designs compared to today's designs. There are many types of visual art that have gown in all areas. Teachers should incorporate themed units that easily relate cross-curriculum studies. Using themed units such as a theme on vehicles can show students early models of cars, trucks, motorcycles, air planes and how they have developed over time in to the models we use today.

Performing art has too developed over time. A great experience for young students is to have a Tribal performer demonstrate for students the dance, and rituals performed by Native American dancers. These dances and ceremonies have evolved over hundreds of years. Students could then compare that performance to a ballet performance and discuss the similarities and differences and how each art has evolved over time.

Whether we express ourselves creatively from the theatrical stage, visually through fine art and dance or musically, appreciating and recognizing the interrelationships of various art forms are essential to an understanding of ourselves and our diverse society.

By studying and experiencing works of fine art and literature and by understanding their place in cultural and intellectual history, we can develop an appreciation of the human significance of the arts and humanities through history and across cultures.

Through art projects, field trips and theatrical productions, students can learn that all forms of art are a way for cultures to communicate with each other and the world at large. By understanding the concepts, techniques and various materials used in the visual arts, music, dance and the written word, students will begin to appreciate the concept of using art to express oneself. Perhaps they can begin by writing a short story which is then transformed into a play with costumes, music and movement to experience the relationship between different art forms.

The arts have played a significant role throughout history. The communicative power of the arts is notable. Cultures use the arts for artistic expression to impart specific emotions and feeling, to tell stories, to imitate nature and to persuade others. The arts bring meaning to ceremonies, rituals, celebrations and recreation. By creating their own art and by examining art made by others, children can learn to make sense of and communicate ideas. This can be accomplished through dance, verbal communication, music and other visual arts.

Through the arts and humanities, students will realize that although people are different, they share common experiences and attitudes. They will also learn that the use of nonverbal communication can be a strong adjunct to verbal communication.

COMPETENCY 33.0 UNDERSTAND CONCEPTS, TECHNIQUES, AND MATERIALS FOR PRODUCING, LISTENING TO, AND RESPONDING TO MUSIC; ANALYZE WORKS OF MUSIC; AND UNDERSTAND THE CULTURAL DIMENSIONS OF MUSIC

Skill 33.1 Compare various types of instruments (e.g., percussion, woodwind, computerized) in terms of the sounds they produce

When we listen to certain music styles, they often connect us to a memory, a time in the past, or even an entire historical period. Very often, classical pieces, such as Bach or Beethoven, create a picture in our minds of the Baroque Period. The historical perspective of music can deepen one's musical understanding.

Throughout history, different cultures have developed different styles of music. Most of the written records of music developed from Western civilization.

Music styles varied across cultures as periods in history. As in the opening discussion, classical music, although still popular and being created today, is often associated with traditional classical periods in history such as the Renaissance.

As world contact merged more and more as civilizations developed and prospered, more and more influence from various cultural styles emerged across music styles. For example, African drums emerged in some Contemporary and Hip Hop music. Also, the Bluegrass music in the United States developed from the "melting pot" contributions from Irish, Scottish, German and African-American instrumental and vocal traditions.

In addition, the purposes for music changed throughout cultures and times. Music has been used for entertainment, but also for propaganda, worship, ceremonies, and communication.

Below is a list of some of the most common categories of musical styles.

Common Musical Styles
Medieval
Classical Music (loosely encompassing Renaissance and Baroque)
Gospel Music
Jazz
Latin Music
Rhythm and Blues
Funk
Rock
Country
Folk
Bluegrass

Electronic (Techno)
Melodic
Island (Ska, Reggae and other)
Hip Hop
Pop
African
Contemporary

Types of Musical Instruments

Instruments are categorized by the mechanism that creates its sound. Musical instruments can be divided into four basic categories.

1. String
2. Percussion
3. Brass
4. Wind

String Instruments

String instruments all make their sounds through strings. The sound of the instrument depends on the thickness and length of the strings. The slower a string vibrates, the lower the resulting pitch. Also, the way the strings are manipulated varies among string instruments. Some strings are plucked (e.g., guitar) while others use a bow to cause the strings to vibrate (e.g., violin). Some are even connected to keys (e.g., piano). Other common string instruments include the viola, double bass, cello and piano.

Wind Instruments

The sound of wind instruments is caused by wind vibrating in a pipe or tube. Air blows into one end of the instrument, and in many wind instruments, air passes over a reed which causes the air to vibrate. The pitch depends on the air's frequency as it passes through the tube, and the frequency depends on the tube's length or size. Larger tubes create deeper sounds in a wind instrument. The pitch is also controlled by holes or values. As fingers cover the holes or press the valve, the pitch changes for the notes the musician intends. Other common wind instruments include pipe organ, oboe, clarinet and saxophone.

Brass Instruments

Brass instruments are similar to wind instruments since music from brass instruments also results from air passing through an air chamber. They are called brass instruments, however, because they are made from metal or brass. Pitch on a brass instrument is controlled by the size or length of the air chamber. Many brass instruments are twisted or coiled which lengthens the air chamber without making the instrument unmanageably long. Like wind instruments, larger air chambers create deeper sounds, and the pitch can be controlled by valves on the instrument. In addition, some brass instruments also control the pitch by the musician's mouth position on the mouthpiece. Common brass instruments include the French horn, trumpet, trombone and tuba.

Percussion Instruments

To play a percussion instrument, the musician hits or shakes the instrument. The sound is created from sound vibrations as a result of shaking or striking the instrument. Many materials, such as metal or wood, are used to create percussion instruments, and different thicknesses or sizes of the material help control the sound. Thicker or heavier materials like drum membranes make deeper sounds, while thinner, metal materials (e.g., triangle) make higher-pitched sounds. Other common percussion instruments include the cymbals, tambourine, bells, xylophone and wood block.

Skill 33.2   Apply common musical terms (e.g., pitch, tempo)

Accent - Stress of one tone over others, making it stand out; often it is the first beat of a measure

Accompaniment - Music that goes along with a more important part - often harmony or rhythmic patterns accompanying a melody.

Adagio - Slow, leisurely

Allegro - Lively, brisk, rapid

Cadence - Closing of a phrase or section of music

Chord - Three or more tones combined and sounded simultaneously

Crescendo - Gradually growing louder

Dissonance - A simultaneous sounding of tones that produce a feeling of tension or unrest and a feeling that further resolution is needed.

Harmony - The sound resulting from the simultaneous sounding of two or more tones consonant with each other

Interval - The distance between two tones

Melody - An arrangement of single tones in a meaningful sequence

Phrase - A small section of a composition comprising a musical thought.

Rhythm - The regular occurrence of accented beats that shape the character of music or dance.

Scale - A graduated series of tones arranged in a specified order

Staccato - Separate. Sounded in a short, detached manner

Syncopation - The rhythmic result produced when a regularly accented beat is displaced onto an unaccented beat.

Tempo - The rate of speed at which a musical composition is performed

Theme - A short musical passage that states an idea. It often provides the basis for variations, development, etc.

Timbre - The quality of a musical tone that distinguishes voices and instruments.

Tone - A musical sound or the quality of a musical sound

Skill 33.3   Relate characteristics of music (e.g., rhythm, beat) to musical effects produced

Variations in air pressure against the ear drum, and the physical and neurological processing and interpretation, give the listener the experience called "sound". Musical acoustics deal with the generation of sound by an instrument, transmitted to the listener through the air, ultimately received as the perception of musical sound.

The musical instrument vibrates and produces sound. The vibrations of a string or wire, a struck membrane, or a blown pipe of the instrument are the usual modes of vibration. Vibrations are motions which may range from the simple to-and-fro movement of a pendulum or the vibrations of a steel plate when struck with a hammer.

Most sound that people recognize as music is dominated by regular, periodic vibrations rather than non-periodic ones, and we refer to the transmission of these vibrations as a "sound wave". In a very simple case, the sound causes the air pressure to increase and decrease in a regular fashion, and is heard as a tone which is distinguished as a musical sound rather than noise.

Skill 33.4   Analyze how different cultures have created music reflective of their own histories and societies (e.g., call-and-response songs, ballads, work songs)

The resources available to man to make music have varied throughout different ages and eras and haves given the chance for a musical style or type to be created or invented due to diverse factors. Social changes, cultural features and historical purpose have all shared a part in giving birth to a multitude of different musical forms in every part of the earth.

Music can be traced to the people who created it by the instruments, melodies, rhythms and records of performance (songs) that are composed in human communities. Starting from early musical developments, as far back as nomadic cave dwellers playing the flute and beating on hand drums, to the different electric instruments and recording technology of the modern music industry, the style and type music produced has been closely related to the human beings who choose it for their particular lifestyle and way of existence.

Western music, rising chiefly from the fusion of classical and folkloric forms, has always been the pocket of a large variety of instruments and music generating new techniques to fit the change in expression provided by the expansion of its possibilities. Instruments such as the piano and the organ; stringed instruments like the violin, viola, cello, guitar and bass; wind instruments like the flute, saxophone, trumpet, trombone, tuba and saxophone; electronic instruments like the synthesizer and electric guitar have all provided for the invention of new styles and types of music created and used by different people in different times and places.

The rites of Christianity during the early middle ages were the focus of social and cultural aspiration and became a natural meeting place for communities to come together consistently for the purpose of experiencing God, through preaching and music. Composers and performers fulfilled their roles with sacred music with Gregorian chants and Oratorios. The art patron's court in the 15th and 14th centuries; the opera house of the 19th century satisfied the need of nascent, progressive society looking to experience grander and more satisfying music. New forms were generated such as the *concerto*, *symphony*, *sonata* and *string quartet* that employed a zeal and zest for creation typical of the burgeoning intellect at the end of the middle ages and the beginning of modern society.

Traditional types and styles of music in America, India, China, throughout the Middle East and Africa, using a contrasting variety of stringed instruments and percussion to typical Western instruments, began a long and exciting merging to the Western musical world with the beginning of widespread colonialism and the eventual integration it would achieve between disparate cultures. Western musical instruments were adopted to play the traditional musical styles of different cultures.

Blues music, arising from the southern black community in the United States would morph into *Rock n' Roll* and *Hip Hop*, alongside the progression of the traditional folk music of European settlers.

Hispanic music would come about by Western musical instruments being imbued with African rhythms throughout the Caribbean in different forms like *Salsa*, *Merengue*, *Cumbia* and *Son Cubano*.

Call-and-response songs are a form of verbal and non-verbal interaction between a speaker and a listener, in which statements by a speaker are responded to by a listener. In West African cultures, call-and-response songs were used in religious rituals, gatherings, and are now used in other forms such as gospel, blues, and jazz. as a form of musical expression. In certain Native American tribes, call-and-response songs are used to preserve and protect the tribe's cultural heritage and can be seen and heard at modern-day "pow-wows". The men would begin the song as the speaker with singing and drumming and the women would respond with singing and dancing.

A ballad is a song that contains a story. Instrumental music forms a part of folk music, especially dance traditions. Much folk music is vocal, since the instrument (the voice) that makes such music is usually handy. As such, most folk music has lyrics, and is descriptive about something. Any story form can be a ballad, such as fairy tales or historical accounts. It usually has simple repeating rhymes and often contains a refrain (or repeating sections) that are played or sung at regular intervals throughout. Ballads could be called hymns when they are based on religious themes. In the 20th century, "ballad" took on the meaning of a popular song "especially of a romantic or sentimental nature".

Folk music is music that has endured and been passed down by oral tradition and emerges spontaneously from ordinary people. In early societies, it arose in areas that were not yet affected by mass communication. It was normally shared by the entire community and was transmitted by word of mouth. A folk song is usually seen as an expression of a way of life now, past, or about to disappear. In the 1960's folk songs were sung as a way of protesting political themes.

The work song is typically a song sung acappella by people working on a physical and often repetitive task. It was probably intended to reduce feelings of boredom. Rhythms of work songs also serve to synchronize physical movement in a gang or the movement in marching. Frequently, the verses of work songs are improvised and sung differently each time. Examples of work songs could be heard from slaves working in the field, prisoners on chain gangs, and soldiers in the military.

COMPETENCY 34.0 UNDERSTAND CONCEPTS, TECHNIQUES, AND MATERIALS RELATED TO THEATRE AND DANCE; ANALYZE WORKS OF DRAMA AND DANCE; AND UNDERSTAND THE CULTURAL DIMENSIONS OF DRAMA AND DANCE

Skill 34.1 **Compare dramatic and theatrical forms and their characteristics (e.g., pantomime, improvisation)**

Students must be able to create, perform, and actively participate in theatre. Classes must be able to apply processes and skills involved in dramatic and theatre. From acting, designing, script writing, creating formal and informal theatre, and media productions, there is a wide variety of skills that must encompass the theatre expression.

Literature in the classroom opens many doors for learning. Reading and rehearsing stories with children allows them to explore the area of imagination and creative play. Students can take simple stories such as "The Three Little Pigs" and act out such tales. Acting allows students to experience new found dramatic skills and to enhance their creative abilities.

Students must understand and appreciate a dramatic work. A school curriculum incorporating dramatic and theatrical forms should include the vocabulary for theatre and the development of a criterion for evaluation of dramatic events. A good drama curriculum should include the following:

- Acting - acting involves the students' ability to skillfully communicate with an audience. It requires speaking, movement, sensory awareness, rhythm and oral communication skills
- Improvisation- the actors must be able to respond to unexpected stimuli in a creative and spontaneous manner and must adapt to any scene that may be previously unscripted
- Drama- a reenactment of life and life situations for entertainment purposes
- Theatre-theatre involves a more formal presentation in front of an audience, typically involving a script, set, direction and production
- Production- this often includes arranging for the entire theatre performance and the production of the whole process
- Direction- Coordinating and directing or guiding the onstage activities
- Playmaking - this involves creating an original script and staging a performance without a set or formal audience
- Pantomime- a form of communication by means of gesture and facial expressions – that is, telling a story without the use of words.

Various areas of art framework should be addressed including but not limited to the following:

- Direction of theatrical productions
- Auditions
- Analyzing script
- Demonstrating vision for a project
- Knowledge of communication skills
- Social group skills
- Creativity
- Understanding the principles of production
- Applying scheduling, budget, planning, promotion, roles and responsibilities of others, knowledge of legal issues such as copyright etc.
- Selection of appropriate works

Skill 34.2   Analyze how technical aspects of drama (e.g., the use of masks, costumes, props) affect the message or overall impression created by a dramatic performance

Lighting

Practically speaking, theatrical lighting makes the actors visible onstage. Artistically speaking, it creates an atmosphere that helps to tell the story being performed be it theatrical or dance. Lighting designers use the color, texture, intensity (brightness or dimness), direction, and movement of light to help create this atmosphere. Light may focus attention on particular areas of the stage or certain actors or dancers. Light is sometimes used to provide transitions in action or scenery. The lighting designer may use variations in colors to create a sense of temperature; for example, yellows and reds to produce a feeling of warmth.

Costumes

A character's costume includes the clothes, make-up, and hairstyle. Costume designers use color, texture, pattern, weight, and style, to convey information about a character - their social class and perhaps personality. The costumes can tell us what time of year it is and where the action is taking place. Costume designers use their craft to express cultural origins, mood and temperament of a character.

Sound

Sound effects and music generate meaning, create mood, and enhance atmosphere or feeling in a theatrical performance. In addition, directors and sound designers often use pre-show music to establish the initial mood of a performance. Does the sound convey a particular time of year or place? Sound, particularly music is often used to create a mood for the action (e.g., relaxing or tense) by using volume and certain styles.

Scenery

Scenery is used to create a visual world for the performer. Scene designers use style, color, mass, form, line, and texture within a defined space (usually a stage) to create an atmosphere. Scenery and props can all be used to create a sense of time, place and mood.

Together, crafts such as lighting, costumes, sound scenery and props work to create an overall message consistent with the story and characters in the drama or dance. These elements can be quite effective when pulled together in this way.

Skill 34.3 Relate types of dance (e.g., ballet, folk dance) to their characteristic forms of movement, expressive qualities, and cultural roles

The various *styles* of dance can be explained as follows:
- Creative dance
- Modern dance
- Social dance
- Dance of other cultures
- Structured dance
- Ritual Dance
- Ballet

Creative dance is the one that is most natural to a young child. Creative dance depicts feelings through movement. It is the initial reaction to sound and movement. The older elementary student will incorporate mood and expressiveness. Stories can be told to release the dancer into imagination.

Isadora Duncan is credited with being the mother of modern dance. **Modern dance** today refers to a concept of dance where the expressions of opposites are developed such as fast-slow, contract- release, vary height and level to fall and recover. Modern dance is based on four principles which are substance, dynamism, metakinesis, and form.

Social dance requires a steadier capability that the previous levels. The social aspect of dance predominates, rather than romantic aspect, representing customs and pastimes. Adults laugh when they hear little ones go "eweeee". Changing partners frequently within the dance is something that is subtly important to maintain. Social dance refers to a cooperative form of dance with respect to one sharing the dance floor with others and to have respect for ones partner. Social dance may be in the form of marches, waltz, and the two-step.

The upper level elementary student can learn dance in connection with historical **cultures** such as the minuet. The minuet was introduced to the court in Paris in 1650, and it dominated the ballroom until the end of the eighteenth century. The waltz was introduced around 1775 and was an occasion of fashion and courtship. The pomp and ceremony of it all makes for fun classroom experiences. Dance traditionally is central to many cultures and the interrelatedness of teaching history such as the Native American Indians dance, or the Mexican hat dance, or Japanese theater that incorporates both theater of masks and dance are all important exposures to dance and culture.

Structured dances are recognized by particular patterns such as the Tango, or waltz and were made popular in dance studios and gym classes alike. Arthur Murray promoted dance lessons for adults.

Ritual dance are often of a religious nature that celebrate a significant life event such as a harvest season, the rain season, glorifying the gods, asking for favors in hunting, birth and death dances. Many of these themes are carried out in movies and theaters today but they have their roots in Africa where circle dances and chants summoned the gods and sometimes produced trance like states where periods of divine contact convey the spiritual cleansing of the experience.

Dancing at weddings today is a prime example of ritual dance. The father dances with the bride. Then the husband dances with the bride. The two families dance with each other.

Ballet uses a barre to hold onto to practice the five basic positions used in ballet. Alignment is the way in which various parts of the dancer's body are in line with one another while the dancer is moving. It is very precise and executed with grace and form. The mood and expressions of the music are very important to ballet and form the canvas upon which the dance is performed.

Skill 34.4   Analyze ways in which different cultures have used drama and dance (e.g., to teach moral lessons, to preserve cultural traditions, to affirm a sense of community to entertain)

From the earliest days of civilization, drama and dance have been a part of human expression across many cultures and throughout the world, serving diverse cultural functions. Worship, the celebration of special events, ceremonies and entertainment are just a few of these functions. Dance was a regular part of religious practices in most major religions and was considered an adjunct to praising with music. Social events and the secular celebrations that were often linked to religious festivals were also marked by dancing, as were formal ceremonies, such as coronations.

Chinese Confucianism and Buddhism incorporate dance as part of religious practices. The trinity of Hindu gods (Brahma the Creator, Vishnu the Preserver, and Shiva the Destroyer) of India are closely associated with dance. Sculptures of Krishna, one of the physical forms or *avatars* of Vishnu often show him with a flute posing in dance positions.

The Hebrews used dance as part of worship and general celebration according to the many references to dance in the Bible's Old Testament.

Dance was and is part of praise, celebration and everyday life among the varied peoples of Africa.

Puppet shows, known as <u>wayang</u>, were used to spread Hinduism and Islam among villagers in Java. Javanese and Balinese dances have stories about old Buddhist and Hindu kingdoms.

Randai is a folk theatre tradition of the <u>Minangkabau</u> people of <u>West Sumatra</u>, usually performed for traditional ceremonies and festivals. It incorporates music, singing, dance, drama and martial arts, with performances often based on semi-historical Minangkabau stories and legend.

Opera, a form of art, which incorporates both music and drama, has been passed down through many generations and many cultures. The Italians, French and Germans are but a few of the cultures to use Opera as a way to entertain and teach moral lessons at the same time.

It is safe to say that drama and dance have been a rich and treasured part of cultural tradition and history in the past and will remain so in the future.

Sample Test

Reading, Language & Literature

1. **To understand the origins of a word, one must study the:**

    A. synonyms

    B. inflections

    C. phonetics

    D. etymology

2. **Which of the following is not a characteristic of a fable?**

    A. animals that feel and talk like humans.

    B. happy solutions to human dilemmas.

    C. teaches a moral or standard for behavior.

    D. illustrates specific people or groups without directly naming them.

3. **All of the following are true about phonological awareness EXCEPT:**

    A. It may involve print.

    B. It is a prerequisite for spelling and phonics.

    C. Activities can be done by the children with their eyes closed.

    D. Starts before letter recognition is taught.

4. **If a student has a poor vocabulary the teacher should recommend that:**

    A. the student read newspapers, magazines and books on a regular basis.

    B. the student enroll in a Latin class.

    C. the student writes the words repetitively after looking them up in the dictionary.

    D. the student use a thesaurus to locate synonyms and incorporate them into his/her vocabulary.

5. **Which definition below is the best for defining diction?**

    A. The specific word choices of an author to create a particular mood or feeling in the reader.

    B. Writing which explains something thoroughly.

    C. The background, or exposition, for a short story or drama.

    D. Word choices which help teach a truth or moral.

6. **Which is an untrue statement about a theme in literature?**

A. The theme is always stated directly somewhere in the text.

B. The theme is the central idea in a literary work.

C. All parts of the work (plot, setting, mood should contribute to the theme in some way.

D. By analyzing the various elements of the work, the reader should be able to arrive at an indirectly stated theme.

7. **Which is not a true statement concerning an author's literary tone?**

A. Tone is partly revealed through the selection of details.

B. Tone is the expression of the author's attitude toward his/her subject.

C. Tone in literature is usually satiric or angry.

D. Tone in literature corresponds to the tone of voice a speaker uses.

8. **The arrangement and relationship of words in sentences or sentence structure best describes:**

A. style

B. discourse

C. thesis

D. syntax

9. **Which of the following is a complex sentence?**

A. Anna and Margaret read a total of fifty-four books during summer vacation.

B. The youngest boy on the team had the best earned run average, which mystifies the coaching staff.

C. Earl decided to attend Princeton; his twin brother Roy, who aced the ASVAB test, will be going to Annapolis.

D. "Easy come, easy go," Marcia moaned.

10. **Followers of Piaget's learning theory believe that adolescents in the formal operations period:**

A. behave properly from fear of punishment rather than from a conscious decision to take a certain action.

B. see the past more realistically and can relate to people from the past more than preadolescents.

C. are less self-conscious and thus more willing to project their own identities into those of fictional characters.

D. have not yet developed a symbolic imagination.

11. **Which of the following is a formal reading level assessment?**

A. a standardized reading test

B. a teacher-made reading test

C. an interview

D. a reading diary.

12. **Middle and high school students are more receptive to studying grammar and syntax:**

A. through worksheets and end -of-lesson practices in textbooks.

B. through independent, homework assignments.

C. through analytical examination of the writings of famous authors.

D. through application to their own writing.

13. **Which of the following is not a technique of prewriting?**

A. Clustering

B. Listing

C. Brainstorming

D. Proofreading

14. **Which of the following is not an approach to keep students ever conscious of the need to write for audience appeal?**

   A. Pairing students during the writing process

   B. Reading all rough drafts before the students write the final copies

   C. Having students compose stories or articles for publication in school literary magazines or newspapers

   D. Writing letters to friends or relatives

15. **The children's literature genre came into its own in the:**

   A. seventeenth century

   B. eighteenth century

   C. nineteenth century

   D. twentieth century

16. **Which of the following should not be included in the opening paragraph of an informative essay?**

   A. Thesis sentence

   B. Details and examples supporting the main idea

   C. A broad general introduction to the topic

   D. A style and tone that grabs the reader's attention

17. **Which aspect of language is innate?**

   A. Biological capability to articulate sounds understood by other humans

   B. Cognitive ability to create syntactical structures

   C. Capacity for using semantics to convey meaning in a social environment

   D. Ability to vary inflections and accents

18. **Which of the following contains an error in possessive inflection?**

    A. Doris's shawl

    B. mother's-in-law frown

    C. children's lunches

    D. ambassador's briefcase

19. **To decode is to:**

    A. Construct meaning

    B. Sound out a printed sequence of letters.

    C. Use a special code to decipher a message.

    D. None of the above.

20. **A teacher has taught his students several strategies to monitor their reading comprehension. These strategies include identifying where in the passage they are having difficulty, identifying what the difficulty is, and restating the difficult sentence or passage in their own words. These strategies are examples of:**

    A. graphic and semantic organizers

    B. metacognition

    C. recognizing story structure

    D. summarizing

21. **All of the following are examples of ongoing informal assessment techniques used to observe student progress EXCEPT:**

    A. analyses of student work product

    B. collection of data from assessment tests

    C. effective questioning

    D. observation of students

22. **A student has written a paper with the following characteristics: written in first person; characters, setting, and plot; some dialogue; events organized in chronological sequence with some flashbacks. In what genre has the student written?**

    A. expository writing

    B. narrative writing

    C. persuasive writing

    D. technical writing

23. Which of the following indicates that a student is a fluent reader?

   A. reads texts with expression or prosody.

   B. reads word-to-word and haltingly.

   C. must intentionally decode a majority of the words.

   D. in a writing assignment, sentences are poorly-organized structurally.

24. Which of the following is an essential characteristic of effective assessment?

   A. Students are the ones being tested; they are not involved in the assessment process.

   B. Testing activities are kept separate from the teaching activities.

   C. Assessment should reflect the actual reading the classroom instruction has prepared the student for.

   D. Tests should use entirely different materials than those used in teaching so the result will be reliable.

Math

25. $\left(\dfrac{-4}{9}\right) + \left(\dfrac{-7}{10}\right) =$

   A. $\dfrac{23}{90}$

   B. $\dfrac{-23}{90}$

   C. $\dfrac{103}{90}$

   D. $\dfrac{-103}{90}$

26. $(5.6) \times (-0.11) =$

   A. -0.616

   B. 0.616

   C. -6.110

   D. 6.110

27. An item that sells for $375 is put on sale at $120. What is the percent of decrease?

   A. 25%

   B. 28%

   C. 68%

   D. 34%

28. Two mathematics classes have a total of 410 students. The 8:00 am class has 40 more than the 10:00 am class. How many students are in the 10:00 am class?

    A. 123.3

    B. 370

    C. 185

    D. 330

29. What measure could be used to report the distance traveled in walking around a track?

    A. degrees

    B. square meters

    C. kilometers

    D. cubic feet

30. What is the area of a square whose side is 13 feet?

    A. 169 feet

    B. 169 square feet

    C. 52 feet

    D. 52 square feet

31. What is the greatest common factor of 16, 28, and 36?

    A. 2

    B. 4

    C. 8

    D. 16

32. If $4x - (3 - x) = 7(x - 3) + 10$, then:

    A. $x = 8$

    B. $x = -8$

    C. $x = 4$

    D. $x = -4$

33. Given the formula $d = rt$, (where d = distance, r = rate, and t = time), calculate the time required for a vehicle to travel 585 miles at a rate of 65 miles per hour.

    A. 8.5 hours

    B. 6.5 hours

    C. 9.5 hours

    D. 9 hours

34. What is the probability of drawing 2 consecutive aces from a standard deck of cards?

   A. $\dfrac{3}{51}$

   B. $\dfrac{1}{221}$

   C. $\dfrac{2}{104}$

   D. $\dfrac{2}{52}$

35. A sofa sells for $520. If the retailer makes a 30% profit, what was the wholesale price?

   A. $400

   B. $676

   C. $490

   D. $364

36. Which of the following is an irrational number?

   A. .362626262...

   B. $4\frac{1}{3}$

   C. $\sqrt{5}$

   D. $-\sqrt{16}$

37. Corporate salaries are listed for several employees. Which would be the best measure of central tendency?

   $24,000 $24,000 $26,000

   $28,000 $30,000 $120,000

   A. Mean

   B. median

   C. mode

   D. no difference

38. Which statement is true about George's budget?

   A. George spends the greatest portion of his income on food.

   B. George spends twice as much on utilities as he does on his mortgage.

   C. George spends twice as much on utilities as he does on food.

   D. George spends the same amount on food and utilities as he does on mortgage.

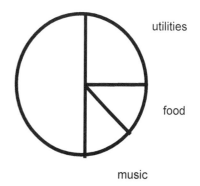

39. Given a drawer with 5 black socks, 3 blue socks, and 2 red socks, what is the probability that you will draw two black socks in two draws in a dark room?

   A. 2/9

   B. ¼

   C. 17/18

   D. 1/18

40. Solve for x. $|2x +3| > 4$

   A. $-\frac{7}{2} > x > \frac{1}{2}$

   B. $-\frac{1}{2} > x > \frac{7}{2}$

   C. $x < \frac{7}{2}$ or $x < -\frac{1}{2}$

   D. $x < -\frac{7}{2}$ or $x > \frac{1}{2}$

41. Graph the solution: $|x| + 7 < 13$

   A.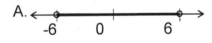

   B.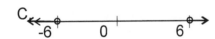

   C.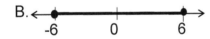

   D.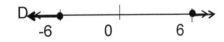

42. A boat travels 30 miles upstream in three hours. It makes the return trip in one and a half hours. What is the speed of the boat in still water?

   A. 10 mph

   B. 15 mph

   C. 20 mph

   D. 30 mph

43. 3 km is equivalent to _____.

   A. 300 cm

   B. 300 m

   C. 3000 cm

   D. 3000 m

44. If the radius of a right circular cylinder is doubled, how does its volume change?

   A. no change

   B. also is doubled

   C. four times the original

   D. pi times the original

Science

45. **Accepted procedures for preparing solutions should be made with _____ .**

   A. alcohol

   B. hydrochloric acid

   C. distilled water

   D. tap water

46. **Enzymes speed up reactions by _____.**

   A. utilizing ATP

   B. lowering pH, allowing reaction speed to increase

   C. increasing volume of substrate

   D. lowering energy of activation

47. **The transfer of heat by electromagnetic waves is called _____.**

   A. conduction

   B. convection

   C. phase change

   D. radiation

48. **Which of the following is *not* considered ethical behavior for a scientist?**

   A. Using unpublished data and citing the source.

   B. Publishing data before other scientists have had a chance to replicate results.

   C. Collaborating with other scientists from different laboratories.

   D. Publishing work with an incomplete list of citations.

49. **Sound waves are produced by _____.**

   A. pitch

   B. noise

   C. vibrations

   D. sonar

50. **Chemicals should be stored _____.**

   A. in the principal's office.

   B. in a dark room.

   C. according to their reactivity with other substances.

   D. in a double locked room

51. In an experiment measuring the growth of bacteria at different temperatures, what is the independent variable?

   A. Number of bacteria

   B. Growth rate of bacteria

   C. Temperature

   D. Size of bacteria

52. Which kingdom is comprised of organisms made of one cell with no nuclear membrane?

   A. Monera

   B. Protista

   C. Fungi

   D. Algae

53. What are the most significant and prevalent elements in the biosphere?

   A. Carbon, Hydrogen, Oxygen, Nitrogen, Phosphorus.

   B. Carbon, Hydrogen, Sodium, Iron, Calcium.

   C. Carbon, Oxygen, Sulfur, Manganese, Iron.

   D. Carbon, Hydrogen, Oxygen, Nickel, Sodium, Nitrogen.

54. Which of the following types of rock are made from magma?

   A. Fossils

   B. Sedimentary

   C. Metamorphic

   D. Igneous

55. What is the most accurate description of the Water Cycle?

   A. Rain comes from clouds, filling the ocean. The water then evaporates and becomes clouds again.

   B. Water circulates from rivers into groundwater and back, while water vapor circulates in the atmosphere.

   C. Water is conserved except for chemical or nuclear reactions, and any drop of water could circulate through clouds, rain, ground water, and surface-water.

   D. Weather systems cause chemical reactions to break water into its atoms.

56. The theory of 'seafloor spreading' explains _____.

   A. the shapes of the continents

   B. how continents collide

   C. how continents move apart

   D. how continents sink to become part of the ocean floor

57. Which of the following is the best definition for 'meteorite'?

   A. A meteorite is a mineral composed of mica and feldspar.

   B. A meteorite is material from outer space that has struck the earth's surface.

   C. A meteorite is an element that has properties of both metals and nonmetals.

   D. A meteorite is a very small unit of length measurement.

58. The measure of the pull of the earth's gravity on an object is called _____.

   A. mass number

   B. atomic number

   C. mass

   D. weight

59. Which parts of an atom are located inside the nucleus?

   A. Electrons and neutrons

   B. Protons and neutrons

   C. Protons only

   D. Neutrons only

History & Social Science

60. Which two Native American nations or tribes inhabited the Mid-Atlantic and Northeastern regions at the time of the first European contact?

   A. Pueblo and Inuit

   B. Algonquian and Cherokee

   C. Seminoles and Sioux

   D. Algonquian and Iroquois

61. Which of the following were results of the Age of Exploration?

   A. More complete and accurate maps and charts

   B. New and more accurate navigational instruments

   C. Proof that the earth is round

   D. All of the above

62. **What was the long-term importance of the Mayflower Compact?**

   A. It established the foundation of all later agreements with the Native Peoples

   B. It established freedom of religion in the original English colonies

   C. It ended the war in Europe between Spain, France and England

   D. It established a model of small, town-based government that was adopted throughout the New England colonies

63. **What intellectual movement during the period of North American colonization contributed to the development of public education and the founding of the first colleges and universities?**

   A. Enlightenment

   B. Great Awakening

   C. Libertarianism

   D. The Scientific Revolution

64. **The first European to see Florida and sail along its coast was:**

   A. Cabot

   B. Columbus

   C. Ponce de Leon

   D. Narvaez

65. **What is the form of local government that acts as an intermediary between the state and the city?**

   A. Metropolitan government

   B. Limited government

   C. The Mayor-Council system

   D. County Commission system

66. **Which one of the following is not a reason why Europeans came to the New World?**

   A. To find resources in order to increase wealth

   B. To establish trade

   C. To increase a ruler's power and importance

   D. To spread Christianity

67. **The year 1619 was a memorable for the colony of Virginia. Three important events occurred resulting in lasting effects on US history. Which one of the following is not one of the events?**

A. Twenty African slaves arrived.

B. The London Company granted the colony a charter making it independent.

C. The colonists were given the right by the London Company to govern themselves through representative government in the Virginia House of Burgesses

D. The London Company sent to the colony 60 women who were quickly married, establishing families and stability in the colony.

68. **The "divine right" of kings was the key political characteristic of:**

A. The Age of Absolutism

B. The Age of Reason

C. The Age of Feudalism

D. The Age of Despotism

69. **During the 1920s, the United States almost completely stopped all immigration. One of the reasons was:**

A. Plentiful cheap unskilled labor was no longer needed by industrialists

B. War debts from World War I made it difficult to render financial assistance

C. European nations were reluctant to allow people to leave since there was a need to rebuild populations and economic stability

D. The United States did not become a member of the League of Nations

70. **Which one of the following would not be considered a result of World War II?**

A. Economic depressions and slow resumption of trade and financial aid

B. Western Europe was no longer the center of world power

C. The beginnings of new power struggles not only in Europe but in Asia as well

D. Territorial and boundary changes for many nations, especially in Europe

71. The belief that the United States should control all of North America was called:

A. Westward Expansion

B. Pan Americanism

C. Manifest Destiny

D. Nationalism

72. Capitalism and communism are alike in that they are both:

A. Organic systems

B. Political systems

C. Centrally planned systems

D. Economic systems

73. The advancement of understanding in dealing with human beings has led to a number of interdisciplinary areas. Which of the following interdisciplinary studies would NOT be considered under the social sciences?

A. Molecular biophysics

B. Peace studies

C. African-American studies

D. Cartographic information systems

74. For the historian studying ancient Egypt, which of the following would be least useful?

A. The record of an ancient Greek historian on Greek-Egyptian interaction

B. Letters from an Egyptian ruler to his/her regional governors

C. Inscriptions on stele of the Fourteenth Egyptian Dynasty

D. Letters from a nineteenth century Egyptologist to his wife

Visual Art

75. Engravings and oil painting originated in this country.

A. Italy

B. Japan

C. Germany

D. Flanders

76. A combination of three or more tones sounded at the same time is called a _____.

A. harmony

B. consonance

C. chord

D. dissonance

77. A series of single tones which add up to a recognizable sound is called a _____.

   A. cadence

   B. rhythm

   C. melody

   D. sequence

78. Which is a true statement about crafts?

   A. Students experiment with their own creativity.

   B. Products are unique and different.

   C. Self-expression is encouraged.

   D. Outcome is predetermined.

79. The following is not a good activity to encourage fifth graders' artistic creativity:

   A. Ask them to make a decorative card for a family member.

   B. Have them work as a team to decorate a large wall display.

   C. Ask them to copy a drawing from a book, with the higher grades being awarded to those students who come closest to the model.

   D. Have each student try to create an outdoor scene with crayons, giving them a choice of scenery.

80. An approach to musical instruction for young children that "combines learning music, movement, singing, and exploration" is:

   A. Dalcroze Eurhythmics

   B. The Kodaly Method

   C. The Orff Approach

   D. Education Through Music (ETM)

81. During the early childhood years (ages 3-5), drama and theatre experiences are especially beneficial to children because they provide the opportunity for students to _____.

   A. apply the concept of turn-taking.

   B. learn the importance of listening skills.

   C. acquire the skills needed to become a proficient reader.

   D. learn early drama skills using their five senses.

82. In the area of Performing Arts, specifically dance, primary grades are expected to have a gross understanding of their motor movements. Which of the following movements would not be age-appropriate?

   A. basic rhythm

   B. early body awareness

   C. imagery

   D. listening skills

83. The history of theatre is important at an early age to describe how theatre has evolved over time. Which of the following is not a vital part of the many time periods of theatre history?

   A. Roman theatre

   B. American theatre

   C. Medieval drama

   D. Renaissance theatre

84. Creating movements in response to music helps students to connect music and dance in which of the following ways?

   A. rhythm

   B. costuming

   C. speed

   D. vocabulary skills

85. Often local elected officials and guest or residents artist are brought into the classroom to:

   A. explain their jobs or trades

   B. observe teaching skills

   C. enrich and extend arts curriculum

   D. entertain students and teachers

86. Early childhood students are expected to be able to complete tasks using basic loco-motor skills. Which of the following would <u>not</u> be included?

   A. walking

   B. galloping

   C. balancing

   D. jogging

87. In visual art studies students are expected to be able to interact in all of the following exercises except one.

   A. Clap out rhythmic patterns found in music lyrics.

   B. Compare and contrast various art pieces.

   C. Recognize related dance vocabulary.

   D. Identify and sort pictures organized by shape, size, and color.

Physical Education & Health

88. The physical education philosophy based on experience is:

   A. Naturalism

   B. Pragmatism

   C. Idealism

   D. Existentialism

89. The modern physical education philosophy that combines beliefs from different philosophies is:

   A. Eclectic

   B. Humanistic

   C. Individualism

   D. Realism

90. A physical education teacher emphasizes healthy attitudes and habits. She conducts her classes so that students acquire and interpret knowledge and learn to think/analyze, which is necessary for physical activities. The goals and values utilized and the philosophy applied by this instructor is:

   A. Physical Development Goals and Realism Philosophy

   B. Affective Development Goals and Existentialism

   C. Motor Development Goals and Realism Philosophy

   D. Cognitive Development Goals and Idealism Philosophy

91. **Social skills and values developed by activity include all of the following except:**

    A. Winning at all costs

    B. Making judgments in groups

    C. Communicating and cooperating

    D. Respecting rules and property

92. **Activities that enhance team socialization include all of the following except:**

    A. Basketball

    B. Soccer

    C. Golf

    D. Volleyball

93. **Through physical activities, John has developed self-discipline, fairness, respect for others, and new friends. John has experienced which of the following?**

    A. Positive cooperation psycho-social influences

    B. Positive group psycho-social influences

    C. Positive individual psycho-social influences

    D. Positive accomplishment psycho-social influences

94. **Which of the following psycho-social influences is not negative?**

    A. Avoidance of problems

    B. Adherence to exercise

    C. Ego-centeredness

    D. Role conflict

95. **Which professional organization protects amateur sports from corruption?**

    A. AIWA

    B. AAHPERD

    C. NCAA

    D. AAU

96. **Which professional organization works with legislatures?**

    A. AIWA

    B. AAHPERD

    C. ACSM

    D. AAU

97. Research in physical education is published in all of the following periodicals except the:

A. School PE Update

B. Research Quarterly

C. Journal of Physical Education

D. YMCA Magazine

98. The most effective way to promote the physical education curriculum is to:

A. Relate physical education to higher thought processes

B. Relate physical education to humanitarianism

C. Relate physical education to the total educational process

D. Relate physical education to skills necessary to preserve the natural environment

99. The affective domain of physical education contributes to all of the following except:

A. Knowledge of exercise, health, and disease

B. Self-actualization

C. An appreciation of beauty

D. Good sportsmanship

100. A physical education instructor anticipates and prevents potential injuries, watches for hidden injuries, and takes an injury evaluation of the entire class. Which of the following strategies to prevent injuries is the teacher demonstrating?

A. Maintaining hiring standards

B. Proper use of equipment

C. Proper procedures for emergencies

D. Participant screening

Answer Key

1.	D	21.	B	41.	A	61.	D	81.	D
2.	D	22.	B	42.	B	62.	D	82.	C
3.	A	23.	A	43.	D	63.	A	83.	B
4.	A	24.	C	44.	C	64.	A	84.	A
5.	A	25.	D	45.	C	65.	A	85.	C
6.	A	26.	A	46.	D	66.	B	86.	D
7.	C	27.	C	47.	D	67.	B	87.	C
8.	D	28.	C	48.	D	68.	A	88.	B
9.	B	29.	C	49.	C	69.	A	89.	A
10.	B	30.	B	50.	C	70.	A	90.	D
11.	A	31.	B	51.	C	71.	C	91.	A
12.	D	32.	C	52.	A	72.	D	92.	C
13.	D	33.	D	53.	A	73.	A	93.	B
14.	D	34.	B	54.	D	74.	D	94.	B
15.	A	35.	A	55.	C	75.	D	95.	D
16.	B	36.	C	56.	C	76.	C	96.	B
17.	A	37.	B	57.	B	77.	C	97.	A
18.	B	38.	C	58.	D	78.	D	98.	C
19.	B	39.	A	59.	B	79.	C	99.	A
20.	B	40.	D	60.	A	80.	D	100.	D

Rationales with Sample Questions

1. D. etymology.
A synonym is an equivalent of another word and can substitute for it in certain contexts.   Inflection is a modification of words according to their grammatical functions, usually by employing variant word-endings to indicate such qualities as tense, gender, case, and number. Phonetics are the science devoted to the physical analysis of the sounds of human speech, including their production, transmission, and perception.

2. D. illustrates specific people or groups without directly naming them.
A fable is a short tale with animals, humans, gods, or even inanimate objects as characters. Fables often conclude with a moral, delivered in the form of an epigram (a short, witty, and ingenious statement in verse). Fables are among the oldest forms of writing in human history: it appears in Egyptian papyri of c1,500 BC. The most famous fables are those of Aesop, a Greek slave living in about 600 BC. In India, the Pantchatantra appeared in the third century. The most famous modern fables are those of seventeenth century French poet Jean de La Fontaine.

3. The key word here is EXCEPT which will be highlighted in upper case on the test as well. All of the options are correct aspects of phonological awareness except the first one, **A,** because phonological awareness DOES NOT involve print.

4. A. the student read newspapers, magazines and books on a regular basis.
It is up to the teacher to help the student choose reading material, but the student must be able to choose where s/he will search for the reading pleasure indispensable for enriching vocabulary.

5. A. The specific word choices of an author to create a particular mood or feeling in the reader.
Diction refers to an author's choice of words, expressions and style to convey his/her meaning.

6. A. The theme is always stated directly somewhere in the text.
The theme may be stated directly, but it can also be implicit in various aspects of the work, such as the interaction between characters, symbolism, or description.

7. C. Tone in literature is usually satiric or angry.
Tone in literature conveys a mood and can be as varied as the tone of voice of a speaker (see D., e.g. sad, nostalgic, whimsical, angry, formal, intimate, satirical, sentimental, etc.

8. D. Syntax.
Syntax is the grammatical structure of sentences.

9. B. The youngest boy on the team had the best earned run average which mystifies the coaching staff.
Here, the use of the relative pronoun "which", whose antecedent is "the best run average, introduces a clause that is dependent on the independent clause "The youngest boy on the team had the best run average". The idea expressed in the subordinate clause is subordinate to the one expressed in the independent clause.

10. B. See the past more realistically and can relate to people from the past more than preadolescents.
Since according to Piaget, adolescents 12-15 years old begin thinking beyond the immediate and obvious, and theorize. Their assessment of events shifts from considering an action as "right" or "wrong" to considering the intent and behavior in which the action was performed. Fairy tale or other kinds of unreal characters have ceased to satisfy them and they are able to recognize the difference between pure history and historical fiction.

11. A. A standardized reading test.
If assessment is standardized, it has to be objective, whereas B, C and D are all subjective assessments.

12. D. through application to their own writing.
The answer is D. At this age, students learn grammatical concepts best through practical application in their own writing

13. D. Proofreading.
Proofreading cannot be a method of prewriting, since it is done on already written texts only.

14. D. Writing letters to friends or relatives
The answer is D. Reading all rough drafts will not encourage the students to take control of their text and might even inhibit their creativity. On the contrary, pairing students will foster their sense of responsibility, and having them compose stories for literary magazines will boost their self esteem as well as their organization skills. As far as writing letters is concerned, the work of authors such as Madame de Sevigne in the seventeenth century is a good example of epistolary literary work.

15. A. seventeenth century

In the seventeenth Century, authors such as Jean de La Fontaine and his *Fables*, Pierre Perreault's *Tales*, Mme d'Aulnoye's Novels based on old folktales and Mme de Beaumont's *Beauty and the Beast* all created a children's literature genre. In England, Perreault was translated and a work allegedly written by Oliver Smith, *The renowned History of Little Goody Two Shoes*, also helped to establish children's literature in England.

16. B. Details and examples supporting the main idea

The introductory paragraph should introduce the topic, capture the reader's interest, state the thesis and prepare the reader for the main points in the essay. Details and examples, however, should be given in the second part of the essay, so as to help develop the thesis presented at the end of the introductory paragraph, following the inverted triangle method consisting of a broad general statement followed by some information, and then the thesis at the end of the paragraph.

17. A. Biological capability to articulate sounds understood by other humans

Language ability is innate and the biological capability to produce sounds lets children learn semantics and syntactical structures through trial and error. Linguists agree that language is first a vocal system of word symbols that enable a human to communicate his/her feelings, thoughts, and desires to other human beings.

18. B. mother's-in-law frown

Mother-in-Law is a compound common noun and the inflection should be at the end of the word, according to the rule.

19. The answer is "B" and again the definition of this word in reading is what you have to know from your coursework.

20 B. Metacognition

Metacognition may be defined as "thinking about thinking." Good readers use metacognitive strategies to think about and have control over their reading. Before reading, they might clarify their purpose for reading and preview the text. During reading, they might monitor their understanding, adjusting their reading speed to fit the difficulty of the text and fixing any comprehension problems they have. After reading, they check their understanding of what they read.

21 B. collection of data from assessment tests

Assessment tests are formal progress-monitoring measures.

22 B. narrative writing
These are all characteristics of narrative writing. Expository writing is intended to give information such as an explanation or directions, and the information is logically organized. Persuasive writing gives an opinion in an attempt to convince the reader that this point of view is valid or tries to persuade the reader to take a specific action. The goal of technical writing is to clearly communicate a select piece of information to a targeted reader or group of readers for a particular purpose in such a way that the subject can readily be understood. It is persuasive writing that anticipates a response from the reader.

23 A. reads texts with expression or prosody.
The teacher should listen to the children read aloud, but there are also clues to reading levels in their writing.

24 C. Assessment should reflect the actual reading the classroom instruction has prepared the student for.
The only reliable measure of the success of a unit will be based on the reading the instruction has focused on.

25. Find the LCD of $\frac{^-4}{9}$ and $\frac{^-7}{10}$. The LCD is 90, so you get

$\frac{^-40}{90} + \frac{^-63}{90} = \frac{^-103}{90}$, which is answer **D.**

26. Simple multiplication. The answer will be negative because a positive times a negative is a negative number. $5.6 \times {}^- 0.11 = {}^- 0.616$, which is answer **A.**

27. Use $(1 - x)$ as the discount. $375x = 120$.
$375(1 - x) = 120 \to 375 - 375x = 120 \to 375x = 255 \to x = 0.68 = 68\%$
which is answer **C.**

28. Let $x = $ # of students in the 8 am class and $x - 40 = $ # of student in the 10 am class. $x + (x - 40) = 410 \to 2x - 40 = 410 \to 2x = 450 \to x = 225$. So there are 225 students in the 8 am class, and $225 - 40 = 185$ in the 10 am class, which is answer **C.**

29. Degrees measures angles, square meters measures area, cubic feet measure volume, and kilometers measures length. Kilometers is the only reasonable answer, which is **C.**

30. Area = length times width (*lw*).
Length = 13 feet
Width = 13 feet (square, so length and width are the same).
Area = $13 \times 13 = 169$ square feet.
Area is measured in square feet. So the answer is **B**.

31. The smallest number in this set is 16; its factors are 1, 2, 4, 8 and 16. 16 in the largest factor, but it does not divide into 28 or 36. Neither does 8. 4 does factor into both 28 and 36. The answer is **B**.

32. Solve for *x*.

$4x - (3 - x) = 7(x - 3) + 10$

$4x - 3 + x = 7x - 21 + 10$

$5x - 3 = 7x - 11$

$5x = 7x - 11 + 3$ The answer is **C**.

$5x - 7x = ^{-}8$

$^{-}2x = ^{-}8$

$x = 4$

33. We are given *d* = 585 miles and *r* = 65 miles per hour and *d* =*rt*. Solve for *t*. $585 = 65t \rightarrow t = 9$ hours, which is answer **D**.

34. There are 4 aces in the 52 card deck.

P(first ace) = $\dfrac{4}{52}$. P(second ace) = $\dfrac{3}{51}$.

P(first ace and second ace) = P(one ace)xP(second ace|first ace)

$= \dfrac{4}{52} \times \dfrac{3}{51} = \dfrac{1}{221}$. This is answer **B**.

35. A. $400
Let x be the wholesale price, then x + .30x = 520, 1.30x = 520. divide both sides by 1.30.

36. A. $500
12(40) = 480 which is closest to $500.

37. B. median
The median provides the best measure of central tendency in this case where the mode is the lowest number and the mean would be disproportionately skewed by the outlier $120,000.

38. C. George spends twice as much on utilities as he does on food
George spends twice as much on utilities as on food.

39. A. 2/9
In this example of conditional probability, the probability of drawing a
black sock on the first draw is 5/10. It is implied in the problem that there is no
replacement, therefore the probability of obtaining a black sock in the second
draw is 4/9. Multiply the two probabilities and reduce to lowest terms.

40. D. $x < -\frac{7}{2}$ or $x > \frac{1}{2}$
The quantity within the absolute value symbols must be either > 4 or < -4. Solve
he two inequalities $2x + 3 > 4$ or $2x + 3 < -4$.

41. A.

Solve by adding -7 to each side of the inequality. Since the absolute value
of x is less than 6, x must be between -6 and 6. The end points are not
included so the circles on the graph are hollow.

42. B. 15 mph
Let x = the speed of the boat in still water and c = the speed of the current.

	rate	time	distance
upstream	x - c	3	30
downstream	x + c	1.5	30

Solve the system:
$$3x - 3c = 30$$
$$1.5x + 1.5c = 30$$

43. D. 3000 m
To change kilometers to meters, move the decimal 3 places to the right.

44. C. four times the original
If the radius of a right circular cylinder is doubled, the volume is multiplied by four
because in he formula, the radius is squared, therefore the new volume is 2 x 2
or four times the original.

45. C. Distilled water.
Alcohol and hydrochloric acid should never be used to make solutions unless
instructed to do so. All solutions should be made with distilled water as tap water
contains dissolved particles which may affect the results of an experiment. The
correct **answer is (C).**

46. D. Lowering energy of activation.

Because enzymes are catalysts, they work the same way—they cause the formation of activated chemical complexes, which require a lower activation energy. Therefore, the **answer is (D).** ATP is an energy source for cells, and pH or volume changes may or may not affect reaction rate, so these answers can be eliminated.

47. D. Radiation

Heat transfer via electromagnetic waves (which can occur even in a vacuum) is called radiation. (Heat can also be transferred by direct contact (conduction), by fluid current (convection), and by matter changing phase, but these are not relevant here.) The answer to this question is therefore (D).

48. D. Publishing work with an incomplete list of citations.

One of the most important ethical principles for scientists is to cite all sources of data and analysis when publishing work. It is reasonable to use unpublished data (A), as long as the source is cited. Most science is published before other scientists replicate it (B), and frequently scientists collaborate with each other, in the same or different laboratories (C). These are all ethical choices. However, publishing work without the appropriate citations, is unethical. Therefore, the **answer is (D).**

49. C. Vibrations

Sound waves are produced by a vibrating body. The vibrating object moves forward and compresses the air in front of it, then reverses direction so that pressure on the air is lessened and expansion of the air molecules occurs. The vibrating air molecules move back and forth parallel to the direction of motion of the wave as they pass the energy from adjacent air molecules closer to the source to air molecules farther away from the source. Therefore, the answer is (C).

50. D. According to their reactivity with other substances.

Chemicals should be stored with other chemicals of similar properties (e.g. acids with other acids), to reduce the potential for either hazardous reactions in the storeroom, or mistakes in reagent use. Certainly, chemicals should not be stored in anyone's office, and the light intensity of the room is not very important because light-sensitive chemicals are usually stored in dark containers. In fact, good lighting is desirable in a storeroom, so that labels can be read easily. Chemicals may be stored off-site, but that makes their use inconvenient. Therefore, the best answer is (D).

51. C. Temperature

To answer this question, recall that the independent variable in an experiment is the entity that is changed by the scientist, in order to observe the effects (the dependent variable(s)). In this experiment, temperature is changed in order to measure growth of bacteria, so (C) is the answer. Note that answer (A) is the dependent variable, and neither (B) nor (D) is directly relevant to the question.

52. A. Monera

To answer this question, first note that algae are not a kingdom of their own. Some algae are in monera, the kingdom that consists of unicellular prokaryotes with no true nucleus. Protista and fungi are both eukaryotic, with true nuclei, and are sometimes multi-cellular. Therefore, the answer is (A).

53. A. Carbon, Hydrogen, Oxygen, Nitrogen, Phosphorus

Organic matter (and life as we know it) is based on Carbon atoms, bonded to Hydrogen and Oxygen. Nitrogen and Phosphorus are the next most significant elements, followed by Sulfur and then trace nutrients such as Iron, Sodium, Calcium, and others. Therefore, the answer is (A). If you know that the formula for any carbohydrate contains Carbon, Hydrogen, and Oxygen, that will help you narrow the choices to (A) and (D) in any case.

54. D. Igneous

Few fossils are found in metamorphic rock and virtually none found in igneous rocks. Igneous rocks are formed from magma and magma is so hot that any organisms trapped by it are destroyed. Metamorphic rocks are formed by high temperatures and great pressures. When fluid sediments are transformed into solid sedimentary rocks, the process is known as lithification. The answer is (D).

55. C. Water is conserved except for chemical or nuclear reactions, and any drop of water could circulate through clouds, rain, ground water, and surface- water.

All natural chemical cycles, including the Water Cycle, depend on the principle of Conservation of Mass. (For water, unlike for elements such as Nitrogen, chemical reactions may cause sources or sinks of water molecules.) Any drop of water may circulate through the hydrologic system, ending up in a cloud, as rain, or as surface- or ground-water. Although answers (A) and (B) describe parts of the water cycle, the most comprehensive answer is (C).

56. C. How continents move apart.

In the theory of 'seafloor spreading', the movement of the ocean floor causes continents to spread apart from one another. This occurs because crust plates split apart, and new material is added to the plate edges. This process pulls the continents apart, or may create new separations, and is believed to have caused the formation of the Atlantic Ocean. Therefore, the answer is (C).

57. B. A meteorite is material from outer space that has struck the earth's surface.

Meteoroids are pieces of matter in space, composed of particles of rock and metal. If a meteoroid travels through the earth's atmosphere, friction causes burning and a "shooting star"—i.e. a meteor. If the meteor strikes the earth's surface, it is known as a meteorite. Note that although the suffix –ite often means a mineral, answer (A) is incorrect. Answer (C) refers to a 'metalloid' rather than a 'meteorite', and answer (D) is simply a misleading pun on 'meter'. Therefore, the answer is (B).

58. D. Weight

To answer this question, recall that mass number is the total number of protons and neutrons in an atom, atomic number is the number of protons in an atom, and mass is the amount of matter in an object. The only remaining choice is (D), weight, which is correct because weight is the force of gravity on an object.

59. B. Protons and Neutrons

Protons and neutrons are located in the nucleus, while electrons move around outside the nucleus. This is consistent only with answer (B).

60 D. Algonquian and Iroquois

The Algonquian and Iroquois nations inhabited the Mid-Atlantic and Northeastern regions of the U.S. These Native Americans are classified among the Woods Peoples. Some of the most famous of these nations are Squanto, Pocahontas, Chief Powhatan, Tecumseh, and Black Hawk. These two nations were frequently at odds over territory. The people of these nations taught early settlers about the land and survival in the new world. They introduced the settlers to maize and tobacco. The settlers and the Native Americans gradually developed respect and opened trade and cultural sharing.

61. D. All of the above

The importance of the Age of Exploration was not only the discovery and colonization of the New World, but also better maps and charts; new accurate navigational instruments; increased knowledge; great wealth; new and different foods and items not known in Europe; a new hemisphere as a refuge from poverty, persecution, a place to start a new and better life; and proof that Asia could be reached by sea and that the earth was round; ships and sailors would not sail off the edge of a flat earth and disappear forever into nothingness.

62. D. Established a model of small, town-based government
Before setting foot on land in 1620, the **Pilgrims** aboard the Mayflower agreed to a form of self-government by signing the Mayflower Compact. The Compact served as the basis for governing the Plymouth colony for many years and set an example of small, town-based government that would proliferate throughout New England. The present day New England town meeting is an extension of this tradition. This republican ideal was later to clash with the policies of British colonial government

63. A. Enlightenment
Enlightenment thinking quickly made the voyage across the Atlantic Ocean. Enlightenment thinking valued human reason and the importance of education, knowledge, and scholarly research. Education in the middle colonies was influenced largely by the Enlightenment movement, which emphasized scholarly research and public service. Benjamin Franklin embodied these principles in Philadelphia, which became a center of learning and culture, owing largely to its economic success and ease of access to European books and tracts.

64. A. Cabot
John Cabot (1450-1498) was the English explorer who gave England claim to North American and the first European to see Florida and sail along its coast. (B) Columbus (1451-1506) was sent by the Spanish to the New World and has received false credit for "discovering America" in 1492, although he did open up the New World to European expansion, exploitation, and Christianity. (C) Ponce de Leon (1460-1521), the Spanish explorer, was the first European to actually land on Florida. (D) Panfilo de Narvaez (1470-1528) was also a Spanish conquistador, but he was sent to Mexico to force Cortes into submission. He failed and was captured.

65. A. Metropolitan Government
Metropolitan Government was the form of local government that acts as an intermediary between the state and the city and comes from the idea of municipal home rule first enacted by Missouri in 1875. As suburbs grew and cities declined a bit, it became more important to have an intermediary between the city and state governments.

66. B. To establish trade
The Europeans came to the New World for a number of reasons; often they came to find new natural resources to extract for manufacturing. The Portuguese, Spanish and English were sent over to increase the monarch's power and spread influences such as religion (Christianity) and culture. Therefore, the only reason given that Europeans didn't come to the New World was to establish trade.

67. B. The London Company granted the colony a charter making it independent.

In the year 1619, the Southern colony of Virginia had an eventful year including the first arrival of twenty African slaves, the right to self-governance through representative government in the Virginia House of Burgesses (their own legislative body), and the arrival of sixty women sent to marry and establish families in the colony. The London Company did not, however, grant the colony a charter in 1619.

68. A. The Age of Absolutism

The "divine right" of kings was the key political characteristic of The Age of Absolutism and was most visible in the reign of King Louis XIV of France, as well as during the times of King James I and his son, Charles I. The divine right doctrine claims that kings and absolute leaders derive their right to rule by virtue of their birth alone. They see this both as a law of God and of nature.

69. A. Plentiful cheap, unskilled labor was no longer needed by industrialists

The primary reason that the United States almost completely stopped all immigration during the 1920s was because their once, much needed, cheap, unskilled labor jobs, made available by the once booming industrial economy, were no longer needed. This has much to do with the increased use of machines to do the work once done by cheap, unskilled laborers.

70. A. Economic depressions and slow resumption of trade and financial aid

Following World War II, the economy was vibrant and flourished from the stimulant of war and an increased dependence of the world on United States industries. Therefore, World War II didn't result in economic depressions and slow resumption of trade and financial aid. Western Europe was no longer the center of world power. New power struggles arose in Europe and Asia and many European nations underwent changing territories and boundaries.

71. C. Manifest Destiny

The belief that the United States should control all of North America was called (B) Manifest Destiny. This idea fueled much of the violence and aggression towards those already occupying the lands such as the Native Americans. Manifest Destiny was certainly driven by sentiments of (D) nationalism and gave rise to (A) westward expansion.

72. C. Utility

As used in the social science of economics, (C) utility is the measurement of happiness or satisfaction a person receives from consuming a good or service. The decision of the student to increase his satisfaction by buying a second candy bar relates to this concept because he is spending money to increase his happiness.

73. A. Molecular biophysics
Molecular biophysics is an interdisciplinary field combining the fields of biology, chemistry and physics. These are all natural sciences, and not social sciences

74. D. Letters from a nineteenth century Egyptologist to his wife
Historians use primary sources from the actual time they are studying whenever possible. (A) Ancient Greek records of interaction with Egypt, (B) letters from an Egyptian ruler to regional governors, and (C) inscriptions from the Fourteenth Egyptian Dynasty are all primary sources created at or near the actual time being studied. (D) Letters from a nineteenth century Egyptologist would not be considered primary sources, as they were created thousands of years after the fact and may not actually be about the subject being studied.

Art

75. D. Based on the history and cultural aspects of artwork found in the Historical and Cultural Context 3.3

76. C. Identifying tones, music, beats etc. can be related to the Artistic Perception module 1.2

77. C. Using crafting and artistic lessons can be related to Artistic Perception 1.2

78. D. Creativity and teaching upper level thinking, reasoning, and creativity lessons can be related to Creative Expression threads 2.1-2.7

79. C. Encouraging artistic creativity can be located in the framework threads 2.2

80. D. Incorporating both musical and movement approaches related to framework of dance and music.

81. D. Students in Early Childhood ages are introduced to drama and theatre using their 5 senses. Using smell, feel, sound, touch, and taste are all senses that even at the earliest ages children know and are able to relate to.

82. C. Early Childhood students are expected to have limited understanding of their bodies and general movement of them. However early imagery is a tool that is only developed once a student begins to mature and doesn't typically happen until late elementary or early middle school age students.

83. B. American theatre wasn't included as a type of theatre in early age drama.

84. A. Students should be able to understand the connections made between movement and music is related by rhythm.

85. C. Teachers often look for outside sources to help aid in their students understanding of lessons and concepts. There are many programs utilized and the artist in residence program is an example of how artists enrich the art program of study.

86. D. Early childhood students are only expected to complete basic motor skills at ages 3-5.

87. C. Dance is not a related area in visual arts.

Physical Education

88. B. Pragmatism. As a school of philosophy, is a collection of different ways of thinking. Given the diversity of thinkers and the variety of schools of thought that have adopted this term over the years, the term pragmatism has become almost meaningless in the absence of further qualification. Most of the thinkers who describe themselves as pragmatists indicate some connection with practical consequences or real effects as vital components of both meaning and truth.

89. A. Eclectic. Are so-called philosophers who attach themselves to no system in particular. Instead, they select what, in their judgment, is true of the other philosophers. In antiquity, the Eclectic philosophy is that which sought to unite into a coherent whole, the doctrines of Pythagoras, Plato, and Aristotle. There is eclecticism in art as well as philosophy. The term was applied to an Italian school which aimed at uniting the excellence of individual intellectual masters.

90. D. Educators use cognitive development goals to describe the act of teaching children in a manner that will help them develop as personal and social beings. Concepts that fall under this term include social and emotional learning, moral reasoning/cognitive development, life-skills education, health education, violence prevention, critical thinking, ethical reasoning, and conflict resolution and mediation. This form of education involves teaching children and teenagers such values as honesty, stewardship, kindness, generosity, courage, freedom, justice, equality, and respect. Idealism is an approach to philosophical inquiry that asserts direct and immediate knowledge can only be had as ideas or mental pictures. We can only know the objects that are the basis of these ideas indirectly.

91. A. Winning at all costs is not a desirable social skill. Instructors and coaches should emphasize fair play and effort over winning. Answers B, C, and D are all positive skills and values developed in physical activity settings.

92. C. Golf is mainly an individual sport. Though golf involves social interaction, it generally lacks the team element inherent in basketball, soccer, and volleyball.

93. B. Through physical activities, John developed his social interaction skills.
Social interaction is the sequence of social actions between individuals (or groups) that modify their actions and reactions due to the actions of their interaction partner(s). In other words, they are events in which people attach meaning to a situation, interpret what others mean, and respond accordingly. Through socialization with other people, John feels the influence of the people around him.

94. B. The ability of an individual to adhere to an exercise routine due to her/his excitement, accolades, etc. is not a negative psycho-social influence. Adherence to an exercise routine is healthy and positive.

95. D. The Amateur Athletic Union (AAU) is one of the largest non-profit, volunteer sports organizations in the United States.
A multi-sport organization, the AAU dedicates itself exclusively to the promotion and development of amateur sports and physical fitness programs. Answer C may be a tempting choice, but the NCAA deals only with college athletics.

96. B. AAHPERD, or American Alliance for Health, Physical Education, Recreation and Dance, is an alliance of 6 national associations.
AAHPERD is the largest organization of professionals supporting and assisting those involved in physical education, leisure, fitness, dance, health promotion, and education, as well as all other specialties related to achieving a healthy lifestyle. AAHPERD is an alliance designed to provide members with a comprehensive and coordinated array of resources, support, and programs to help practitioners improve their skills and in turn, further the health and well-being of the American public.

97. A. Each school has a PE Update that publishes their own periodicals about physical activities. It aims at helping the students to catch-up on what is happening around them. The school produces this update to encourage their students to become more interested in all of the physical activities that they offer. School PE Updates, however, do not include research findings.

98. C. The government treats the physical education curriculum as one of the major subjects. Because of all of the games that we now participate in, many countries have focused their hearts and set their minds on competing with rival countries. Physical education is now one of the major, important subjects and instructors should integrate physical education into the total educational process.

99. A. The affective domain encompasses emotions, thoughts, and feelings related to physical education. Knowledge of exercise, health, and disease is part of the cognitive domain.

100. D. In order for the instructor to know each student's physical status, she takes an injury evaluation.

Such surveys are one way to know the physical status of an individual. It chronicles past injuries, tattoos, activities, and diseases the individual may have or had. It helps the instructor to know the limitations of each individual. Participant screening covers all forms of surveying and anticipation of injuries.

XAMonline, INC. 21 Orient Ave. Melrose, MA 02176

Toll Free number 800-509-4128

TO ORDER Fax 781-662-9268 OR www.XAMonline.com

CERTIFICATION EXAMINATION FOR OKLAHOMA EDUCATORS - CEOE - 2007

PO#   Store/School:

Address 1:

Address 2 (Ship to other):

City, State Zip

Credit card number_____-_____-_____-_____   expiration_____

EMAIL _____

PHONE   **FAX**

13# ISBN 2007	TITLE	Qty	Retail	Total
978-1-58197-781-3	CEOE OSAT Advanced Mathematics Field 11			
978-1-58197-775-2	CEOE OSAT Art Sample Test Field 02			
978-1-58197-780-6	CEOE OSAT Biological Sciences Field 10			
978-1-58197-776-9	CEOE OSAT Chemistry Field 04			
978-1-58197-778-3	CEOE OSAT Earth Science Field 08			
978-1-58197-794-3	CEOE OSAT Elementary Education Fields 50-51			
978-1-58197-795-0	CEOE OSAT Elementary Education Fields 50-51 Sample Questions			
978-1-58197-777-6	CEOE OSAT English Field 07			
978-1-58197-779-0	CEOE OSAT Family and Consumer Sciences Field 09			
978-1-58197-786-8	CEOE OSAT French Sample Test Field 20			
978-1-58197-798-1	CEOE OGET Oklahoma General Education Test 074			
978-1-58197-792-9	CEOE OSAT Library-Media Specialist Field 38			
978-1-58197-787-5	CEOE OSAT Middle Level English Field 24			
978-1-58197-789-9	CEOE OSAT Middle Level Science Field 26			
978-1-58197-790-5	CEOE OSAT Middle Level Social Studies Field 27			
978-1-58197-788-2	CEOE OSAT Middle Level-Intermediate Mathematics Field 25			
978-1-58197-791-2	CEOE OSAT Mild Moderate Disabilities Field 29			
978-1-58197-782-0	CEOE OSAT Physical Education-Health-Safety Field 12			
978-1-58197-783-7	CEOE OSAT Physics Sample Test Field 14			
978-1-58197-793-6	CEOE OSAT Principal Common Core Field 44			
978-1-58197-796-7	CEOE OPTE Oklahoma Professional Teaching Examination Fields 75-76			
978-1-58197-784-4	CEOE OSAT Reading Specialist Field 15			
978-1-58197-785-1	CEOE OSAT Spanish Field 19			
978-1-58197-797-4	CEOE OSAT U.S. & World History Field 17			
			SUBTOTAL	
	FOR PRODUCT PRICES GO TO WWW.XAMONLINE.COM		Ship	$8.25
			TOTAL	

CPSIA information can be obtained
at www.ICGtesting.com
Printed in the USA
BVHW011523250119
538684BV00003B/147/P